AUTOBIOGRAPHY
VOLUME 1

I KNOCK AT THE DOOR

Each volume in the evocative and richly entertaining autobiography of Sean O'Casey is essential reading for a proper appreciation of this major Irish dramatist whose plays were among the most exciting developments in modern drama.

Born in the back streets of Dublin, suffering from weak and diseased eyes, he lived in poverty and physical hardship for many years. In his late teens he became a manual labourer and after working on the roads or in the docks from five in the morning to six at night he would spend his evenings helping the cause of the Gaelic League and Sinn Fein. He became Secretary of the Irish Citizen Army and a founder member of the Irish Labour Party. Although his first published work was in 1907, not until the success of *Juno and the Paycock* in 1925 did he give up manual work and become a full-time writer.

Sean O'Casey wrote his autobiography in six volumes over more than two decades, recreating in Volume 1 the days of his Dublin childhood. Volume 2 tells of his coming to manhood and includes episodes later used by the playwright in *Red Roses for Me*.

The photograph, 'Quais' by Evelyn Hofer, reproduced on the cover, is from *Dublin: A Portrait* by V. S. Pritchett and Evelyn Hofer, published by The Bodley Head.

By the same author in Pan Books

AUTOBIOGRAPHY (VOLUME 2):
PICTURES IN THE HALLWAY

AUTOBIOGRAPHY
VOLUME 1

I KNOCK AT THE DOOR

SEAN O'CASEY

UNABRIDGED

PAN BOOKS LTD : LONDON

First published 1963 in a three-volume edition
of the Autobiographies in St Martin's Library series
by Macmillan and Company Ltd.
First published 1971 in this form by Pan Books Ltd,
33 Tothill Street, London, S.W.1

ISBN 0 330 02716 6

Printed in Great Britain by
Richard Clay (The Chaucer Press), Ltd, Bungay, Suffolk

CONTENTS

I KNOCK AT THE DOOR

Knock, and it shall be opened unto you

To Breon and Niall

A CHILD IS BORN

IN DUBLIN, sometime in the early 'eighties, on the last day of the month of March, a mother in child-pain clenched her teeth, dug her knees home into the bed, sweated and panted and grunted, became a tense living mass of agony and effort, groaned and pressed and groaned and pressed, and pressed a little boy out of her womb into a world where white horses and black horses and brown horses and white-and-black horses and brown-and-white horses trotted tap-tap-tap tap-tap-tappety-tap over cobble stones, conceitedly, in front of landau, brougham, or vis-à-vis; lumberingly in front of tramcar; pantingly and patiently in front of laden lorry, dray, or float; and gaily in front of the merry and irresponsible jaunting-car:

Where soldiers paraded, like figures taken out of a toy-box, wearing their red coats with yellow breastpieces; blue jackets with white breastpieces; and tight trousers with red stripes or white stripes or yellow stripes down the whole length of each leg; marching out on each royal birthday of the Queen to the Phoenix Park for a Review and Sham Battle, with guns and lances and swords and cannons; going by the Saluting Point at a quick march, or at a trot, and lastly, at a gallop, with a thunder of hoofs and a rattle of shaking cannon, that made all hearts quiver with hope for a new war; while the soldiers having got back to barracks when the fun was all over, rubbed down their sweating horses or cleaned their rifles, murmuring all the time against the birthdays of queens that gave them all so much mucking about for nothing:

Where a great poet named Tennyson, anticipating Hollywood, had built up in the Studio of his mind, his Come into the garden, Maud, the black bat night has flown; and had sent his cardboard kings and warriors and uncompromising virgins out into the highways and byways that sprinkled the lawns of the welltodo, men bowing low to the knights as they went galloping by like the wind in a hurry; and the maidens smiled and beckoned and sighed as the knights careered about among the roses and the holly-hocks, gathering on the points of their lances lovely little bunches of rosemary and rue:

Where energy was poured out in Bibles and tracts and hymns; and sweet little stories, swinging little boys and girls up to heaven or down to hell; where the hosts of heaven, embattled, assembled for the fray on a croquet lawn; and all the passion, frightfulness, laughter, strife, tears, peace, defeat, victory, agony, and bloody sweat of heaven's war with hell sank into a delicately scented, gently moving, sweet conversing, pink and mauve and cream-coloured garden party:

Where it was believed that when children died of croup or consumption or fever, they were simply not, for God took them:

Where Ruskin, with his delicate mind and Christianly crafted hands, modelled his figures of speech with mud and tinsel; and Mr Poynter, President of the Royal Academy, summoning up all his powers of imagination, and summing all that ever had been or would be in art, painted the *tour de force* and cul-de-sac of a visit to Æsculapius:

Where almost all found all in all in God on Sundays; and the rest of the week found all in all in bustles, Bibles, and bassinets; preaching, prisons, and puseyism; valentines, victoria crosses, and vaccination; tea fights, tennis, and transubstantiation; magic lanterns, minstrel shows, and mioramas; music-halls, melo-dramas, and melodeons; antimacassars, moonlighting, and mid-wives; fashions, fenians, and fancy-fairs; musk, money, and monarchy:

Where every shrubbery in every pet-of-heaven house held a monkey, stuck there by Darwin, a monkey that stretched out a sudden paw to rip a bit of fragrant lace from the petticoat of any lady stooping down to pull a sprig of lavender, sending the ladies flying with fear into the churches to pull and pull the bells, making all the clergy run like hell into the pulpits to yell Peace, be still, for there is nothing revealed that cannot be hidden away; and so queen and consort, peers, clergy, commons, and people buried deep this monkey bone of our bone and flesh of our flesh, thick edge of the wedge, whereby millions of years were thrust between themselves and other people and God, jerking away a sense of nearness so obliging that it put a latch-key into the pocket of every Catholic and Protestant for a private gateway into the kingdom of heaven.

And the woman in child-pain clenched her teeth, dug her knees home into the bed, became a tense living mass of agony and effort, sweated and panted, pressed and groaned, and pressed and pressed till a man-child dropped from her womb down into the

world; down into a world that was filled up with the needs,
ambitions, desires, and ignorances of others, to be shoved aside,
pressed back, beaten down by privileges carrying godwarrants of
superiority because they had dropped down into the world a
couple of hours earlier. The privileges were angry and irritable;
but the round-bellied, waggle-headed, lanky-legged newborn
latecomer kicked against the ambitions, needs, and desires of the
others, cleared a patch of room for itself from the trampling feet
and snapping hands around it; was washed, napkined, and fed;
added on three, four, or five ounces of weight every week, taking
most of it from its mother and a little from the life around it;
and so grew gradually, and gathered to itself the power, the
ignorance, the desire, and the ambition of man.

Forty years of age the woman was when the boy was three, with
hair still raven black, parted particularly down the middle of the
head, gathered behind in a simple coil, and kept together by a
couple of hairpins; a small nose spreading a little at the bottom;
deeply set, softly gleaming brown eyes that sparkled when she
laughed and hardened to a steady glow through any sorrow, deep
and irremediable; eyes that, when steadily watched, seemed to
hide in their deeps an intense glow of many dreams, veiled by the
nearer vision of things that were husband and children and home.
But it was the mouth that arrested attention most, for here was
shown the chief characteristic of the woman: it quivered with
fighting perseverance, firmness, human humour, and the gentle,
lovable fullness of her nature. Small strong hands, hands that
could slyly bathe a festered wound or scour a floor – wet cloth
first, then the brush soap-foamed, tearing the dirt out, then wet
cloth again and, finally, the dry cloth finishing the patch in back
and forward strokes and twisting circles of rhythmic motions. A
sturdy figure carried gracefully and with resolution; flexible, at
peace in its simple gown of black serge, with its tiny white frill
round the neck that was fair and unwrinkled still. A laugh that
began in a ripple of humour, and ended in a musical torrent of
full-toned mirth which shook those who listened into an irresis-
tible companionship.

And all this was seen, not then, but after many years when the
dancing charm and pulsing vigour of youthful life had passed her
by, and left her moving a little stiffly, but still with charm and still
with vigour, among those whose view of the light of life had
dimmed and was mingling more and more with a spreading
darkness; and vividly again, and with an agonized power, when

she was calmly listening to the last few age-worn beats of her own dying heart.

This had been the shake of the bag, and she knew that she would never have another child. She had had seven before – three boys and one girl living, and one girl and two boys dead. Each of the two dead boys had been called John, and her husband said that this last boy's name was to be John, too. She thought for a long time. It seemed to be a challenge to God to do that, to give the name of John to this new child. He was undoubtedly her last child, and she wanted him to live. The two born before that had been called John, had died, died of the same thing, died of croup.

She remembered how the first had died, died before she knew he was dying, died of croup. Then after another two years, another boy had come, and they had called him John. Her husband had said we must have a boy called John. Her husband with doggedness and she with misgiving had called him John. He had been vigorous enough, and had sprawled and kicked a twelve-month way into the world, when suddenly he seemed to get a feverish cold, a little cough, and a watering from the eyes. Then one evening on her way to his bedside she stopped, frightened by the sound of a hard choking cough. Prompted, at first, by fear to go away and refuse to hear, she went slowly through the room to the bed, and found him struggling from under the clothes, his arms moving wildly, his eyes staring, his face bluish, and his breath coming in short and cluttering gulps. She remembered that, in a panic, she had slapped a bonnet on her head and a shawl round her shoulders, had gathered the little body into a blanket, rushed out of the house, down the street, climbed into a passing cab, calling on the driver for God's sake to drive fast, fast, fast to the Abercorn Hospital.

—He can do it, if He wants to, she murmured in the cab all the way to the hospital, He can save the child; the other died, but this won't, this won't, won't, won't die. With a thought, God can take this choking lump from the little child's throat, and give him back his healthy happy breathing.

And the child got it harder and harder to get its breath, and the choking effort of the child to breathe whistled agony into her brain. She tore up the steps of the hospital, rang and rang and rang the bell, pushed past into the hall when the door was opened.

—Get the doctor, she said, pantingly, to the porter, get the doctor, get him quick to look at this child of mine quick, to treat this little child of mine, quick please, for he's dying, but can easily be saved if the doctor comes quick, bring me quick to the doctor or let him come quick to me here, there's no time to be lost, for it's the croup he has, and he's dying fast and will be dead if the doctor doesn't come quick, go and get him, go and get him, go, go and get him quick.

And she had walked up and down, down and up the hall, waiting, waiting for the porter to bring the doctor, afraid to look at the convulsed little face hidden under the shawl, and trying to hear less clearly the choking cadences of the shivering cough shaking the little figure sheltering in her arms.

The porter came back and told her that the doctor was attending a patient, and would be with her in a brace of shakes.

—This child can't wait, she answered threateningly; and he must be treated at once, the other patient must wait, but this child is choking and may die any moment, man; where's the doctor, and I'll bring the child to him myself?

She ran over to a passing nurse, held the child firmly to her bosom with one hand, and caught the nurse's arm tightly with the other.

—A doctor for this child, nurse, before it's too late, she pleaded, for this child that's dying with the croup. See, his face is getting black with the choking; nurse, quick, please, for he's getting less and less able to breathe, and I'll hold the hospital responsible for anything that happens to him; for I've been left here waiting too long, too long, and the child choking, without any attention; for it's the croup he has, and I'm afraid he's dying.

The nurse led her gently over to a side of the hall, and pressed her gently down on a seat.

—Sit down, on the bench there, sit down, she said softly, and I'll get the doctor to see the child. She had shouted after the departing nurse, This'll be my second Johnny that'll have died of the croup, if you don't hurry.

And again she had asked God to help and hurry the doctor so that her child wouldn't die in her arms.

Suddenly she held her breath as she heard a curious rasping sigh, and her bosom shuddered as she felt the little body in her arms give a mighty straining stretch; then she knew that what she wanted to keep away had come to her; and she pressed to her breast a dear possession that had emptied itself of life. She had sat, stricken dumb, motionless for some moments, then she had laid the little form down on the bench, and looked at the rigid little face tinged with purple; she had closed the shades of the staring eyes, placed two pennies on the lids, and bound them there with her handkerchief.

Some time after, the doctor, followed by the nurse, came up the corridor, and she had called out to them, You came too slow, for God came quicker and took the child away. The doctor had come over to her, put his hand over the child's little heart, murmuring, Yes, he's gone; but no skill of ours could have saved him. And she answered bitterly, None of you broke your heart trying.

She had taken up the dead form in her arms, and said to the nurse and to the doctor, Open the door, now, that I may pass out, and leave you all in peace.

The doctor had laid his hand on her arm to say, You can't carry the dead child home with you like that; better leave him in the deadhouse for the present.

She had answered hotly, I will bring him home, and lay him out at home, and bury him from the home where he lived and played out his little life, and let whosoever will try to stop me.

They had opened the door, and as she passed out the nurse whispered, Have you got your cab fare? but she passed out without giving the thanks of an answer.

She nodded to a cab on the rank opposite; when it came over, she got in carefully, hugged the body to her breast for a few moments, then laid it down on the seat opposite, stretched the little legs straight, placed the arms tightly down the body, instead of folding them over the breast in the form of a cross as the Roman Catholics were in the habit of doing. She kept her hand with a loving pressure on the breast of the child, for the jolting of the cab over the stones of the street made the body lie uneasy on the seat. She hadn't cried, but she pressed her lips tightly together, and with the fingers of one hand dressed the fair hair neatly back from the dead-cold forehead. This would be another painful halting-place in her own and her husband's life. All usual things would stand still till this was over. Had she come in a victoria, a brougham, or a landau, all the bells in the hospital would have been ringing attendance on her. Even the food eaten by her and her husband would taste of sorrow till his body had been buried, and they felt that their little boy's soul was getting accustomed to God.

In the agitated state of her mind she tried to think of a portion of the Bible that would soften a little the hardness of her trouble.

She could think only of the widow, the widow's little son, and of Elijah. But there was no Elijah now to take this little son out of her arms, and stretch himself upon the boy, call three times upon the name of the Lord, and bring the living soul back again to the dead body – only a doctor who had delayed his coming, and a deadhouse.

Such a bright little youngster as he was too. Everybody admitted that he was far ahead of most children of his age. Peculiar look in his eyes that showed intelligence. Curious quick and alert manner he had. Not much movement in him now. In her heart she was glad that he had been baptized, though the Roman Catholic idea of original sin was ridiculous and laughable. Imagine that little child stretched there consigned to hell, or limbo, or whatever they called it, because he hadn't had a drop of water sprinkled over him. Terrible religion to believe in a thing like that.

She heard, subconsciously, the playing of a band and the sound of many voices, and the steady regular sound of many marching feet. Then the cab stood still. The sound of the band got louder, and the sound of the voices and the marching feet came close. The driver got down from his seat, and stood beside the window of the cab.

—We'll have to go a roundabout way, he said, or wait here till God knows when, for a fly couldn't get through a crowd like this, much less an animal like a horse. They're bringing Charlie Stewart Parnell to the Rotunda with bands and banners, where he's to speak on the furtherance of Home Rule for Ireland. That band knows how to rattle out The Green Above the Red, I'm telling you. They've the best belly-drummer in the whole bloody country. My God Almighty, looka the way that fella's twirlin' the sticks! He's nothin' short of a genius at it.

Then she heard a rolling roar of cheers breaking out that held on for many minutes, the cab-driver waving his hat, and yelling out a fierce and excited approbation.

—That's Parnell himself that's passed, he said, when the cheering had subsided, Ireland's greatest son. I'd sell me hat, I'd sell me horse an' cab, I'd sell meself for him, be Jasus, I'd nearly sell me soul, if he beckoned me to do it. He's the boyo'll make her ladyship, Victoria, sit up on her bloody throne, an' look round a little, an' wondher what's happenin'.

She shrank back into the shadow of the cab, and looked at her dead child lying stiff on the seat-cushions, stained with spots of tobacco and smeared with spilled beer. She waited dumbly for the crowds to pass, longing to get home so that she might bring her husband within the compass of her sorrow.

—The soldiers are all confined to barracks, went on the cab-driver; an' it's just as well, for we're in no humour to be lookin' calmly on at the red coats on their backs and the crowns an' roses in their caps, noddin' misrule and persecution to the whole of us. Parnell has taken from England's strength so that his name stands big in Ireland, an' that God'll keep him sthrong's a prayer that keeps on in an echo dying away to begin in a powerful prayer again.

—I happen to be a loyal woman, she had said, with all my hopes gathered round the person and the throne, though, she thought, it hasn't rendered me much, it hasn't rendered me much. God Almighty, heavenly Father, you might have spared this little son of mine.

She had been a good woman; she had done her daily round and common task, tainted with only a little grumbling; she had worshipped Him in spirit and in truth; she had held fast to the faith once delivered to the saints; her husband knew his Bible well, most of it in the letter and all of it in the spirit; always arguing and proving popery was dangerous and repugnant to the plain word of scripture; that the sinner could always go straight to God without passing round saints or angels, there being only one mediator between man and God, the man, Jesus Christ. After all, He might have let this occasion of the chastening of those whom He loveth slide aside from the smiting of her harmless innocent baby.

Or, even if He had taken the little boy when the boy was at home with his father and mother; or in the hospital with the doctor striving to help him, and the nurse watching the failure of the doctor's skill; it would have been more bearable and better than to have wriggled into death in her arms, and go off, with no one she knew near enough to give her the pity of relationship or friendly company.

—Now, suddenly said the cab-driver, the procession's endin' an' we can follow on, crawlin' cautiously at the tail-end of it.

He jumped up on his seat again, said yep to the horse, and went on slowly, halting now and halting again whenever anything intervened to interfere with the progress of the crowd who marched with pride and defiance, carrying in their midst the Leader who symbolized the body, spirit, and soul of the marching people. On crept the cab following hundreds of flaming torches reddening the excited faces of the marchers, the glow forming a huge smoky golden halo above the heads of the crowd. On crept the cab after the mighty yellow and green banners that each section of the crowd carried, the bands playing with a reckless crash and blare that, for many, fashioned drab thoughts of risk into a vision of men gathering to the trumpet-call of God.

Slipping, at last, down a side turning, the cab passed through several streets, and then stopped outside her door. Stepping out of the cab, she bent down and in, lifted the little stiff shawled figure in her arms, and asked the driver the fare. One an' a tanner, he said, and added that he hoped there wasn't much wrong with the child, ma'am. Then as he caught sight of the little face as it slid from the fold of the shawl, he ejaculated, Jasus Christ, the kid's dead!

He took the one and sixpence silently, lifted his hat, mounted to his seat, gathered the reins in his hands, and quickly cantered away.

She brought the body in, laid it down on the bed, then went out to her husband. He had looked at her, and murmured, Oh, is he worse, then? They had gone into the room together; she had pulled off the handkerchief tied over the face of the little child, and the two of them had gazed at the rigid little face silently and long.

—He has stretched a lot, she said.

—When did he go? he asked.

—In the hospital, lying in my arms, before one came to look at him, she answered.

She felt his arm round her, pressing tenderly.

—Dear Sue, he said, my poor dear Sue.

She had quivered a little, and murmured brokenly, He is the second Johnny that has been taken from us. Perhaps we didn't do well, when the first died, to call the second one John.

The circling arm tightened round her. She looked up at him, and saw his face form into a fresh and firmer tightness.

—Sue, he answered, we may yet have another child; that other child may be a boy; if we should have another child, and that other child should be a boy, we shall call his name John.

FIRST THE GREEN BLADE

THE THIRD Johnny, passing by the doggedness of his father and the superstitious anxiety of his mother, crawled a little farther into life. Delicately and physically undecided, he crept along. He has a stout heart, said his mother, the first five years are the worst, and, if he can get over them, God is good. With ever-verdant care, she watched him. She gave him his full share in the attention she had to pay to others, and the little leisure she snapped now and again from her household work was crowded with thoughts for Johnny's fuller and firmer settlement in the world. She had nursed him viciously through an attack of bronchitis when he had made but a six months' journey into the world; but no cough had lingered, and he ran about and laughed like other children; so where there was life there was hope, and God was good. The others murmured, it's Johnny here and Johnny there; but she reminded them that they were well into the thick of the world, while Johnny had only started. But God had not forgotten, and the trial was sent at last.

When he was five, his mother noticed a look of torment in his eyes. They harboured a hot and torturing pain that made him rub them vigorously, and cry long and wonderingly in the sunny hours of the day and through the long dark hours of the night. Small, hardy, shiny, pearly specks appeared on the balls of his eyes. He began to dread the light; to keep his eyes closed; to sit and moan restlessly in the darkest places he could find. For many weeks life became a place of gloom, streaked with constant flashes of pain. They folded a big white heavy handkerchief into a bandage, and wound it round his head, like a turban, to guard his eyes from the touch of whatever sunlight tottered in through the little windows of the little house.

Johnny had no sense of danger, no fear of any possible loss, no idea that something was happening which would mean agony for many years, and be a persistent and inscrutable handicap to him throughout the rest of his life. He felt only a curious resentment that he wasn't as others of his age were, and as he himself had been, able to run, to shout, to rejoice when the sun shone; to go to bed tired and full of sleep when the sun went down, getting strength for another and another chance to run, to laugh, and to rejoice in the middle of the sun's encouragement towards

merriment and play. It was a time when eye troubles were
thought little about, nor any weakness of the body when the
weakness didn't pin the body to the bed. Pennyworths of golden
ointment, zinc ointment, zinc and rosewater were the eye
remedies of the people, except when an eye was cut asunder by an
accident.

Such things as smallpox, typhoid fever, diphtheria, and scarlet
fever were the only blights that stimulated the doctors to rush
about, hair-tossed and coatless, to blow on the bugles of alarm,
forcing the people to close up their houses, seal themselves away
from the fresh air, and burn sulphur in their rooms, filling the
place with fumes, like incense rising from an altar in hell.

It was a time when every infant on some day in each passing
week had to be filled with castor-oil, and dosed with syrup of
squills, first having their chafed buttocks rubbed with stuff that
had the grittiness of powdered steel. A time when only a few brave
men separated themselves from this dung-like heap of ignorance,
and, in a few bare corners of the world, sought to learn more about
the mysteries of life, disease, and death, rather than seek safety
with the crowd that ambled and arsed its way easily and nicely
about through the hours of life; life under cocked hats, red
gowns, and black gowns, droning out the laws of men; life under
snowy surplices droning out the laws of God; and life under silk-
scented gowns droning out the laws of love.

So his eyes grew worse and the pain waxed sharper. His mother,
from an eggcupful of zinc and rosewater, with a tiny piece of rag,
bathed them three times a day, and at night smeared the lids
heavily with golden ointment taken from a penny box; but no
strength crept into the weakness and no softness into the pain.
The others, irritated by his crying, warned his mother that the
habit of crying would only make them worse, and told the boy
that his eyes were beginning to look like two burnt holes in a
blanket. His mother, recommended to it by a neighbour, applied
a poultice of sodden tea-leaves, a remedy that had once cured the
neighbour's child of a horrid redness of the lids; but no strength
crept into the weakness, nor did any softness creep into the pain.

Then a friend of one of his brothers said that if the boy's head
was plunged into a bucket of cold water and the eyes held open
beneath the water for five minutes or so at a time, several times
a day, this would bring hardiness to the most stubborn weakness
any eye ever had. Johnny was seized and, screaming protests,
his head was pushed down into a bucket of dead cold water till

the eyes were underneath; and he was vehemently called upon to open his eyes, open his eyes, damn it, couldn't he open his eyes, and let the water get at them. When he struggled, cold and frightened, they pushed him farther down till the water flowing through his nostrils gurgled down his throat, almost choking him, leaving him panting for breath, shivering and wet, in the centre of reproaches and abuse because he had kept his eyes fiercely closed underneath the water. Threats, thumps on the back, failed to make him promise that he would open his eyes under the water; and all round him despaired of the remedy, saying it was waste of time if he wasn't made to open his eyes under the water, not worth a curse so long as he keeps his eyes shut; if he goes blind, it'll be his own fault; while Johnny stood there obstinately, with his head bent down on his breast, shocked and shaken, the water from his saturated hair trickling, by way of his neck, steadily down his back, and by way of his cheeks, dripping down to his belly; crying over and over again, The bandage, the bandage, put the bandage over me eyes again, they're paining me terribly. And so no strength crept into the weakness, neither did softness creep into the pain.

Then they all forsook him, saying, Leave him to the pain, then, since he won't do the one thing that will do him good; he has been pampered too much for anyone to pity him. Only his mother harassed her mind for help; only she, with deep pity and un-breakable patience, stood between him and the chance that his sight might go, leaving him helpless in the hands of man and no nearer to God; only she raised the banner of fear for him in the face of everyone she met, and pried everywhere for assistance to save him from the evil of perpetual darkness.

One day his mother suddenly remembered that she had heard a sister make mention of a kid having sore eyes going to some place or another, getting treatment, and getting well again. So out she set with the bandaged Johnny to see her sister, going a third of the way by tram and the rest by foot, to a low-roofed white-washed cottage stuck in a place by the back o' beyond in the Tenters' Fields, where they used to bleach the linen, over by Dolphin's Barn. There she and Johnny had a nice tea with home-made scones well warmed in the oven, melting in your mouth before you'd time to sink your teeth in them.

—Johnny's a case for a doctor, said the sister. You cart him off to St Mark's Ophthalmic Hospital for Treatment of Diseases of the Eye and Ear, that's in Lincoln Place, just beside the back enthrance of Trinity College. Everyone who isn't a pauper pays sixpence for a ticket, lasting for a month, with attendances three days in each week. Go on Monday, or Wednesday, or Friday, for on any one of these days you're sure to see Mr Story, who's the greatest of living men, knowing how, when, and where to fiddle with the eyes. It's safer to go early at nine if you want to get away quick, for it's getting more and more crowded every day, an' everyone has to take his turn; an' sometimes the doctors take a long time over a case, especially if it is an ear; and you can do nothing better than to bring Johnny there to hear what they say and to see what they can do for him.

And Johnny's mother got up, and thanked her sister, and said she'd have to be goin', but she'd bring Johnny to the hospital the first thing on Monday morning. And Johnny's mother's sister kissed him, and put a new penny quietly into his pocket, and said God wouldn't let him lose the sight of his eyes.

Then they departed, and, going through The Liberties, came to where Meath Street meets Thomas Street. There Johnny and his mother took a tram which sailed along merrily as far as the top of Cork Hill, and was there stopped by a crowd.

—It's the Ball, said the conductor, the Vice-Regal Ball with all the gulls o' Dublin gawkin' at the notabenebilities flockin' in to a fine feed an' a gay night in Dublin Castle.

—An' we'll be stuck here for ages, said a woman in the corner.

—We might as well have a decko at the grandeur that's keeping the country going, before Mister Parnell and his poverty-stricken dupes reduce us all again to a state of nature, said a genteel-looking man, with a watery mouth and a drooping moustache, sitting in the centre of the car, as he got up from his seat, and climbed down nicely on to the street.

—The day isn't far distant, said the conductor, when that gent that's just gone out'll doff his hat to another tune, or hang as high as Gilderoy; and leaning against the entrance to the tram, he hummed:

Oh, black's your heart, Clan Oliver, and coulder than the clay!
Oh, high's your head, Clan Sassenach, since Sarsfield's gone away!
It's little love you bear us, for the sake of long ago,
But hould your hand, for Ireland still can strike a deadly blow.

Johnny's mother got up, climbed down, and helped Johnny off the tram.

—Little Protestant boys should never listen to Fenian songs, she said to him; whenever you hear one, you must always murmur God Save the Queen to yourself.

Mingling with the crowd, they couldn't get out of it, and were carried along to a spot almost beside the entrance to the Castle where they found Ella and Archie gleefully watching the glory passing in to the fine feed and the gay-grand night of dancing.

—Come here, in front of me, said Ella, pulling Johnny beside her, and stay quiet and stand still and don't stir, till we see all the lovely lords and ladies tripping and trotting into the Castle.

—I'm bringing Johnny to a special hospital for the eyes and ears only, on Monday morning, said Johnny's mother to Archie.

—He ought to be brought somewhere, said Archie, for his crying by day and his crying by night is becoming more than most of us can stick.

—When I was on me way along, said Ella, the carriages stretched from the Castle Yard, down Dame Street, Westmoreland Street, through Sackville Street, and right into Cavendish Row. Oh, look at the oul' fogey in blazing blue, with a pile of gold braid on his chest, and a slip of a girl nearly on his knee, in that brougham just gone by us.

—Stuck fast in the arms of a pleasure he'll never feel, murmured Archie.

—I'll get Johnny up early on Monday, said the mother, and bring him to the hospital, whatever happens.

—Th' oul' fogey, said Ella, had a jewelled star hanging be a blue ribbon in the middle of the pile of gold braid – Order of the Garter, I suppose.

—Not the Garter, said Archie, for only a few, outside of princes of the Royal Blood, get the Garter. Mantles of purple velvet lined with silk the knights wear. Musta been the Order of St Patrick you seen, for it has a blue ribbon an' the motto, *Quis Separabit*; but if they'd only known the right way to do things here they'd have gone the whole hog an' made the ribbon green.

—I wish I hada known about this hospital before, said the mother, for Johnny might have been saved a lot of pain by gettin' attention in time.

—Looka' the kids over there, ejaculated Ella, all in their bare feet an' without a flitther on them. Shame for their mothers to let them look on at a sight like this.

—The whole thing gives a great amount of employment, said

Archie encouragingly. Even the photographers benefit, for the whole crowd get their photos taken after the ball is over, after the break of morn, after the dancers leaving, after the stars are gone, to be able to look back at themselves in their old age in their gala get-up.

—Sixpence a month, with three visits a week, isn't a lot to charge, if they can do anything at all for Johnny, murmured the mother.

—Some of the dresses of the duchesses cost hundreds an' hundreds of pounds, said Ella.

—And sweet goodbye to the kingdom, the power, and the glory, if we get Home Rule, added Archie.

—Well, we'll see what they can do for Johnny on Monday, said his mother, putting her hand protectingly on his head.

—Here's a crowd of them coming, said Ella excitedly, here's a great crowd of them coming quick and fast, thick and last, comin' thro' the rye, comin' thro' the streets, comin' to

The Castle Ball

As far as the eye could see or the mind wander, the Dublin streets were a running stream of landau, victoria, coupé, brougham, coach, and cab forcing a way to the Castle Yard, each vehicle heavy with the precious bodies and souls of earls, barons, bishops, ambassadors, judges, privy councillors, right honourables, most honourables, honourables, archdeacons, spiritual pastors, and masters and mistresses,
  Sailor goo-goos in blue, white, and gold,
  Soldier goo-goos in black, scarlet, and gold.
Top-heavy and stern in shakoo or busby, in helmet or bearskin,
  finished off with a hackle or ball, a spike or a plume,
not a speck of the dust of the earth on their skin or their
  clothes,
all the others cock-hatted, knee-breeched, and sword-girded,
exhilarant all on their way to their master,
with their ladies in silks and their ladies in satins,
or swathed in poplin all finely brocaded,
and wearing rich lace from Valenciennes city,
made haughty by living through hundreds of years,
straight to the core of the Castle they streamed,
or they sauntered at ease talking lightly of things that had
  passed or were present,

while soldiers saluted or stood to attention,
stood stiff to attention,
busy blasting the lot though their lips never moved,
stood blasting the stir that kept them alert standing stiff to
    attention,
while heavy police in dull blue and bright silver
and glossy belts buckled too tight on their bellies,
moved hither and thither all puffing and sweating,
encircling the flurried showpieces of men,
escorted and sorted the highly-priced rabble across the
    courtyard,
safe into the arms of fine far-seeing footmen
all padded in plush, yellow, red, and plum-coloured,
satin coats of cerise and warm brown on their backs,
fatted calves swathed tight in the whitest of silks,
and their heads periwigged, merriwigged, and beribboned,
whose bowing shoved all the gay sheep to a shepherd,
a man made by God in a hurry and tired and eager to get the
    thing over and done with,
new-fashioned with orders by man and made mighty,
with his ugly shape tailored away in a suit of the best of black
    velvet,
knee-breeches he wore,
and his snowy-white shirt had a rainbow of ribbons,
a sword with rare gems in the hilt hanging cold by his side,
with his funny face pale with importance and pride,
he modelled a tentative waddle into a parade,
he toddled along with a fair rod in his hand,
like a message from God he came back and went forward,
and gestured and motioned and beckoned them on,
with O'Donnell then, fight the good fight again,
sons of Tirconnell, all valiant an' thrue,
make the false Saxon feel Erin's avengin' steel,
on for your counthry, O'Donnell aboo,
(someone was singing round a near corner),
went forward and backward and beckoned them on,
ambassadors bringing fair words from far lands,
and blue-hooded barons with hell-baiting bishops,
having after them tails of archdeacons and deans,
with everything honourable, hot with excitement,
trotting tense and refined neck and neck with the judges,
aligned with the elegant sailor geegaws and soldier gawgews,

with their ladies in poplins and satins and silks,
armed with flounces and fans, followed after the rod
held high in the hand of the figure dressed up
in the richly-made suit of the best of black velvet,
followed firm
on a fine and immaculate carpet of crimson,
on, Marmion, on, up the stairs, on again,
and on and on up to the room where the throne was,
where the man in the suit of the best of black velvet
litanied loud the great names of the land,
and the men bending low bent down to their bellies,
while the flounces and fans bent waist and bent knee,
slid back on a heel sinking into a curtsey as brave as you like,
in honour of kingship viceregally there,
and standing agley and agloom on the throne,
the well-pampered minds of the flounces and fans all fevered
    with fear,
for the slightest false movement in showing how well
they knew how to support and comport themselves there
in front of the blue-gartered leg of a goose,
would shatter and shame them,
in front of a blue-gartered leg of a goose,
whose little bow swallowed big bows and the bending.
Having learned fitly sless blessed to give than it is to receive,
the ambassadors wise and the archdeacons holy,
with all the great barons and judges most upright,
followed hard by all the right and left honourables,
tacked on to the soldier and sailor gewgaws,
hurried past hurried fast hurried on to the ballroom,
where the silks and the satins flourished flounces and fans,
in the chippendaled, palm-spotted, chandeliered ballroom,
there the couples were welting away on the floor in a giddy
    gavotte,

> *My wife and I lived all alone*
> *in a little log hut we called our own,*

legs lift and look from flying flounces and a bustle on each
    backside bounces,

> *She loved gin and I loved rum,*
> *I tell you what, we'd lots of fun,*

while the right reverends, most reverends, and reverends sadly mouched round the chippendaled, sheratoned banks of the room, spiritually dead to the rollicking music of the red-coated, gold-braided, heavy-epauletted, tight-trousered military band making things merry and bright for the world,

> *Ha, ha, ha, you and me,*
> *little brown jug don't I love thee,*

while those known for their learned and godly conversation meandered along by the margin of the river of jollity veiling a holy vision against the sight of baroneted eyes peering and judicial eyes glancing and right and left honourable eyes gleaming and soldier and sailor eyes sparkling at the view of bare shoulders and sweet and white breasts getting bigger and bigger as they popped in and popped out from the bantering bodices worn by the right lovely damsels aglow with delight at the shame of showing their partners nice things to be remembered when the glee was over,

> *Oh I could ride a ride a ride a ladie,*
> *a certain ladie,*
> *in a lilac-scented room all warm and shadie,*
> *hooks and eyes will come undone with little aidie,*
>
> *Ha, ha, ha, you and me,*
> *little brown jug don't I love thee,*
>
> *On a sofa all but everything displaydie,*
> *Venus showing off the sweet tricks of her tradie,*
> *working hotly haydie, hotly hotly haydie,*
> *we'd soon make something quick that wouldn't fadie,*
> *yes I could ride a ride a ride a ride a certain ladie,*

lifting legs from flying flounces all the time the spiritual pastors and masters moped restlessly under the palm trees thinking dumb spiro speriodically towards the tempered truth that the one way to keep their flocks any distance from the danger of hellfire was to persistently hold a red-hot poker tight to their arses, while outside under the Milky Way and the Pleiades, the landau, brougham, victoria, coupé, coach, and cab drove through the Castle gates into the yard paved with good and bad intentions, like the road to hell, defended with horse, foot, and artillery, courtyard of England's faithful garrison in eirinn of the saints and scholars and scuts and the glorious round towers and the dear little shamrock so green with the wolf-dog lying down and the harp without the crown and the sun-burst of Ireland between ourselves, be Jasus, the counthry is in a nice way between the two of them, while heavy policemen in dull blue and bright silver, and leather belts round their waists, buckled tight over their bellies, moved hither and thither, sweated and puffed, escorted and sorted the gorgeous high-jinkers of Irish society carefully along to the narrow red way that led them safe into the arms of the figure, dressed up in a suit of the best of black velvet, who ushered them to the throne and to the one who sat upon the throne, like unto a jasper and sardine stone, having a rainbow round his feet like unto red rubies, white pearls, and blue sapphires, while from many elders having crowns on their heads, seated round the throne, proceeded the thundering of voices singing Hearts of oak are our ships, hearts of oak are our men, who always are ready, and steady boys, steady, for we'll fight and we'll conquer again, and again, the soldiers saluted and stood to attention, stood stiff to attention, blasting by God, though their lips never moved, the ravishing stir that kept them alert, standing stiff to attention, Until the day break and the shadows flee away, we ought to go now for the last lone cab has gone in and the gates are shut and darkened, while the dances of them that make merry cannot be seen, neither can the voices of them that make merry be heard any longer, linger longer Louisiana Lou, and now we're back to where we started, said Archie, as they streeled home.

Two more nights of misery limped slowly by for Johnny, sitting up in bed, squirming his body and grinding his teeth; while his mother, with an old topcoat round her shoulders, stood over him in the shadowy light of a candle, holding old cloths saturated with cold water to his eyes, trying to mollify the pain, her face white with suppressed sympathy whenever he implored her to do something to take the pain away, murmuring that the hospital would do all that and more for him, and that he had only to stick it for two more short days; and when many hours had crept slowly and ashamed away, exhaustion lulled the pain, the saturated head of the boy sank more deeply into the drenched pillow, his mother put an arm around him and hummed a hymn, There's a Friend for little children above the bright blue sky, a Friend who never changes, whose love will never die; our earthly friends may fail us, and change with changing years, this Friend is always worthy of that dear name he bears; and the two of them slumbered together.

THE HILL OF HEALING

AT HALF PAST eight in the morning, washed and dressed, with a thick handkerchief over his eyes, Johnny, helped by his mother, ate sparingly of his bread and tea, for he was soon to be given over to a power that could do many things to hurt and frighten him, and force him to suffer a fuller measure of pain.

He went down the street, holding his mother's hand, as slowly as he could, so that what was going to come to pass might not come too quickly. Opposite the end of the street, he heard a tram stop, and felt his mother lifting him inside and helping him on to a seat, and saying, if he was good and gave the doctor no trouble, she'd buy him a sponge cake, and they'd take the tram home again. The tram, pulled by patient, muscle-wrenched horses, jingled along, stopping now and again to take passengers on and let passengers off, each pull, to get the tram restarted, giving the horses a terrible strain. The conductor came along, with his money-bag and gleaming silver punch, and gathered the fares, tuppence for his mother and a half fare of a penny for him. He heard the punch ring with a clear shrillness as the conductor holed the tickets which were given to Johnny by his mother to hold, a red one for her, she said, and a yellow one for him; an' maybe you'll be able to look at them when we're comin' back, for the doctors may do you so much good that you may be able to fling the bandage off when we leave the hospital.

They got out at Westland Row, and his mother led him down Lincoln Place till they came to the hospital, a timid shabby-looking place, having a concrete path, with a few beds dotted with geraniums, before the entrance which wasn't any bigger than the two windows that would form the front of a grocer's shop. Over the big shop-like windows, in big letters, were the words, St Mark's Ophthalmic Hospital for Diseases of the Eye and Ear. Going inside, they found themselves in a long narrow hall, divided in two by a barrier of polished pine. At the upper end were two doors, one to let the patients in to the doctors, and the other to let them out when the doctors had finished with them for the time being. The hall was furnished with long, highly-polished, golden-coloured pitch-pine benches on which a number of men, women, and children were sitting, slowly moving up to the door leading to the room where the doctors were. Near the entrance was a huge stove, and near this stove was a table on which, like an offering on an altar, was a big book enshrining the details of the patients' names, homes, and occupations. At this table sat a big, heavy, stout man of sixty-five with a white beard, a short bulgy neck, an incessant cough, a huge head, the skull of which was bald and hard and pink and polished like the pine benches. He was called Francis.

Johnny's mother gave the details asked for – his age, where he lived, and that he suffered from a disease of the eyes; and when Francis was told that the boy's father was dead, he shoved the word orphan into the space required to denote the father's occupation. The sixpence was handed over, and they were given a ticket of admission which would also be used by the doctor to write down the prescribed remedies to be applied to the diseased eyes. These were made up and handed out to the patients at the dispensary, a little closed-in booth-like space with a sliding panel, stuck in a corner of the hall. They got, too, a large sheet fixed in a cardboard protector, having on it diagrams of the eye, so that the doctor could record the origin, nature, and progress of the ailment, to be filed and retained by the hospital for future reference. They sat down on the bench among the patients, and waited for their turn. The people were being admitted in batches of five or six at a time, the rest moving up nearer as the others went in. As they waited and moved up and waited, his mother read what was written on the ticket:

St Mark's Ophthalmic Hospital for Accidents
and Diseases of the Eye and Ear

—

Out-patients attending this Institution, under the care of
MR STORY
are to attend on
Mondays, Wednesdays, and Fridays
before ten o'clock
Each person (not a pauper) will pay sixpence for a
ticket which will last for one month from date of
issue. This Ticket must be kept clean, and presented
open at each visit, and preserved when the attendance ceases.

Johnny heard the people round him talking of their complaints, their pain, and their hopes of improvement.

—I have to go months yet, he heard a voice say, before there'll be any improvement. Steel chips in a foundry flew into me eye, an' they had to get them out with a magnet. They made me jump when they were doin' it, I can tell you.

—He had to cut the sthring, said a voice a little nearer, to separate the bad blind eye from the good one, an' now he's breakin' his arse to cut the blind one out altogether, sayin' that it's no use havin' a dead eye in your head; but I have me own opinion about that, for the dead one isn't so disfigurin', if you don't examine it too closely, so it 'tisn't.

—It's wonderful, murmured another voice, what a lot of things a man can do without, accordin' to the doctors.

—Some o' the buggers would give up the spendin' of the first night with a lovely woman he was after marryin' for a half-hour's hackin' at a man, said the first voice.

—The first real touch o' spring is comin' into the air at last, said a soft voice, a little lower down; in the people's park yesterday the main beds were a mass o' yellow daffodils. The whole time I was gettin' a mug o' tea an' a chunk o' bread down me, I was lookin' at them.

—Geraniums, red geraniums for me, said an answering voice, every time, every time.

—I don't know, I don't rightly know, answered the soft voice; to me, red geraniums or geraniums of any other colour seem to have a stand-offish look, always, while daffodils seem to welcome you to come in and walk about in the midst of them.

There was a moment's silence, then Johnny heard the second voice saying, maybe you're right, but I still hold to the red geraniums.

—See that man sittin' opposite, said a woman to his mother, have a glance at his ticket, and you'll see it's printed in red – don't look over too sudden – see?

—Yes, he heard his mother say, I see it's printed in red, while ours is printed in black. Why is that, now?

—Because he's a pauper, and doesn't, as we do, pay for his treatment.

Johnny felt a glow of pride. He wasn't a pauper, and he held the card of admission out so that all could see it was printed in black.

Suddenly they found themselves in the doctor's room, and a nurse made them sit down on a special bench to wait for Mr Story. It was a room full of a frightening light, for the whole north wall was a window from side to side, and from floor to ceiling. There was a ceaseless sound of instruments being taken from trays and being put back again. Tinkle, tinkle, tinkle, they went, and cold sweat formed on Johnny's brow. All round the wall terrible pictures of diseases of the eye and ear were hanging. A nurse, in a blue calico dress, with narrow white stripes, was hurrying here and there, attending to the doctors; and everywhere there was a feeling of quiet, broken by a man's moan, or by a child's cry, that made Johnny tense his body with resentment and resistance.

At last, Mr Story, a tall thin man, with a sharp face and an elegantly-pointed reddish beard, came over to them, and said shortly, bring the boy over to the window. Johnny was led over to the window, and the bandage taken from his eyes: the light, the light, the cursed, blasted, blinding light! He was seated on a chair; he was fixed between the doctor's legs; his head was bent back as far as a head can go; he could feel the doctor's fingers pressing into his cheek just below his eyes: the light, the light, the cursed, blasted, blinding light!

—Open your eyes, said Story, and look out of the window; go on, open your eyes, like a good little boy.

—Open your eyes for the doctor, Johnny, said his mother.

—Open your eyes, said Story, sharply, open your eyes, at once, sir.

But the cursed, blasted, blinding light flooded pain in through the lids, and he kept them tightly closed. His mother nervously shook his arm.

—Open your eyes, you young rascal, she said.

But he sat, stiff, firm, and silent, and kept them closed.

Story beckoned to two students. One of them held his head from behind the chair, the other held his arms, but still, firm, and silent, he kept them closed. His obstinacy forced them into fierceness; they took him out of the chair, while his mother, embarrassed, threatened him with all sorts of violence when she got him home. They stretched him, on his back, froglike, on the floor, students holding his legs, nurses holding his arms, while Story, kneeling beside him, pressed his fingers under his eyes firmly and gently, till with an exasperated yell, Johnny was forced to open them, and Story, from a tiny glass container, instantly injected into his eyes a tiny stream of what looked like cold water, which spread like a cooling balm over the burning ulcerated surface of his eyeballs.

Silently, then, he submitted to a fuller examination in a pitch-dark room, filled with little cubicles, in each of which a gas-jet flared; and from a mirror-like instrument strapped on the doctor's head, Story searched his inner eye for a fuller indication of the disease that took from his life the sense of sight in agony and sweat. After two hours of examination and treatment, Story returned to his desk, and beckoned to Johnny's mother to come over to him. She came, slowly and anxiously, and listened to what the doctor had to say.

—The boy will not be blind, he said, writing rapidly on the case-sheet, but getting him well's going to be a long job. Bathe the eyes regularly in water as hot as he can bear it, afterwards with a lotion they will give you at the dispensary. Most important of all, some of the ointment, as much as will fit on the top of your finger, is to be inserted underneath the lids – not on, mind you, but underneath the lids – every night and every morning; and the boy will have to wear a bandage for a long time. He is to be given nourishing food, and he is to take a teaspoonful of Parrish's Food, after each meal.

—Can he go to school, doctor? asked the mother.

—No, no school, he said snappily. His eyes must be given absolute rest. No school for a long, long time.

—If he doesn't go to school, sir, he'll grow up to be a dunce.

—Better to be a dunce than to be a blind man, said the doctor. The boy must be brought here on each Monday, Wednesday, and Friday till an improvement removes the necessity for attendance oftener than once a week. Get these remedies at the dispensary, he added, giving her the prescription, do all that I've told you, be patient, and don't let the boy go to school; and Mr Story, with his elegant white hands, his red pointed beard and his morning coat, hurried away, followed by a flock of students, to attend to another patient.

—Me eyes must be pretty bad, said Johnny to his mother, as she was being fitted out with ointment, lotion, syrup, and bandage, at the dispensary, when he won't let me go to school.

Not to have to go to school – that was a thought full of a sweet savour. No schoolmaster, no lessons, no wear and tear of the mind with reading, writing, and arithmetic. He was saved from being one of the little slaves of the slate and satchel.

—It won't be nice, he murmured to his mother, if, when I grow up, I amn't able to read and write, will it ma?

—No, said she, it would be terrible; but, please God, you'll soon be well enough to go, for it might easily be as well to be blind as not to be able to read or write.

Then a nurse heavily bandaged his eyes, and his mother led him forth from the hospital, having finished his first day with an Institution that was to know him so well in the future that the doors nearly opened of their own accord when they saw him coming.

HIS DA, HIS POOR DA

AND ALL this time and for many months before, he who was called Michael, the old man, his mother's husband, the father that begot him, was lying in a big horsehair-covered armchair, shrinking from something that everybody thought of, but nobody ever mentioned.

Out of Limerick he had come, walking the roads to find a job, and settle down in Dublin. Down in Limerick, a Catholic man had married a Protestant maid; all the children had been reared up in the thick of the Catholic religion; but the Catholic father had died when Michael was an infant, so his mother had taken the chance to bring up her last-born in the true Protestant faith once for all and once for ever delivered to the saints. When Michael had grown up into a young man, his mother had been taken up to heaven. Then his Catholic brothers and sisters began to quarrel bitterly with Michael over the things that Jesus said and the things that Jesus did and the meanings that were hidden in the things that Jesus did and Jesus said, and by all accounts, Michael had a pretty tough time of it. So one fine day, without as much as a goodbye or a kiss me arse to the rest of them, he set his face towards Dublin, and turned his back on the city of Limerick for ever and ever, amen.

> *Brandenburgh the ditch has crossed*
> *And gained our flank at little cost,*
> *The bastion's gone – the town is lost;*
>
> *Oh! poor city of Luimneach linn-ghlas.*
> *Out, with a roar, the Irish sprung,*
> *And back the beaten English flung,*

Till William fled, his lords among,
From the city of Luimneach linn-ghlas.

'Twas thus was fought that glorious fight,
By Irishmen, for Ireland's right --
May all such days have such a night
As the battle of Luimneach linn-ghlas.

Up he came to Dublin, and married Susanna, who became the mother of his children, with Johnny as the shake of the bag. He was known to the neighbours for many years in his simple suit, half-tall hat, and blackthorn stick, bringing home his two pounds, weekly, to his wife, like clockwork; liked by many, a little feared by all who knew him, having a sometime gentle, sometime fierce habit of criticism; and famed by all as one who spat out his thoughts into the middle of a body's face. A scholar he was to all, who was for ever poring over deep books, with a fine knowledge of Latin, and a keen desire that others should love learning for its own sake, as he did.

And here he was now reclining in a big horsehair-covered armchair, shrinking from something that everybody thought of, but no one ever mentioned.

A ladder on which he stood, it was said, had slipped from under him, and, in falling, his back had struck a chair, and his spine had been injured. Doctors came in by the door, examined him, asked him what was wrong; and he annoyed the doctors by replying that the doctor had been sent for to find out. The doctor ordered that the patient should be rubbed all over with fine lard, and then left, as wise as he was when he first came in. So the delicate sensitive face, fringed by a soft brown beard, grew paler and thinner day by day, the white shapely hands moved more restlessly over the rests on the chair, and the reading of his beloved books became a burden too heavy to bear. He wanted Ella to read Shakespeare to him, for Sue, his wife, wasn't much good at anything above Dickens (though she knew all about Falstaff); but Ella wouldn't, for Ella, studying to be a teacher, was too busy, and the dad, anyhow, had crept a little too close to the grave to be pleasant or interesting. And death was death and life was life and Ella was Ella.

There was a little more give and take in life, too, since his dominance had been confined to the armchair. The boys could stay out a little later; return, too, with a whiff of drink off their breath, and stand square-shouldered and proud-mannered in front of their mother, knowing that the probing eyes were dimming in the other room, and were trying to see through a darkness that buried in its silent blackness the coming call of God; and that lips that might have framed a message of scorn were now sadly forming messages claiming kinship with Jesus, son of man, and son of God, who came into the world to save sinners.

There was one comfort that, if he died, he would die in the midst of his books. There they were in the big bookcase, snug in a recess to the side of the fireplace. Marshalled tightly together, there they were, the books he used to read, pore, and ponder over: a regiment of theological controversial books, officered by d'Aubigné's *History of the Reformation*, Milner's *End of Controversy*, Chillingworth's *Protestantism*, holding forth that the Bible, and the Bible alone, is the religion of Protestants, with an engraving of the fat face of the old cod stuck in the front of it; Foxe's *Book of Martyrs*, full of fire and blood and brimstone, *Popery Practical Paganism, Was St Peter Ever in Rome?* having in it a picture of divines battering each other with books, and SS Peter and Paul, in the clouds of heaven, looking down and laughing at the fighters, actually saying, if pictures could speak, Go it, boys, give each other socks. Like inspection officers, the English Bible, the Latin Vulgate, and the Douai Testament stood pompously together, and, to the right, *Cruden's Concordance* acting as orderly officer; a neatly uniformed company of Dickens', Scott's, George Eliot's, Meredith's, and Thackeray's novels; Shakespeare's Works; Burns', Keats', Milton's, Gray's, and Pope's poetry; on the top shelf, six or seven huge volumes, like podgy generals, of *The Decline and Fall of the Roman Empire*; and leaning idly by their side was Locke's *Essay on the Human Understanding*; and a whole crowd of school books that had been used by the boys and Ella, with a number of camp followers consisting of prizes they had won at Sunday school, such as *I and Jesus with the Zulus*; *Little Crowns and How to Win Them*; *Boys and Girls of the Bible*; *Gospel Garlands for Little Girls*; *The Sieges of Gibraltar*; *From Crécy to Tel-el-Kebir*; while in the corner was a shy little book calling itself *Creation's Testimony to its God*; and locked away in a drawer, forbidden to be touched by anyone save the head of the house, lay a mysterious book which the father said confined the dangerous teaching of a Bishop Berkeley; and, mother added, was all about nothing being real, and that all things we saw were only images of our own ideas, and that such books were only to be read and thought of by minds big enough to understand that they were rubbish.

Her husband had spent most of his life among his books, and though it was nice to know that the whole neighbourhood respected your father as a great scholar, and at home with the Latin, said Ella, yet what use was it all when the time came for you to hand in your gun? Locke's *Essay on the Human Understanding* was all balls, said Mick, for the very look of the thing was enough to start you praying to God that the human mind would never become anything like what it was represented to be in the book.

Several times only, Johnny had come into touch with his father. When he was old enough to know about things, his father was ill, and he was bad with his eyes; and his father hated the thought that, because of his eyes, Johnny would grow up to be a dunce, a thing that was an abomination in the sight of the lord, his father, so the two seldom came together. Once when nobody was in the house, save his mother, and she busy in the sick room, he had been sent out to buy an ounce of Cavendish cut plug.

—The dunce will forget what he's been sent for before he's halfway there, his da had said, as his mother carefully fixed his cap on his head while his little body vibrated with anxiety and importance.

—No, he won't forget, said the mother, for he isn't quite the dunce you think he is, and bending down, she had whispered in his ear, now, remember, say it to yourself all the way to the shop, ounce of Cavendish cut plug, ounce of Cavendish cut plug.

And he had run swiftly and anxiously to the little shop three streets away, gripping closely the money in his little fist, murmuring rapidly, constantly, and breathlessly, ounce of Cavendish cut plug, ounce of Cavendish cut plug, ounce of Cavendish cut plug. Then he had run back as rapidly, anxiously, and breathlessly to his mother, who examined the little parcel carefully, and pronounced it to be good. She brought him in to his father so that he might deliver it himself, and his father took it from him silently and wearily, as he sat in his chair. Johnny stood with his head bent down, looking at the bony knees giving angles to the black trousers, and the small firm feet, thrust into slippers, nestling together on a small red and black rug stretched before the fire.

—Now, his mother said, expectantly, now you see, father, he didn't make any mistake after all.

Then the wasted sensitive hand left the arm of the chair, and

Johnny felt it resting on his head, as his father said softly and sadly, No, he is a brave little fellow, and his father's son.

Shy, without the power to raise his head to look at his father, Johnny left the room, joyous and triumphant, murmuring, ounce of Cavendish cut plug, ounce of Cavendish cut plug.

Once again, when the parlour door had been left open, Johnny, passing by, had ventured to peep into the room. There he was sitting stilly in the large gorse-hair horse-hair armchair, rimmed with mahogany, the armchair that, after his father had died, had fallen asunder. All that Johnny could see was a thin white wasted hand resting grimly on the arm of the chair, and a patch of intensely black hair beneath a cricket-cap made of red, white, and blue segments. There was his poor da, or, his father, as Johnny's mother spoke of him to his brothers and sister, sitting facing the fire, with the little coloured mermaid in a glass bowl on a little table to his right, and a picture of Queen Victoria in her coronation robes on the wall to his left.

He must have sensed the boy peering in at him, for the head in the cricket-cap suddenly turned, and the boy caught a frightening glimpse of a white, wasted, agony-lined face, jewelled with deep-set eyes now gleaming with appealing anger at the boy who was looking in at him. Johnny saw the blue veins swell in the delicate hand that rested on the chair, and his ears were shocked by the sound of the low weak voice trying to shout at him, Go away, go away, you, and shut the door at once – this is no place for little boys.

Johnny had closed the door quick, had run for his life through the hall out into the street, full of the fear of something strange, leaving his da, his poor da, shrinking from something that everyone thought of, but nobody ever mentioned.

HIS FATHER'S WAKE

ONE VERY cold morning Johnny's mother wakened him up, saying, Get up, Johnny, get up, me poor boy; there are many things to be done, and you must be washed, and take your breakfast a little earlier than usual.

He rubbed away some of the matter that clung to his eyes, and shivered in his thin shirt.

—Ugh, he muttered, it's cold, it's very cold.

—There'll be many a cold morning to face from this out, said his mother, as she helped him on with his trousers, and rearranged the crumpled bandage on his forehead. Tell Ella, she went on, to give you a clean bandage.

—Not Ella, he said, you, mother: Ella's rough, and Ella doesn't care.

—Ella will have to do it this morning, she said, for I have to stay with your poor father.

He groped his way to the kitchen, and Ella caught him by the arm, saying, Come on here, till I bathe your eyes and wash your face. She sponged the caked matter from the lids of his eyes in water as hot as he could bear, grumbling most of the time she was doing it.

—It won't be long now till you'll have no servants to be dancing attendance on you. Cuddling's over, now, and you'll have to fend for yourself.

She washed his face and neck with particular vigour, combed his hair determinedly, twisted and bound a fresh bandage round his left eye, buttoned a collar round his neck, fixed his coat on, and brushed it briskly.

—Now, she said, sit down, take your breakfast, and give God thanks you have it.

He sat down by the deal kitchen table, the top worn thin by continual scouring, which had a white loaf in the centre, a drop of butter in the middle of a plate, seemingly miles from the rim, a cup and saucer, and, on the hob, a brown teapot that sparkled with the reflection of the flames that shot up every second from a warm coal fire. Tom was standing moodily by the fire, with one elbow leaning on the mantelpiece; Archie was drumming softly with his fingers on the window that looked out into the backyard; and there seemed to be a curious silence in the house; a silence that flooded in and flooded out whenever a door was opened; a silence that made the whole house feel silent and solemn.

—Four minutes past three, this morning, said Archie, just said to the mother, put your arms round me, Sue, and before she had time to call anyone, he was gone.

—I'm glad, murmured Ella, that mother has decided on having a closed-in hearse, for people that are anything at all always use a closed-in hearse.

—We've got the ground in perpetuity, said Archie, and no one, bar ourselves, can ever be buried in it.

Something had run up against them, and had jolted them from one uncertainty into another. Not knowing exactly how to take it, they took it in silence; for the few words they said were invisible fingers pointing out the silence. They were harnessing, in ritual of word and manner, the disturbance and silence on to God, though His name was not mentioned. God would be present to help as long as they had to think of these things, for He was a very present help in time of trouble: Come in the evening, come in the morning, come when you're called, or come without warning.

The thing that had jolted them lay in the parlour, the little parlour, kept perpetually swept and garnished for visitors that demanded some ceremony, and were entitled to see all the best that the family had. The room with the horsehair-covered furniture, the polished mahogany cabinet, dainty little brackets, supported by little pillars, decorated with mirrors, that was called an overmantel; ecru lace curtains, girded in the middle with crimson knitted cords, on the windows. On a little table, by the window, a large glass bowl filled with clean water in which floated a coloured glass mermaid, with yellow hair, black spots for eyes, big breasts, with scarlet nipples on them, and a blue, yellow, and green tail, shaped like the tail of a fish. The mermaid had a golden comb in her hand, and she stared out of her glass bowl at all who came into the room and at all who went out of the room. Now her little black spots of eyes were staring at something that lay very still in a bed at the opposite side of the room. On the wall over the bed was a big picture of Lord Nelson Bound for Trafalgar's Bay, all his orders aglitter on his breast, and he stepping out like a whole man for his last scrap in this world. Beside him walked a man in a white beaver hat, green cutaway coat, and brown plush knee-breeches. He was looking up into Nelson's face with a look of worship for the great one who had inspired The boy stood on the burning deck whence all but he had fled, the flame that lit the battle's wreck shone round him o'er the dead; while with one hand the same man in the cutaway coat and the brown plush knee-breeches, in the same picture, pushed aside a stout enthusiastic fishwoman who was trying to get close to the sailor hero, wellaway and lack-a-day, on his last road to do battle for his England, home, and beauty. Facing Nelson on the opposite wall was a picture of Queen Victoria, all decked out in her coronation robes, with none of the fun and all of the pomp, power, wealth, and parade of her colonial and Indian empire peering out of her bulgy blue eyes.

Here in the same room, under the stare from the paper faces of Lord Nelson and Queen Victoria, protected by the rear-guard of his beloved books, lay Michael O'Casside from Limerick. Stretched out he lay, his firmly-closed eyes staring backwards, arms and hands lying straight down by his sides, his dark beard so neatly trimmed that there wasn't a hair astray, nicely folded up for heaven beneath a snowy sheet, a sharply-cut outline of stiffening flesh and bone: thought, education, toil, laughter, tears, sex, turned into dust and ashes.

Cold, stiff, and quiet the thing lay, while life outside hurried about settling everything for it, rushing to the registrar of deaths; going to leave an order for an open grave; selecting the coffin, heavy oak, with heavy brass plate and handles; hiring a four-horsed hearse; telling the clergyman the time of burial so that he would be on the spot to spread the rumour of the resurrection; letting people out who had seen the body and letting people in who hadn't; listening to and answering the murmur of questions.

—Hardly althered a bit although he was twelve and more months lying, but thank God that gave him a peaceful end to the end of it all, for he was a good man and quite happy now wherever he may be, sayin' that it was nothing short of hypocrisy to blame the romanists for veneratin' the relics of the saints when we ourselves snatched handkerchiefs an' tore them into shreds as sacred souvenirs because Moody and Sankey had wiped their brows and their noses in them after gassy speeches and holy serenades in the Rotunda or Christian Union buildings filled with souls packed like sardines together busy beseechin' that their sins bein' red like crimson might be made as white as snow, an' now when I look at him the nose seems a little thinner, no, yes just a shade, though you'd hardly notice it if you didn't look close from where I'm standin'; he simply put his arms round Sue's neck she says, says Dear Sue, dear dear Sue, sighed and stretched and stretched and sighed again a little, and went away where the good niggers go a little pale an' haggard-lookin', but she's bearin' up wonderfully under it all, was a cruel blow but God will lessen the knock in it in His own good time an' in His own peculiar way, for I nearly dropped when I heard her sayin' such a thing to a woman still weak with the first impressions after losin' her husband only a few moments before holdin' Sue's hand in a vicey way, out of place an' terribly ignorant, underminin' the sympathy simmerin' in your soul for the sorrow starin' you in the

face with her folds shall be full of sheep and the valleys shall stand
so thick with corn that they shall laugh and sing, makin' a conun-
drum of the connexion between what she was sayin' and the
mystery of the stiffness that's stretched out undher the snowiness
of the death linen, unheeding Sue telling her of the sore that
spread over the butt of his spine and the doctors looking anxiously
couldn't make it out having come quietly after he lay down on the
bed he's dead in now, following the giving under him of his legs
getting thinner an' thinner every day that passed by with Sue his
wife never ending tending to him, larding his limbs every night
regular in the hope of some movement coming into them out of a
doctor saying that you couldn't tell what would happen if you
tried hard enough, thinking of what she'd do if he died with an
unreared child clinging to her, and the gameness of him refusing
to have any clergyman near him in his last moments, holding on to
the fact there's no mediator between God and man save only the
man Jesus Christ, messing about trying to twist the thoughts of a
man to things of no account, slipping soft and slow into the arms
of Jesus like the winds that blow from the south sighing so soft
and low, whisper their secrets sweet, whisper and I shall know
that he never missed sending his children as regular as clockwork
to church, Bible class, and Sunday school, keeping them from
spoiling the sabbath by singing hymns in the twilight when the
lights were low and the flickerin' shadows softly come and go
whenever the weather stopped them from going to worship God
in His holy temple, showing that he was in favour of worshipping
in spirit and in truth wherever two or three are gathered together
in His name, hardening infancy into the ways of the Lord who is
the rock himself an' not Peter, at all, who forgot himself whenever
anything crossed the confidence and quietness of his mind by a
torrent of curses that must have made the hair of the other
apostles who weren't use to it stand on its end, listening to the
crowing of the cock as he warmed himself at the fire and hearken-
ing to the little maid saying that his voice showed plainly he
must have come from Galilee, hiding himself frantically away
from what he was, which is as bad as shoving on to show yourself
forth for what you're not, like that Katie Johnston over there,
trying to plunder attention from everyone round her with her
bustle so pronounced as to form a swell altogether too lavishly
extended over her behind, disturbing the gaunt and sober decency
of the forms and signs gathered together in a house that has a
stiff dead man lying in one of the rooms giving a species of

serenity even to the pictures of Nelson and Queen Victoria hanging on the walls, who came up from Ballina only a couple of years ago wearing the airs and graces of having lived in Dublin all her life, though a city-cut skirt on a pair of country hips only helps to accentuate the difference between them, with the dry cough and the red-glazed cheeks tellin' of a comin' dissolution that'll happen vividly in the full knowledge of the present generation which should recommend to her, if anything ought, the marrying of the lunatic asylum attendant who's a bit queer himself, coming into constant contact with the mad people, and her mother making much of him in season an' out of season an' Katie keeping him at arm's length when she finds him thrilled and panting with the saucy delusion of getting him to tie her shoe beneath a skirt lifted to show a leg fading deliciously up under a cloud of white fancy flounces, or fastenin' a brooch slyly sliding out of her breast, purposely done to let him fiddle longingly with her diddies, an' after a little while when he was hot an' full of a choky sensation, puttin' the pin back in its place herself an' tellin' him an' thankin' him that would do nicely, gigglin' up in his face when she saw that he had gone far enough to try an' tear off every stitch she was wearing and fling her flat on the floor in front of the eyes of all in the room, shy at the sight of fifty-four years of experience gesturin' in frantic emotions that were only the resuscitation of a withered imitation of youth's spring, and go for a woman young enough to be a daughter as old as possible for the man to have, though it's not easy to blame a supple-legged lassie of twenty-three for thinking twice before takin' on the dhry, unlively, lack-pressure embraces of an old cod controlled by his years from doing anything desperate in the way of fanciful lovemaking which are unsuitable considerations for the occasion here present with us, sitting as we now are pressing the hard seats of chairs with tender bottoms burnin' for something soft under them while we are waiting for the men to come with the coffin so that the dead man may be made snug and ready before he goeth to his long home far away from this one where he'll nevermore have a portion, nor in anything that is done under the sun we all hope'll be shining when the poor body's taking its last tour through the streets, following the horses wearin' a resigned and determined look on their faces of no turning back while they're pulling their little cargo of what was once a man like meself, though I'm really a woman an' different in every way after gettin' down me a dollop of tea, I'll thry to forge to the front in

the rush at the end of getting close to the clergyman doing the
needful at the rim of the grave makin' the best of a bad bargain
with God, tellin' Him of the words spoken by the mouth of His
own apostle that appearances didn't matter a damn and that death
had lost its sting and that the grave has been swallowed up in victory.

HIS FATHER'S FUNERAL

JOHNNY WATCHED the cabs coming into the street, eager to
pick up those who were going to his father's funeral: red cabs
with black linings, black cabs with yellow linings, green cabs with
red linings, and blue cabs with brown linings. The first stopped
near the house where his dead father lay, and the rest formed up
behind, one after the other, stretching like a string down the
street, waiting for the rush to come when the body would be
carried out to be packed into the hearse which hadn't arrived yet.
The drivers of the cabs dismounted from their seats and leaned
against the walls of the houses in twos and threes, forming a
grotesque, shaggy, lurching frieze on the face of the sun-mellowed,
rain-stained bricks of the houses. A crowd of friends and neighbours had gathered near the door of the house, and waited, standing still and standing silent. There was a low murmur as the
hearse, like a huge, black, decorated gothic casket, drawn by four
black horses, each with a black plume on its head, came slowly
trotting up the street in state, and sidled with dignity into a space
right in front of the waiting cabs. The driver of the hearse and his
assistant, wearing big, black, tall hats, and long, heavy, blue silver-
buttoned coats, climbed quietly down from their high-up seats,
and hovered about near the door, waiting for the call to come in
and nail the coffin down.

A cab suddenly swept round the corner, came at a rapid trot
up the street, pulled up in a line parallel with the hearse; and
the driver, jumping down, joined two other drivers, who stood
smoking and leaning and talking together against a wall near the
window of the house. The newcomer took off a hard bowler hat
and wiped his forehead.

—The belly-band broke on the way, he said, an' be the time I
put a stitch of twine in it, I thought he'd be planted, an' all the
prayers said.

One of the other two drivers took a pipe from his mouth, spat on the path in front of him, and answered, Plenty of time, Jim – he hasn't been screwed down yet. Curious how long people take to say goodbye to a dead man.

—I'll give them another quarter of an hour, said the third driver, who wore a yellow muffler round his throat, if some good Jesuit 'ud come along an' give me a joram o' malt to lower down into me belly – didderay didderee didderum, he hummed.

—Me an' Jack, said the driver who had come in a hurry, had a great night yesterday. Afther dockin' t'animals, we opened with a couple o' pints in Dempsey's, then we had three more in the Bunch o' Grapes, slung another five into us in Henessey's, an' ended with the last o' three more in The Royal Oak as the shutthers were comin' down at the tick of eleven o'clock.

The man wearing the yellow muffler rubbed his hands together, and envy glistened in his eye.

—Not a bad sackful for a man to get down him in the latther end of a night, he murmured – didderay didderee didderum.

Johnny, standing by the heads of the hearse-horses, saw the boy Connor, who went to school with him, standing beside his mother, watching him, and leering whenever he caught Johnny's eye. Johnny moved nearer to him so that Connor could get a better view of him standing cockily near the hearse-horses, impatiently scraping the road with their feet and shaking the black plumes whenever they tossed their heads. Connor moved till he was just beside Johnny, though, sly enough, he held on to his mother's skirt, which he had stretched out as far as it could go. Johnny felt his head beside his shoulder, and heard him whisper in his ear, Go an' put your hand on a horse if you're as brave as you're thryin' to look.

Johnny stiffened with pride and stroked the band of crisp crêpe on his arm as he saw kids in the crowd watching him and Connor. Stretching out a hand timorously, he stroked the haunch of the nearest horse. The animal gave a shuddering start, and kicked viciously, making the hearse shake and Johnny jump away from him in fright.

—Gaaaa, you mischeevous little bastard, roared the driver wearing the yellow muffler, gaaaa, out o' that, an' leave th' animal alone, or I'll go over an' kick the little backside off you!

Johnny slunk away a little, and turned his back to Connor, so that his shamed and frightened face couldn't be seen.

—Fifteen pints between eight and eleven, said the driver

wearing the bowler hat, I wouldn't ask anything betther, even on the night of me first daughter's weddin'. We got home, he went on, we got home, but it took two hours to do it, where it should ha' taken only twenty minutes: two solid hours o' mighty sthrivin', but we done it in the end.

—They ought to have the old man warmly folded up be this, said the man wearing the yellow muffler, didderay didderee didderum.

—The both of us were rotto, went on the driver wearing the bowler hat, the two of us strugglin' together, him helpin' me an' me helpin' him, whenever help was needed. We sung The Heart Bowed Down all the way home, fall an' up again, fall an' up again; I'd call it a red-letther night, even afther a day of thinkin'.

—Last week was a rotten one with me, said the third driver; a few roll-an'-tea-for-lunch laddies, who are always lookin' for the return of their fare in the change.

Johnny felt Connor beside him again, and whispering at him over his shoulder.

—Mother says, he whispered, that in a week or so you won't be so cocky.

—You're not comin', anyway, answered Johnny, for I heard me mother saying that she hoped the Connors wouldn't thry to shove their noses in at the funeral.

—Yah, sneered Connor, you're shapin'. Just because your father's dead you think you're big in your black suit, but me mother says it isn't new at all, but only dyed.

Johnny turned slantwise, looked at Connor in the eye, and murmured, If it wasn't for me father bein' dead, I'd go round the lane with you, an' break your snot.

—On the way home, said the man wearing the bowler hat, we met two lovely big-diddied rides, and they were all for us going home with them, but neither of us could let go his hold on the other, and so we had to keep everything buttoned up.

—Wonder they didn' thry to lift yous, said the third driver.

—We were so dhrunk, went on the man wearing the bowler hat, that we didn't know our own religion, but we weren't dhrunk enough for that.

—I'd ha' done something, said the man with the yellow muffler, even if I hadda lie down to do it, didderay didderee didderum.

A woman came running to the door of the house, looked about her, saw Johnny, beckoned excitedly to him, and shouted,

You're to come in, Johnny, an' give your poor father a last kiss before he's screwed down.

Johnny stood still, shivered, and gaped at the woman standing in the doorway. He retreated a little, and caught hold of Mrs Connor's skirt.

—I won't go, he said. I don't want to go in.

—Here, come in at once, sir, said the woman in the doorway, roughly, an' pay the last respects to your father, who's in heaven now, an' watchin' down on all your doin's, an' listenin' to all your bold sayin's.

—I'll not go in, he repeated plaintively. I'm afraid, an' I'll not go in.

—*I* wouldn't be afraid, Johnny heard Connor say, to kiss me father, if he was dead, would I, mother?

—Don't be afraid, son, said Mrs Connor, patting Johnny's head, your father wouldn't do you any harm, an' when you're grown up, you'd be sorry you hadn't given him a last kiss.

—Come in, you little rut, when you're told, shouted the woman at the door, an' don't be keepin' every one waitin'.

She ran towards him, but he dodged her, and made off down the street, running full tilt into the man wearing the yellow muffler, trampling on his foot, and hitting his head into the man's belly.

—Jasus, me foot! yelled the man, you lightning-blooded little bastard, where the hell are you goin'!

—He's the dead man's little boy, said the woman, getting hold of Johnny's arm, an' he's wanted to give his dead father a last kiss before he's screwed down.

—An' he was makin' off, snarled the man, an' knockin' the puff out o' people . A nice way of showin' his love for his father.

—Let me go, let me go, screamed Johnny, kicking viciously at the woman's legs, as she dragged him towards the house. I won't go, I don't want to kiss him.

—Your mother'll have a handful in you when you grow up, me boy, she said, as she gathered him forcibly into the house in her arms.

She held him tightly in the midst of the crowd in the room waiting for the coffin to be screwed down. His mother turned round when he began to scream again, came over, and caught his hand in hers.

—Let him down, let him down, Mrs Saunders, she said to the

woman. Then she bent down over him, putting her arm round his trembling body and kissing and kissing him, she murmured, There, there, hush, nothing is going to happen to you.

He circled her with his arms, pressed his face into her skirts, and she felt his fingers cleaving through her skirt to the flesh of her thighs.

—I couldn't, I couldn't, he sobbed. Don't ask me, mother, don't ask me to kiss him, I'm frightened to kiss a dead man.

He felt a gentle, sympathetic pressure of an arm around him, and softened his sobbing.

—No one'll ask you to do it, she said. I'll kiss him goodbye for you myself. Just touch the side of the coffin with the tip of your finger.

She gently drew out his arm, and he shuddered deeply when he felt the tip of his finger touching the shiny cold side of the coffin.

—That's the brave little son, she murmured; and now I'll give your father a last kiss from his little boy.

She bent down and kissed the thing in the coffin, and he heard her say in a steady whisper, Goodbye, my Michael; my love goes with you, down to the grave, and up with you to God.

She stepped back, and he felt her body shaking. He looked up and saw her lips quivering in a curious way, as she said quietly to the waiting hearsemen, You may put the lid down on top of him now.

The hearsemen stepped forward and lifted the coffin lid from where it was resting behind the coffin against the wall, silently and quickly fitted it on, and, with things they took from their pockets, began to turn the screws, filling the tense quietness with the harsh grinding sound of the screws tearing their way down through the hard oak of the coffin. When the screws had been driven home, the hearsemen went out and stood beside the hearse. Six men, two at the head, two at the feet, and two in the middle, lifted the coffin up on their shoulders, and, in a curious body-bending way, carried the corpse, feet first, from his home to the hearse that waited outside to carry the body to the grave.

The man wearing the yellow muffler rubbed his hands gleefully together.

—We ought to be soon bowling along merrily to the boneyard, now, he murmured expectantly, didderee didderay didderum.

The three of them suddenly caught sight of the end of the coffin appearing in the doorway. They took their hands out of their pockets, and went with a hurried ambling run to the doors of their cabs, and sought their fares from the crowd that came pouring out after the coffin. There was a rapid noise of opening cab-doors, another rapid and sharper noise of the doors closing when the fares had climbed inside. The six men carrying the coffin, their arms locked over each other's shoulders, heads turned sideways to prevent the coffin edge from scraping their necks, walked slowly and rhythmically to the back of the hearse; the two leaders, stooping, rested their end of the coffin on rollers laid on the floor of the hearse, the middle couple bent down and slipped from under the coffin, the last couple pushed their end, and the revolving rollers carried the coffin into the hearse, and a hearseman closed the door.

Johnny was lifted into the mourning-coach by his mother, who followed after with his three brothers and sister, and they all settled themselves on the seat of the coach. The cab-drivers mounted to their seats, gathered their faded rugs of blue and green and red from the backs of the horses, folded them with a deft motion round their knees, sat down, took the reins in their hands, waited for the hearse and the mourning coach to pull out into the centre of the street, and then with a Yep, eh, yep, there, to the horses, followed, one after the other, and went with an easy, ambling trot down the street, wheeling round the first turning, wheeling again at the next turning till they were back in the street they had first left, slowing down to a walk as they passed the dead man's door, and then away at a trot again towards the cemetery miles and miles away.

Johnny, hedged in between his sister and brothers, edged towards the window, but his sister pulled him back as he was trying to let the window down.

—Sit easy, can't you? she said, you can't go looking at things out of the window at your father's funeral! Keep quiet with those feet of yours, or you'll pull the dress off me.

—Let him come over here, said his mother, and he can keep quiet and look out of the window at the same time.

His mother guided him beside her, so that with a little stretching of his neck he could see the world as it was passing by. They went slowly by the piece of waste ground at the end of the street where a huge Gospel tent was standing. He caught a glimpse of the long red scroll stretched over the entrance with the word Welcome in big letters on it. He thought of the night that he had timidly crept down and lifted the flap of the tent to have a squint at the crowd of faint figures filling the place, dimly shadowed out by the smoky light from many oil lamps. He remembered how he had struggled and shouted out, Let me go, let me go, or I'll tell me mother, when a dark-bearded little man, with a pale face and cloudy eyes, had grasped him by the arm and had tried to pull him inside, saying in a curious, sneaky way, Another loved and little lamb for Jesus.

Hearse, mourning-coach, cabs, and cars, threaded their way through the tenement-hedged streets where swarms of boys and girls played and fought in front of the gloomy houses that had once, his mother told him, sheltered all the great lords and ladies of the land. Round into Cavendish Row where the houses were high and still mighty, with stately doors and flashing windows. Outside of some of them maids, with black or blue dresses and white aprons and caps with floating streamers, were polishing brass plates, letter-box flaps, and heavy knockers of bronze or brass.

—Dublin houses of the gentry when they come to town, said his mother.

—They have to die the same as all of us, said Ella, his sister. Dust they were and dust they shall become.

—It would hardly be fair for God to let them live for ever, said his mother. We're passing through Aungier Street, now, she added, glancing out of the window.

—Haven't we a long way to go still? Johnny asked her anxiously.

—No, she said, not a very long way now.

—But it'll take a long time to get there, won't it; a long, long time, really?

—We'll get there all too quickly, she said softly.

—There'll be quite a crowd at the graveside, said Ella.

—The full up of three carriages, twenty-six cabs, and six side-cars, said Michael.

—The number that's attendin' the funeral show the respect every one had for him, said Ella.

—An' yet he rarely spoke, and never mixed with any one, murmured the mother.

—It won't be very long till we begin to feel his loss, said Archie.

—We'll all only have to pull together, an' things'll be easy enough, said the sister.

—I'm the only one that'll miss him, said the mother, me an' Johnny.

—We'll look after you both, never fear, said Ella, so keep your pecker up.

—Steadily, shoulder to shoulder, steadily, blade by blade, added Tom.

The coach stopped opposite the cemetery, they climbed out, and, in a moment, the pathway swarmed with the crowd that had emptied itself out of the cabs and off the side-cars. From a carriage that had immediately followed the mourning-coach a tall, thin, black-bearded clergyman stepped, and hastened on in front to the vestry, provided for the robing of the clergy by the cemetery authorities.

The hearse pulled in through the central gates on to the main path, which cut the cemetery into two huge sections. One of Johnny's brothers took some documents from his pocket and handed them to a fat, pompous-looking, little man, wearing a big tall hat and black gloves, and who had a face like a frozen image. The little man took the documents, examined the brass plate on the coffin to see that the body therein was related to the person docketed and scheduled in the papers. He nodded assent, and the coffin was placed on a low car covered with flowing black draperies, and pulled by a well-groomed, gentle-looking black horse, enveloped in a black gown heavily embroidered with silver, so that only the eyes, the ears, and the feet of the animal were visible. A tall black plume rising from his forehead made him look like the nag that the Black Prince rode at the battle of Crécy. Overhead in a grey sky, spotted with timid-looking blue patches, dark heavy clouds were being tossed and pushed along by a northerly wind blowing steadily and reasonably, except that now and again it gathered strength and swept by fiercely, filling the cemetery with a mad rustle and a cold swish-swish from the bending branches of the trees as it went sweeping by. At intervals a sulky beam from a peevishly-hiding sun would dart out from a corner of the sky, flooding patches of the graveyard with a jeering, flippant brightness, rippling and dancing slowly over the head-stones and the floral flotsam that Christians scatter about a cemetery to make the place look as jaunty, as merry, and as unconcerned as possible; then, after flushing the place with a timid brightness, the sun would glide away, slip back into itself behind the clouds, and the dismal gloom that was slinking round would press forward and cover up everything again. Elegant beeches, ivy-trunked oaks, dark, well-tailored cypresses, looking like guardians keeping things in their proper places, and fan-

branched yews, looking like shy, saintly, Georgian ladies dancing
a quiet, secret minuet to themselves, were ranged along the
avenues and paths. Tombstones, tall and squat, square and round,
old, middle-aged, and new, spread themselves everywhere, with
an occasional lanky obelisk, like a tall boy peering over the
shoulders of the others, seemed to gather closer together, stiffen,
stretch, and stare and stare at the newcomer that had come
to be planted, wondering who he was, whence he came, and
whether what was coming would add to the dignity and ease
of the dust that lay buried there.

Off the contingent started, the little fat man, with the tall hat
and the face like a frozen image, leading in front of the bier, with
the documents in his hand, directing the way to Section F, Plot B,
Grave OX5432/2345, where the cargo of decaying flesh was to be
stored against the day of the resurrection of the dead; after the
black-palled bier, pulled by the black-palled horse, came the
mother and Ella, with Johnny walking between them, then, close
up, the various relatives of the dead man; and spreading out in a
long procession behind, the friends of the family, silent and
solemn-faced, marched up the main avenue towards the vestry
where the clergyman stood, robed and ready to receive the body
of his brother for committal to the clay. The silence was broken
only by the soft fall to the ground of the horse's padded feet, the
coo-cooo of a pigeon, the rustling of the leaves on the trees, or
the cold swish-swish of the bending branches as a stronger wind
went sweeping by.

The clergyman, with the big black beard, wearing a white
surplice and a black stole, holding a prayer-book in his hand,
open at the Service for the Burial of the Dead, waited till the bier
came close, then turned and marched by the side of the little fat
man with the face like a frozen image, and recited in a loud and
serious voice:

I am the resurrection and the life, saith the Lord: he that
believeth in me, though he were dead, yet shall he live: and
whosoever believeth in me shall never die.

We brought nothing into this world, and it is certain we can
carry nothing out. The Lord gave, and the Lord hath taken
away; blessed be the Name of the Lord.

Coming to Section F, the cortège wheeled to the right, off the
main avenue, and midway in a narrow path, a little to the left,

they came to a heap of newly dug earth piled up beside an open grave. The coffin was lifted from the low black-palled car by four heavy-featured grave-diggers, who put ropes round it, and set it down by the side of the open grave. The black-bearded clergyman, walking carefully between the other graves so as not to step on one, slipped on a damp sod of grass, and was pitching into the grave, when one of the grave-diggers caught him, pulled him back, and set him on his feet again.

—A narrow shave, sir, he said, as the clergyman tried, with a hasty brush of his hand, to remove a hand-pattern of clay which the grave-digger's grip had left on his white surplice.

Johnny saw the sudden look of fright that had crossed the face of the clergyman when he was slipping, and thought how funny it would have been had the clergyman fallen into the grave, and the fun they'd have had pulling him out again by his white surplice and his black stole. He giggled. His mother roughly pulled him by one arm and his sister by the other, and he was pushed behind them, red-faced with fear and shame. The looks on their faces told him that there would be nothing funny in a clergyman with a white surplice and a black stole falling into an open grave. The clergyman straightened himself up, opened the book again at the proper place, and began to read, as a pigeon coo-cooed, and the branches of the trees, bending, gave a cold swish-swish as a stronger breeze came sweeping by.

Man that is born of a woman hath but a short time to live, and is full of misery. He cometh up, and is cut down, like a flower; he fleeth as it were a shadow, and never continueth in one stay.

The grave-diggers lowered and lowered the coffin into the grave, and took the ropes from under it. One stood back a little distance, and the other stood near the edge of the grave, hatless, with a fistful of earth in his hand, waiting. The clergyman went on:

Forasmuch as it hath pleased Almighty God of his great mercy to take unto himself the soul of our dear brother here departed, we therefore commit his body to the ground; earth to earth [the grave-digger threw some of the clay from his fist down on the coffin], ashes to ashes [more of the clay fell on to the coffin], dust to dust.

The grave-digger threw what remained of the clay in his fist down on the coffin; then he left the side of the grave and joined his comrade, the two of them throwing their eyes round, Johnny heard afterwards, to try to pick out the one that would be likely to give them a tip. The clergyman went on:

> I heard a voice from heaven, saying unto me, Write, From henceforth blessed are the dead which die in the Lord: even so saith the Spirit; for they rest from their labours.

> *Lord have mercy upon us.*
> *Christ have mercy upon us.*

The grave-diggers hurried forward and rapidly began to shovel the pile of clay into the open grave in a strict and tense silence, again broken only by the pigeon's coo-cooo, and the cold swish-swish from the bending branches of the trees as a strong breeze went sweeping by. Johnny looked up at his mother standing stiffly watching the grave-diggers filling the grave, and he saw that tears were streaming down her cheeks. He crept closer and closer to her, wrapped his right arm round her left one, squeezed it, caught her hand in his and pressed and pressed and pressed it.

The clergyman lingered looking down at the clay falling on the coffin, his hands entwined in front of him, eager, possibly, for the thing to come to an end, sick of the dampness of the grass oozing through the thin soles of his boots, making his feet feel dead, dreading a cold to come, shivering a little whenever the trees gave a swish-swish as a stronger breeze went sweeping by; thinking of the bright fire in his study at home, with life and warmth filling every corner, and tea, hot and richly brewed, poured into dainty cups, with his wife dividing life into two parts by talking of the things that belonged unto her home, and the things that belonged unto her husband's parish.

The grave was filling up now – the men were working rapidly – and in another few minutes they would be topping it, and he could quietly slip off, remembering the sudden rise in shares this morning that meant a gain of one hundred and thirty-five pounds and a few odd shillings, which wasn't too dusty when you came to think of it – at the evening service on Thursday he must remember to speak finally to the church charwoman about pawning the two hassocks that had been newly covered only a few days before – she might lay her hands on other things – only a few feet from the top now, feet numb and hands raw and nipped with the damp of the whole place, shivering and sodden with desire of decay and death and darkness and drooping – the shovels are tapping the top of it now – so goodbye for the present, dear sorrowful sister in Christ, and comfort remember is His to bestow, for your husband's in heaven and happier far than we can be here, who are seeking a city that's hidden away, and Sion's its name, shining for ever with light everlasting, out-ageing the sun and the moon and the stars that gleam through the day and glitter at night, and never forget when God's city's in bloom, the sun and the stars and the moon will only be dust in the streets, frail dust in the streets of the city of God – so hurry your thoughts through your grief to the day when Christ on the clouds shall come sweeping again through the sky from His Father, and the dead that were bless'd by a union with Him shall come out of their graves and stand to attention, saluting their Lord, this when they have done, they'll seek out the loved one they've lost and the ones they have left sporting on in the flesh, and remember, unbroken unbent in the faith, you will gather your loved one yourself to your breast, to enjoy him for ever fresh-robed in a glorified body, unsickened by thoughts of the past or thought for the future, for these shall be merged and forgot in the sun and the moon and the stars which shall only be dust in the streets in the city of God, and His mercy shall keep you till then; so farewell for the present, dear sister in Christ, for the tea is at hand and the crumpets are ready and I must be vanishing now.

Heavily, for his feet felt puffed and softly numb with the damp that had oozed through the thin soles of his boots; stiffly, because his joints had tightened with the cold, the clergyman picked his path through the graves, crossed the main avenue, and dived into the vestry. As his mother lingered by the grave arranging the flowers that had been hastily placed there, Johnny saw him come out of the vestry, swinging a little leather case in his right hand, and hurry away till the trees hid him from view.

Ella touched her mother's arm, and said, You just come along now, Ma, and try to keep your pecker up; but her mother went on silently arranging the flowers on the grave, so Ella stole away to join her brothers strolling slowly along towards the main avenue.

For a long time Johnny waited and waited, till his mother turned away from the grave, and he saw that tears were streaming down her face. He crept up closer and closer to her as they slowly moved away, caught her hand in his and pressed and pressed and pressed it in a dead silence broken only by a pigeon's coo-cooo and the cold swish-swish of branches bending as a stronger breeze went sweeping by.

WE ALL GO THE SAME WAY HOME

THEY SAUNTERED down the main avenue, uneasy, and fearful of the change that the leaving of an intimate thing behind them for ever would bring into the thought, life, and action of the family. Death had dunted into the family life, and had stunned its functions for the time being. Nothing would be exactly the same again. There would have to be a new grouping and a new laying out of all things.

Suddenly Johnny saw the red coat of a soldier in the midst of the crowd who wore their dark-toned suits as if they were vestments.

—Look at the soldier, Ma, look at the soldier with a drum and crossed gold guns on his arm! he cried.

Johnny saw Ella's face go red, and his brothers grinning, as his mother hushed him, and said no one must raise a voice in a cemetery.

Johnny stared at the red-coated soldier who had a lovely epaulette, like a sickle moon, on each shoulder, covered with white braid, sprinkled with little red crowns, and white braid all over his breast and down his arms, all dotted with the little red crowns. And over his back and shoulder there ran a cord which met just above his left breast and then fell down in two big lovely tassels of blue, yellow, and green plaited cords.

He's a bugler, thought Johnny, a bugler that blows the Reveille every morning to rouse all the other soldiers out of their deep sleep, as one day the angel Gabriel will blow his own trumpet to wake up all the dead who lie around us here in thousands: Little Boy Blue, come blow your horn, the cow's in the meadow, the sheep's in the corn.

He saw his brother Tom go over and shake hands with the soldier; he saw Ella's face redden again as the soldier's eyes stared over to where she was walking along with her mother.

—He should never have come to the funeral, Johnny heard his

mother say to Ella; you know the state your poor father'd have been in had he known you knew him – he would never sanction a soldier. For goodness' sake, don't speak to him here.

Johnny saw Ella tossing her head, but she said nothing.

Tom came to their side again, and, looking back, Johnny saw the soldier following them afar off.

—It's wonderful, the long sap-swollen grass that grows in a graveyard, said Tom.

—The best grass that grows anywhere, grows in a graveyard, said Archie. They must make a tidy bit out of the hay they get from it. Everything is money here, and nothing goes to waste. No one ever yet saw a balance-sheet from a cemetery.

When they had passed through the big gate, and had come to the mourning-coach, Tom held back while the others climbed into it.

—I think I'll jog along back with Bugler Benson, he said, when the others had settled themselves in the coach; we'd be a bit crowded, if I came in.

—Oh no, Tom, said his mother complainingly; do come in, and for this one day, at least, let us all go the same way home.

—Johnny hummed silently to himself as Tom, with a disappointed scowl on his face, climbed into the coach, and squeezed himself into a corner.

We all go the same way home
All the whole collection, in the same direction,
All go the same way home, so there's no need to part at all,
And we'll cling together like the ivy on the old garden wall.

The coach delayed while the driver mounted and settled himself in his seat. Johnny, glancing towards the window of the coach, saw it curtained with a sparkling blue sky, cut clean in two by a deep black poplar, like a dark angel standing taut in a tight suit of blackest velvet, guarding 'gainst disturbance of the sleep of the dead.

The coach moved on, and then he watched the others sitting for a while silent, thinking of the upset and scattering that death had given to the even ordering of things. He seemed to feel that the sorrow that filled the coach was all in his mother's heart. This death was a curious business. Who killed cock robin? I, said the sparrow, with my little arrow, I killed cock robin. He could see the picture in the book, with the robin stretched out on his back, his knees tightly gathered into his red breast from which an arrow stuck out wickedly, and his little beak stiff and gaping open. And in a corner in a tree, on a bough, an evil-looking sparrow with an eye and a leg saucily cocked as if he had just done something grand. There he perched and stared and jeered in a tree, on a bough, with a little bow held wickedly under a wing.

—The grave looked to be one of the deepest I have ever seen, said Ella.

—It must be dug deep enough to hold four, said Michael, for that's the number allowed to go in when the plot's bought outright.

—It's our family property, altogether, now, isn't it? asked Tom.

—Absolutely, responded Archie; we hold the plot in perpetuity.

—Mother, said Johnny suddenly, if a bird wanted to shoot a boy with an arrow, how hard would he have to pull?

—Oh, I couldn't say, she said.

—Why don't you try to think of what you're going to say, said Archie to Johnny; for you mean how hard would a boy have to pull if he wanted to shoot a bird with an arrow?

—No, said Johnny to Archie, no, I don't. How hard would a bird have to pull if he wanted to shoot a boy with an arrow? For a boy to shoot a bird with an arrow, he wouldn't have to pull hard at all.

—Silly kid, said Tom, a bird couldn't hold a bow to shoot an arrow.

—How do you know he couldn't? questioned Johnny.

—Oh, do be quiet, said Ella.

—But how does he know a bird couldn't shoot an arrow?

Tom glared at him, and said, because we know he couldn't.

—But supposing, only supposing a bird could, went on Johnny, how hard would he have to pull?

—That, laughed Archie, would depend on whether the bird was a cock or a hen.

—Nice kind of talk, this, and father only a few minutes in the grave.

—This comes of letting him go to the funeral, complained Michael. He's getting twice too old-fashioned for his years.

—You'll have to keep very quiet for a few days, said his mother, till your father's been a little while with God.

—But why a little while, Mother, Johnny asked, when Sunday-school teacher says that a moment and a million years is all the same to God?

—Oh, try to keep your little gob shut for a second or two! said Ella irritably.

Johnny fell silent. He hated, hated all these people, all, except his mother, with their big heads, big faces, big hands, and big feet. He was angry with them; but they were too big to fight, for one of them could easily stamp him under his big feet. He wanted to spit at them, to answer them back, but he shut his little mouth tight, and answered them never a word. But in his mind he sang, and sang loudly: And the birds of the air went a-sighing and a-sobbing when they heard of the death of poor cock robin, when they heard of the death of poor cock robin. If his da was as happy as they were eager to make out, getting warmed up again in Abraham's bosom, and sure of everything going where he was gone, why did they all sit so still and stiff and stony? How they all loved to cheat a kid out of anything he had a thought to do. And, anyhow, if they only knew, Who killed cock robin was a funeral song, wasn't it? Of course it was, of course it was.

Johnny, from the window, watched the jingling horse-drawn trams going up or down the street, the drivers holding the reins with one hand, and resting the other on the hand-brake. The coach was travelling twice as quick home as it had travelled to the cemetery, and soon they were passing between Trinity College and the Royal Bank of Ireland.

—I wonder will the Home Rulers ever be able to turn the Royal Bank of Ireland into an Irish House of Parliament? murmured the mother, as she glanced out of the window.

—God forbid they'd ever be able to turn such a beautiful building into a rendezvous of rowdyism, said Ella fervently.

—Parnell's the only gentleman in the whole gang, said Tom. They were watching their chance for years, and Kitty O'Shea is only an excuse for downing him. If they throw him over, clowns and pantaloons in a pantomime parliament are all that they can hope to be.

—He should have more respect for himself than to go and carry on with a married woman, said Ella.

—If all that's said about him is true, he should do the decent thing, and resign at once, said Archie.

—Ay, said Tom, and give the guttermen the power.

—They're not all guttermen, said Archie, and even if they were, they deserve all the more credit for lifting themselves out of it.

—There's no credit going to them, said Tom, for it's Parnell, the man they're hounding, that lifted them out of the gutter, and planted them on their feet.

—Why doesn't he get hold of some single woman, inquired Ella, and leave the married women alone?

—The people are showing what they think of Parnell, anyway, said Michael.

—Ay, the ignorant superstitious country gulls who walk in daily dread of their parish priests, said Tom scornfully.

—How do you know they're in dread of their parish priests? asked Michael.

—What about the priest who threatened to turn into a goat anyone that dared to say a word in favour of Parnell? Read the papers, man. And Tom spat out of the window.

—What about the men that are standing by him – are they in dread of the parish priests?

—Read the papers, read the papers, man.

—He has no right to make a fool of himself over a married woman, persisted Ella.

—Oh, we all know, said Michael, turning fiercely on Ella, that he has no right to make a fool of himself over a woman, married or single, so pocket that stuff and button it up, and let him answer the question of whether or no those who are standing up for Parnell are in dread of their parish priests?

—What about the priests preaching against Parnell from off the althars? asked Tom.

—Name the priests, name them! said Michael loudly; what althars, which althars, whose althars?

—Read the papers, repeated Tom; you wouldn't be so ignorant if you read the papers.

—I suppose you think you are the only one who was brought up to be able to read the papers?

—Read the papers, read the papers, man, chanted Tom.

—Oh, said the mother pleadingly, don't let us have any argument on our way home from your father's burial.

They sank into silence again, and sat moody till the coach pulled up at the door of their home, and silent and stiff and stony they went into the house. Tom gave a shilling to the driver who said Thank you, sir, and sorry for your trouble, before he drove away.

Johnny lingered outside, but his sister came out, caught him by the arm, and brought him inside, saying, Come in, come in; you can't be seen knocking about outside on the day your poor father was buried, and you'll have to behave like a different boy for a week or two. They went into the room where his mother and father had slept together, and where he had lain sick for over a year, and where he, at last, had died. The blind on the one window was still down, and the room was dark and solemn. His mother pulled a cord which sent the blind rattling up, and the light leaped in, touching with a curious brightness the dreariness that sickness and death had gathered, and that still loitered around the things sickness and death had left behind them.

—This room'll have to be well aired for a day or two, said Ella, as she and her brothers sat round a fire that the neighbours had kept going while they were away at the funeral.

Johnny wandered over to the window, and watched the redness of the sun in the sky over the house opposite.

—The damp and cold of the cemetery has gone right through me, said Ella, as she lifted her skirt to warm her legs.

—Look at the sun, look at the sun, Mother, cried Johnny, how red he is. Why is he so red?

—Oh, said his mother, glancing out of the window, I suppose he was feeling a little cold, and God wrapped a scarlet cloak around him.

—Does God like red, Mother?

—Oh, yes, yes, He likes red; there are quite a lot of flowers and things in the world that are coloured red.

—Does God like the colour red the best, Mother?

—Oh, I couldn't rightly say, Johnny; I think He likes all colours, really.

—And yellow, too; for look at the buttercups, the primroses, the cowslips, the daffodils, and, and the dandelions; He must be very fond of yellow, too, mustn't he, Mother?

—Yes, He must be very fond of yellow, too, Johnny.

—But I don't think He cares a lot for blue, Mother, for there's only the violets and the bluebells – but I forgot about the sky, the blue of the sky that's everywhere on a fine day. He must be specially fond of blue, mustn't He, Mother?

—What about a cup of tea, or something, said Archie, and never mind the colour choice of God?

—Lay the table, Ella, said the mother, and we'll have some tea, an egg each, and some cold meat that's left over.

—He seems to cotton on a good deal, too, to white, went on Johnny; for look at the daisies, the hawthorn, and the clouds. Curious that God likes white. Why does He like white – it's not much of a colour, is it, Mother? And black, too, for look at the dark night; but then He always softens that a little with a golden moon or the silver stars.

—Oh, chuck it, Johnny, chuck it, boy, broke in Michael, who felt uncomfortable, as they all did, with the name of God dangling around; half an hour's enough with God for one day.

—You mind your own business, said Johnny, fiercely turning on him; you're always trying to stop me when I say anything, but I'm not asking you, anyhow.

—Just you chuck it when you're told, said Michael angrily, and give me none of your lip.

—What would you do if I didn't chuck it? asked Johnny defiantly.

—Chuck it, chuck it, shouted Michael. You're getting just a little bit too crabby for Michael.

His mother went over to Johnny, and, bending down, whispered to him, Keep quiet, Johnny, and some other time when no one but ourselves is here, we'll talk of all those things.

Johnny turned away from her, full up of a feeling to cry, but he shut his teeth together tight, and looked out of the window at the redness of the sun in the sky over the house opposite, making the roofs of the houses look like polished bronze. Big heads, big hands, big feet, big voices, bitter snap and bitter snarl. If he was only up to their size, or they down to his, he'd give them snarl for snap and snap for snarl. He drummed softly, then sharply, with his fingers on the window-pane, murmuring to himself, There was a little man, and he had a little gun, and up the chimney he did run, his belly full of fat, and his old cocked hat, and pancakes in his bum, bum, bum.

—Oh, stop that drumming, drumming, for God's sake, screamed Ella. We've had enough to bear today without having that kind of noise dashing through our brains.

—Oh, don't be always nagging at the child, remonstrated the mother, suddenly and angrily. You're all at him, if he only stirs. He can't be expected to sit or stand all days with his hands folded and his tongue still.

—You shouldn't take his part when you know he's in the wrong, retorted Ella.

—It's dangerous to open your mouth about him, grumbled Michael.

They all sat round the table, Ella cutting the bread and butter, while the mother poured out the tea. She gave an egg to each, keeping the smallest for herself. She filled out a cup of tea, which, with several slices of bread and butter, she placed on a little table beside the window, saying to Johnny, Take this quietly here, now, where you won't be in anybody's way.

—Mother, he whispered, am I not going to get any egg?

—I'm going to give you half of mine, she said.

And right enough, when she'd broken and peeled the top of the egg, she spooned out the most of it, and spread it over several slices of the bread she had given to him. This was a treat, for it was nearly a year since he had enjoyed the taste of an egg, and he guessed that such a joy would not come near him again till Easter morning came. Eating his egg and drinking his tea, he watched the big heads and big hands guzzling down their eggs and tea and meat.

—Not much to be got out of an egg, muttered Archie; a dozen of them wouldn't make a fair meal for a man.

When they had finished, they grouped themselves round the fire, the men smoking, and Ella reading *The London Story Paper*. The mother brought in a basin of hot water, and began to wash up the things. Johnny climbed on to a chair, and helped her, handing her the cups to be rinsed, and then taking them from her and arranging them on the table when they had been rinsed and dried. He helped her to carry them out to be placed in neat rows on the dresser shelves in the other room. Johnny was feeling more comfortable. Life was resuming its old way. His father's death hadn't changed things a whole lot, after all.

When everything had reached its proper place, and they returned to the other room, Ella had her coat on, and was fixing her hat on her head before a tiny mirror hanging on the wall.

—You're not going out, are you? asked her mother.

—I am, for an hour or so, replied Ella, and Johnny saw her face go red; I'm going for a walk, I want a walk, I feel the need of a little air and exercise.

—The one thought in my head is the man I want to wed, that's my little, little drummer boy in red, grinned Michael from the corner of the fireplace.

—I think it would be better, remarked the mother, if you stayed at home for this evening.

—I'm going out, said Ella; and turning to Michael she snapped, You cock your thoughts on yourself, and never mind me.

She left the room, and they heard her close the door noisily as she went out into the street. There was silence for some minutes afterwards; then the mother took the cloth from the table, shook the crumbs into the fireplace, rolled the cloth up, and carrying it with her, went away into the other room.

Michael took his pipe from his mouth, and mixing a leer with a grin on his face, said, Ella'll have to keep her eyes skinned, or the wind'll blow her clothes up. Then he tapped his pipe on the hob, and hummed:

> *The Drummer-boy in red to his little girl said,*
> *Come.*
> *When I've had a little fiddle*
> *With your little diddle middle,*
> *Then I'll play a tarradiddle*
> *On your middle liddle diddle*
> *White bum.*
> *When I'm fed up with the fiddle,*
> *This red-coat'd drummer kid'll*
> *Start a rapid tarradiddle*
> *On your liddle diddle middle*
> *White bum!*

Tom tittered knowingly, and said, Now, Mick, now that's enough. Halt, the Buffs! What about going down to Nagle's for a few quiet pints?

—No sooner said than done, answered Michael; what have you got on you?

—Enough for tonight, said Tom.

Then they rose up from sitting before the fire, the three of them, and began to put their heavy coats on.

—I wonder, said Michael, how you'd get to know whether God Almighty likes blue, green, yellow, or red the best?

—Oh, shut up, Mick, said Tom, and let the kid alone.

—Red, I think, went on Michael, red like the red on a monkey's arse.

—No more talk like that in front of the kid, said Tom, tittering.

—Oh, shag the kid! said Michael, he'll have to learn about these things some day.

They planked their hats on their heads, called out to the mother that they were going out for a spell, Tom lingering to put his hand shyly on Johnny's head as he passed, and to say, Don't mind Mick, Johnny; you're all right, boy.

Johnny watched them going by the window, eager, talking with a strut in the tone of their voices; off to take their quiet pints of porter at Nagle's counter in Earl Street, well in sight of Nelson's Pillar.

Johnny watched the little lamplighter running, with his little beard wagging, carrying his pole, with a light like a sick little star at the top of it, hurrying from lamp to lamp, prodding each time a little yellow light into the darkness, till they formed a chain looking like a string of worn-out jewels that the darkness had slung round the neck of night. His mother returned to the room as he was stretching to see how far he could see down the street, and how many of the lights he could count. Going over to the fire, she sat down, and gazed steadily into the blaze.

—I was just thinking, Mother, he said, that green must be a great favourite of God's, for look at the green grass, and the leaves of bushes and trees; and teacher said that green stands for life, and God loves life.

He waited, but his mother did not answer him. He turned, and saw her gazing steadily into the blaze of the fire. He stole over and sat down beside her, and took her hand in his. And there they sat and stared and stared and stared at the flame that gushed out of the burning coal. Suddenly he looked up and saw the flame from the fire shining on tears that were streaming down her cheeks.

RIP

At the age of forty-six the father had died. The old man was dead, the old man was buried, buried deep in a quiet corner close to a cypress tree, a tree that faded away into the darkness of the night and came again to life with the sun in the morning. And the shadow of the cypress tree, on a sunny day, kindly covered the place where the dead man's face lay, veiling from the closed eyes the new things that were being done by those whom the dead man had brought up in the nurture and admonition of the Protestant Lord, and in the strength of the best education the means of the fearless and honest dead man could give them.

—My children, he would say, raising himself up stiff and defiant in his chair, will get the best education my means, and the most careful use of those means, will allow. It isn't the best that's going, but it is the best that can be got by me for them. They will be, at least, fit for jobs that will give them a decent and fair living as things go with such as we are; and on themselves will then rest the chance of making a good position better, with the knowledge they have gained from a few men and a lot of books; and, later on, by the wisely-used experience gathered from things said and done by those with whom they'll move, and live, and have their being, they will be fit to fight in the fight of life when it comes to face them. Shield and spear shall they have when the day comes for them to go forward.

And so Michael and Tom had gone without a lagging step to Number 1 school, under Professor J. L. Ryan, principal of the five schools that formed the Central Model Schools of Dublin, where small fees were paid by parents; where teachers stood higher than teachers who taught elsewhere; where the books were dearer and superior to most of the others used in the ordinary National Schools. There they all were, schools, teachers, books, and pupils busy as hell, hunting out of their systems the danger of learning a single thing about their own country and their own people, save that the seventeenth of March was called St Patrick's Day, and that it was morally permissible, all things considered, to sing The Harp that once thro' Tara's Halls the soul of music shed, provided the song was sung as if you were an' you weren't singing it, and that you were a little surprised to be hearing it sung at all, and especially surprised if you heard it gettin' sung be yourself, seeing that the harp was hangin' on the wall with all its music mute and its soul fled and its glory gone and its day over; so that you somehow felt it hardly decent to mention its name even at a late hour when the sun had long since gone down, and sleep was heavy even on the eyes of the young and hardy; an' if it was to be sung at all be Protestant people, then it certainly should be sung *sotto voce* in the spirit prescribed by the articles, canons, and catechism of the church, and the laws and regulations of the viceroy and the officers and non-commissioned officers of the Royal Irish Constabulary.

Archie went to Number 2 school, under Mr Boyd, Presbyterian principal, and red-bearded Mr Galleher, Catholic assistant, who used to say, when he had a few jars in him, that Presbyterians were decent men, but damned bigots. Mr Boyd, on the other hand, when he was quite sober, as he always was, used to choose as often as he decently could when he held religious

instructions, the text as a password to higher things, Ephraim –
meaning Mr Galleher – is joined to idols, let him alone.

So, after many days, the two eldest had to face the facts of life
built up by the canons, articles, and creeds of the Church, the
traditions carried on by his excellency the viceroy – hard put to
live on twenty-five thousand pounds a year – and the rules of the
officers and non-commissioned officers of the Royal Irish Constabulary. Michael, at the age of fourteen, was a rare hand with
the pencil. Pictures of a dog lying down by the lock of a canal,
and one of a girl with a bird on her head, called The Kestrel, had
been so admired by the dead man that he had had them framed
and hung on the wall for all to see; and all who came saw, till
one day Michael took them out to show them off, and never
brought them back again – selling them for a bob or two, as
the story went round a long time afterwards. If I only had had
the money, the dead man had murmured one day when he was
showing the pictures to a friend, I'd have made an architect of
him, but the fees were too heavy; so he'll have to be satisfied to
do his duty in that state of life unto which it shall please God to
call him. So Michael took second place in an examination, and
became a telegraph clerk; and Tom took first place in an examination, and became a sorter in the General Post Office of Dublin.
There they had been working for some time before their father's
death, orderly, peaceable, and respectable, wearing their trim
little bowler hats, the badge of all their tribe; nicely-cut ready-to-
wear suits; Michael, something of a dandy at the time, adding a
curl to the quiff in his hair, a pin in his tie, and a slim cane under
his arm, each, after contributing to home expenses, furnished
out of his princely pound a week, as being poor, yet possessing
all things.

Strange faces began to be seen in the Casside household, faces
that stared for a few moments at Queen Victoria who stared back
with her thinly blue eyes, and at Nelson, for ever bound for Trafalgar Bay; strange faces that peered for a moment or two at the
lonely little glass mermaid floating in her little sea gathered into
a glass bowl; faces that eyed the array of books left behind by the
poor dead man, looking wan and out-of-place where thoughts
were fashioned into quick words about things that were born,
lived, and died in the passing hours of a day; and when they had
looked, they turned away to sit by the fire for a smoke, a drink,
a chat, or a sing-song on a Sunday evening to the tune of the
church bells that called and cried for all to come and worship,

and fall down, and kneel before the Lord their Maker, seeing that they were the people of His pasture, and the sheep of His hand; called and cried to all to come and acknowledge and confess their manifold sins and wickedness, to the end that they might obtain forgiveness of the same, by God's infinite goodness and mercy; and win the approval of the canons and catechism of the Church, the viceroy, and the officers and non-commissioned officers of the Royal Irish Constabulary, and the Dublin Metropolitan Police.

But the crying and the calling of the bells went in through one ear and out through the other, as sounds unasked for, and sounds unanswered. The altar now was the kitchen table, and in the midst of the candlesticks, a huge gallon can filled with porter, with Michael and Tom as swaggering altar-boys, and the red-coated drummer, with the blue, yellow, and green tassels dangling on his breast, pouring the beer skilfully into any empty tumbler that wanted to be filled; while Johnny sat in a corner drinking ginger-beer, never noticing his mother sitting in the opposite corner, silently knitting, looking up with a wan smile on her face on hearing the red-coated drummer giving a pretended yelp when Ella pinched his thigh, or Ella giving a real scream when he pinched hers; her peaceful and firm face dimmed by the tobacco smoke that curled from the pipes of the smoking men. Silent she sat, knitting, and thinking, maybe, of a silent man lying in a quiet corner out under the cold stars, and the last hopes of her life but a few dying blooms on a lonely grave; while Tom was singing, in a harsh and staggering voice, a song of bustling battle:

> *Side by side, in the crimson tide,*
> *In the days not long ago,*
> *On we dashed, and our bayonets flashed,*
> *As we conquered every foe.*
> *One by one, as the fight was won,*
> *I saw my comrades fall,*
> *An' I was the only one left to answer the last roll call!*

With all the others joining in, and the voice of the red-coated drummer loudest of all, to sing the sad brave words a second time, their hearts swelling with desire to fight, to fight, aye to fall under the Union Jack for any cause that a single thought could say was worth a fight; Ella looking fondly at her drummer, as she dangled on her lap a fine white hand having on one finger a slender ring decorated with a circle of what was called seed pearls, and in the midst of the white seed pearls, a tiny red speck that was called a ruby, bought in a pawnbroker's with money won as a prize in a shooting competition; for Ella's drummer was best shot in his regiment, and wore crossed gold guns on his sleeve, and a little, blue-and-white drum with yellow heads on the arm of his coat above his elbow, causing Ella to feel that nothing was too good to be kept from her drummer, as she dangled her ring about on her lap while Tom's staggering voice was singing his song of bustling battle; and the mother sat in her corner silent, knitting and thinking, maybe, of a man whom God had taken from her and put to lie in a quiet corner out under the cold stars, her thoughts mixing with the tune of the church bells crying and calling on all people to come and worship, and fall down, and kneel before the Lord their Maker.

Her Michael was in heaven, anyway, resting in sure and certain and undivided peace; maybe looking down on her, and telling her, silently, to be brave. Things, too, might easily be a lot worse. As long as her two boys were working, even though Ella would lose her job when she married, her little Johnny wouldn't want; and that was something to go on with and remember, please to remember the fifth of November, of gunpowder, treason, and plot; but God stepped in, and saved the nation from a terrible calamity, and God would step in, and save her, and would never let her be confounded.

She cocked her ear, for that mouth of a drummer was saying something. His eyes were hazy, for they had lowered a second gallon of beer between them.

—The Army's the greatest life goin', he said; if a man wants to see life, let him take the Queen's shillin'.

—The life here, said Michael, isn't even worth spittin' on, so we're well out of it, Tom, me boy – I one of the Queen's Sappers and Miners, an' you one of the Queen's Old Toughs.

—Can't help rememberin', broke in Tom, excited and glowing, the look on the kissers of the two superintendents when we told them to stick their jobs where the monkey put the nuts.

—Write to us, says I to them, said Michael, when we're lyin' under a foreign sky, an' the lads all pressin' round to bid us a long farewell.

—Here, at home, said the drummer, balancing his tumbler of beer in his hand, or afar in the wilds of India, Canada, Afghanistan, or Burma, what does it matter so long as we're faithful to the Queen, and honour the flag? A drink, boys, a drink to the soldiers of the Queen!

And the three of them, lifting their glasses, shouted, Soldiers of the Queen! and gulped down their beer.

Their mother's fingers ceased to move among the needles. That was why they had been so excited for the last few days; and so silent. They were leaving her, they were lost to her, they had 'listed. The gay, gaudy uniforms dished out to her soldiers by the Queen with the thinly blue eyes, had taken two sons from their mother. So she sat there staring at them drinking to the Queen's soldiers, while her hands ceased to move among the needles.

Tom noticed her staring at them, and, coming over, he put a hand gently on her shoulder.

—You've two sons soldiers, now, Mother, he said; but don't you worry, for neither of us, here at home, or far away in a foreign land, will ever forget the old woman. You'll be a proud woman when your son comes home in his red coat and his busby; ay, an' maybe with medals on his chest too.

They were leaving her, they were lost to her, they had 'listed. She tightened her sensitive mouth, nodded and smiled to the company, bent her head over her knitting, and the active fingers began again to move rapidly among the needles.

Leaving a parting pat on his mother's shoulder, Tom returned a little unsteadily to his place beside the drummer, took up his glass of beer, and gazed excitedly about him.

—The Royal Dublin Fusiliers, he said a little thickly, the Old Toughs, by the right, quick march for foreign lands where dusky faces grin and threaten, where spears are flung and shots are heard, where wounds are got and cheers are given, where swaddies fall and England conquers. But we are here to fill the vacant places; and huskily he sang a song, and huskily they sang it with him:

On the banks of the Clyde stood a lad and his lassie
The lad's name was Georgie, the lassie's was Jane.
She flung her arms round him, and cried, Do not leave me,
For Georgie was going to fight for his Queen.

—Raise it higher, said Michael; altogether, an' let the buggerin' chorus go; and so they did; Johnny, with a will, singing with the best of them:

Over the burnin' plains of Egypt, under a scorchin' sun,
He thought of the stories he'd have to tell to his love when
  the war was won.
He treasured with care her dear lock of hair,
For his own darling Jennie he prayed;
But his prayers were in vain, for she'll ne'er see again,
Her lad in the Scotch Brigade!

—Michael, my Michael, murmured the mother to herself, as her fingers moved among the needles, it is good that you cannot hear your boys and girl singing in their hearts that there is no sorrow, but sorrow will come, though I have not your clear mind to tell them how. You will not know, for you are safe from knowledge where the weary cease from troubling, and the wicked are at rest; but the beginning of your dear peace has meant the end of mine.

And Tom went on huskily singing his song of love and war, and huskily all the rest of them sang it with him.

HAIL, SMILING MORN

ELLA FOUND it hard to even doze during the night before the smiling morn that was to see her married to her man. The hilarious ecstasy in store for her tomorrow night was too much in her mind to let her close her eyes for long, for her beloved is white and ruddy, the chiefest among ten thousand. His locks are bushy, and black as a raven. His mouth is most sweet: yea, he is altogether lovely. So she longed for the night to end and the day to come, so that the day might end, too, and the night come again at last.

She had heard the bells of St George's Church chime the hours, one after the other, one after the other, Jesu! she had heard the bells chime at midnight; and now she was listening to them chiming the hour of six in the morning; six in the morning, an' all's well, so she'd soon have to be getting up in order to be ready an' in good time for everything.

It would never do to keep the holy clergyman waiting. He was also the manager of her school, and to be kept on her hands as long as possible, if she wasn't to be kicked out of her job as

teacher the minute she was married; for even a few more weeks'
work would pay something off the hired furniture, though, in a
lot of ways, she'd be glad to be rid of the whole of them, and so
be able to devote herself to her home and her husband.

Let her think, now. Yes, everything was ready – the gold half-
sovereign for the fee; though what a well-off clergyman wanted
with a shining half-sovereign that she needed so badly herself
she couldn't guess and daren't argue about, for it was here, and
there, and gone, like Hamlet's ghost; gone, but not forgotten,
either, was the gold wedding-ring that she herself was minding,
to be given to her love when she met him at the front door of the
church; the new dress, with its leg-of-mutton sleeves, carefully
laid out over the back of a chair; the new frilled white petticoat
carefully laid out over the dress; the snowy drawers, with deep
flounces sweeping out around the edges, carefully laid out over
the petticoat; the garibaldi blouse prettily folded on the seat of
the chair, and the pink stays nesting on the blouse; and her new
high boots going half way up the calves of her legs, under the
chair, and vivid blue bustle hanging by its ribbons from a hook
in the wall – all well conserved for weeks in layers of lavender to
entice and make glad the heart of the leading side-drummer in the
first battalion of the King's Liverpool Regiment, best shot in the
regiment, and regimental haircutter to the men.

And fine the drummer'll look in his red coat with its white
braid and crescent epaulettes, his spiked helmet on his dear
dark head; and the blue, yellow, and green bugler's cord slung
around his breast an' back, with the two gorgeous tassels cas-
cading down from his left shoulder; and with his short cross-
hilted sword hanging from his hip he'll look like the knight of the
burning pestle, or a peacock turned into a moving man, with a
heavy square face, dimly lighted by two deep-black eyes, a
thick dark moustache, jet-black hair carefully parted in the dead
centre, and on the left turned into a jauntily curled quiff. A
broad-shouldered body, short, thick, and sturdy legs, and a jerky
and conceited way of walking like a peacock turned into a moving
man.

From tomorrow on – though she'd have to put in an appearance
now and again till her job was gone – she'd no longer have to
sing in the parish church of St Mary's. She'd sing, now, only for
her drummer-boy; and Johnny, maybe, when he came on a visit
to them after the two of them had settled down. No longer the
rector would have the right to hold her tight as a teacher in the

infants' school of St Mary's at twenty-five Lower Dominick
Street, the biggest house in Dublin, with its five storeys up and
five windows across; teaching a hundred and ten score kids from
three to seven years old in a huge hall at the other end of a big
yard, a hall as big as hell and as high as heaven, heated in the
winter be a big stove that got red-hot an' gave out stifling fumes;
savin' ourselves from suffocatin' be puttin' a galvanized bucket,
filled with water, on the flue, an' moidered trying to keep the
children from burnin' themselves, the way they'd be runnin'
to see the sulphur blobs dancin' on the surface when the water
boiled; and the windows stuck up near the roof to deliver the
kids from the temptation of leppin' out through them whenever
the lessons got too hard; to be opened, you had to strain at a
long rope, though if you once got it opened you'd never get it
shut, an' if you once got it shut you'd never get it open, so there
they stayed tight and taut the whole year through the time that
Johnny learned his ABC here, an' how to read an' spell words of
two letters, so me he we be my no go to up it is or of ox an at
am as in if us on, is it an ox? it is an ox, is it my ox? if it is an
ox it is my ox, so go up to the ox as it is my ox, I am at the ox,
with a little song to cheer him up in the winter when the north
wind doth blow and we shall have snow an' what will the robin
do then, poor thing, oh he'll run to the barn to keep himself
warm an' hide his head under his wing, poor thing, to be runnin'
round after a surplice for forty pounds a year bursting me lungs
with the dint of singin' O be joyful in the Lord, all ye lands serve
the Lord with gladness an' come before His presence with a
song of sixpence for it is He that hath made us an' not we ourselves, an' we are His people an' the sheep of His pasture, never
failin' to hear the baa-baas of the white sheep or even the baa-
baas of a black sheep astray in the wilderness stumbling up an'
stumbling down the mountains wild and bare, far off from the
gates of gold opened for all with a wide welcome in the first of
only two sacraments, namely baptism by which infants even are
grafted into the Church as is laid down in the twenty-seventh
article, and are therein made members of Christ and signed with
the sign of the Cross in token that they shall never be ashamed
to confess Christ crucified but continue His faithful soldiers
and servants unto their lives' ending, with a cough from the stout
Protestants present to show they realized only too well that this
business of the signing of the cross is but a fond thing vainly
imagined and partaking in its essence and application of an

echo of the profane and old wives' fables believed in and loved
by the unfortunate Roman Catholics downsunk deep in grievous
and deadly superstitions winked at by the pope and bishops,
pretendin' that they came straight out of the mouth of the holy
apostles starin' outa the stained-glass windows at us all singin'
at the top of our voices that the Lord hath done marvellous things
an' callin' on the round world an' all dwellin' therein to sit up
an' take notice of me real mind dwellin' on a scarlet coat decorated gay with white braid dotted with little red crowns an' the
green, blue, an' yellow woven tassels hangin' on his breast, an'
the bugle hangin' at his side'll make him look like Let me like a
soldier fall upon some open plain, his breast expandin' for the
ball to blot out every stain, as we go up the aisle facin' the altar
to be reverently an' discreetly an' advisedly buckled together for
ever an' ever till death do us part from that day forward for
better'n worse an' richer or poorer in sickness or health to love
an' to cherish, to hate an' to perish, me Ma says if I marry him,
for he's rough and uncouth, but the love of a good woman'll
make him gentle an' meek an' mild, an' even if all the gilt an'
braid an' swingin' tassels are hidin' ignorance, after we've been
married a day or two, a lesson a night for a year'll learn him more
than a swift way of picking out the coloured letters of the alpha-
bet, and taking of a lower number from a higher one will be less
of a strain, for him to give up the drink, too, after a loving talk
before we go to sleep for the night is far spent an' the day is at
hand when me Ma'll realize how wrong she was in thinkin' he
knew nothin' more than how to beat a roll on a drum an' blow
a few bugle-calls, after her goin' into ecstasies herself at the con-
cert when she heard Nicholas on the stage, an' another soldier
in the back of the gallery unseen be any, with a muted cornet
playing the Alpine Echoes with a tenderness overpowerin' to
anyone having anything even approachin' a heart to feel that in
love certificates for French an' music an' freehand drawing are
but little things that are here today an' gone tomorrow, for love
can give up a lot without missin' anything as long as his heart
beats true to me his love, ready to follow after him saying Whither
thou goest I will go, where thou lodgest I will lodge, an' where
thou diest will I die rather than turn an ear to the old woman's
croakin' about the risk, I'm takin' it all like the gipsy's warning
not to trust him gentle lady, though his voice be soft an' sweet,
heed him not who kneels beside thee softly pleading at thy feet,
now thy life is in its morning, cloud not this thy happy lot, to be

saying prayers an' chantin' psalms an' singin' hymns an' teaching a crowd of chiselurs who can pick up the truth the whole truth and nothing but the truth that the top of the map is called the north the lower part the south the right-hand side the east and the left-hand side the west only be having it stung into them with the constant encouragement of the cane, with a few sweet cuts added to give good measure and to hurry them off the broad way that leadeth to destruction on to the narrow way that leadeth to a sure an' certain way of gettin' on in the world when they grow up into fair women and brave men whose hearts beat happily when the music arises with its voluptuous swell an' soft eyes speak love to eyes that speak again unto the children of Israel that they go forward to do the thing I have to do once me mind is made up, for with his strong arms he'll be well able to keep and protect me from all evil and cares not like the dawny white-collared mickeys only fit for perchin' on soft-cushioned office-stools from nine till four an' comin' home at the end of the week with barely enough in their pockets to help towards payin' the rent while they're lookin' forward the whole year through towards the one decent meal they allow themselves when the bells are ringin' in Christmas Day an' the herald angels are singin' an' salutin' the happy morn whereon was born a Saviour who is Christ the Lord bringin' peace on earth to every country save only this unhappy land soaked in superstition an' ignorant of all things belongin' to its peace, hard set in a mad race after Home Rule with Parnell at the head of the hunt hallooin' them on who ought to know better being as he is a Protestant an' the only gentleman among the gang of guttersnipes he's gathered round him muckin' up the dignity an' grace of the House of Commons an' eager to undo all the fine work done durin' the past few centuries in civilizin' the wild Irish, showin' them how decent an' handsome life may be made when it gets to know the truth as it is in Christ Jesus an' Protestant an' loyal activities in general, I'd say that if these Home Rule gentry got their way there wouldn't be a Protestant cathedral left standing an' we'd go about all our days wallowin' in blasphemous fables an' dangerous deceits fully set forth in the Romish Mass by which the very words of our Saviour are twisted into a meaning they were never intended to have, any understandin' at all is to know that the Irish must be kept down for their own good, for if once they got the upper hand the people who matter would immediately be made unsafe in the positions they are entitled to hold under the Union Jack which is the only

flag left that for a thousand years braved battle an' the breeze an'
has brought joy an' security to all who live under it an' remain
respectable, shown be the fact that Victoria is known as the
Great White Mother by all the peoples under her sway, excludin'
the Fenians cruelly callin' her the Famine Queen, but we'll never
let the Fenians or the followers of Parnell be anything more than
spouters at a meeting or two or singers of God Save Ireland at
night in their cabins with the windows closed an' the doors shut
tight, which is only fair seein' that this is a free country an' everyone has a right to his own opinions, an' trying to keep people
down only makes matters worse, like the damned English with
their No Irish Need Apply after the Park murders, even though
it was well known that it wasn't the English Protestant Cavendish
the Invincibles were after but the Irish Catholic Burke who was
noted as a prime boyo for preventin' the people from budgin' an
inch beyond a common prostration he himself thought proper
be hints quietly placed in his ear from the judges an' generals of
Dublin Castle puttin' mounted Constabulary on the main road
of the Phoenix Park after the deed was done, an' Marwood the
hangman dancin' gaily around the giant Joe Brady while his
assistant was tying him up for the drop with the rope placed fair
an' nice around Brady's neck an' he marchin' on, never listenin'
to the priest sayin' the prayers for the dyin', but only murmurin'
Poor ould Ireland, poor ould Ireland with only less than a minute
left to prepare to meet his God, leavin' behind him the unfortunate Irish lookin' an' roarin' for what they know they can't get
an' traducin' themselves early an' late by their figaries on the
floor of the House of Commons, with the great Marquis of
Salisbury, if it wasn't for Parnell, well able to keep them under
his thumb an' constantly laughin' at them an' shakin' his head
when he heard of Fanny Parnell wavin' a newspaper over her
head an' rushin' in to her mother to say with a cheer that Arabi,
ara be jabers, Arabi Pasha had beaten the British in Egypt,
forgettin' that many of her own brave people were sheddin' their
blood to keep up England's glory in spite of all the agents an'
bailiffs an' landlords who were meetin' with a sharp an' sudden
end in followin' their lawful rights an' duties, which hardly bears
thinkin' about seein' that it might well have been my own
Nicholas who is to become one with me before tomorrow's sun
sets that had been cut clean in two by a double-handed dervish
sword, soakin' the hot sands of the desert with his blood an'
his fadin' ears full of the yells of the heathen tramplin' on his

poor body, carryin' the black flags of the Mahdi an' his hordes pourin' outa the Soudan after puttin' the finishin' touch on General Gordon, with ould Gladstone cuttin' down a tree under the eye of the mornin' an' warmin' his well-slippered feet be the fire in the hush of the evenin', failin' to lift a finger in organizin' a column to go to the relief of the men who were fightin' their last fight for their Queen an' Country'll never forget them and the memory of the great things done will be green for ever, from now on I'll have to be settin' these things aside to concentrate on things far more important than Gladstones an' Gordons who are here today an' gone tomorrow where the good niggers go, so put up de shovel an' de hoe for there's no more work for poor uncle Ned for he's gone where de good niggers go, and the rest is silence as Shakespeare says, so it behooves your humble servant to tamper only with the change tomorrow's bound to bring about in the things I think an' the things I do from the day forth so help me God, to measure how I'm goin' to live on what I get an' what I give outa what I get while he's in the Army for the next year or more before his twelve years with the colours are up an' he gets his deferred pay of twenty-one pounds to give us a start off, with his regimental pay an' hair-cuttin' allowance amountin' to not more than fifteen shillin's a week all told, it'll be a tough job to keep goin' without even allowin' for common emergencies that are sure to crop up while he's there an' I'm here waitin' for tomorrow's darkness when a girl that never lifted her clothes an inch above her ankles'll have to take them all off an' give everything she holds dear to the man of her choice in spite of me mother for ever pickin' at me because poor Nicholas isn't anything higher than a drummer, as if rank mattered in any way to a true-hearted an' pure girl who truly loved a man, an' furthermore if you look at their pictures what real difference is there between Nicholas with his gay red coat on his back an' his bugle by his side an' his spiky helmet on his head an' the Prince of Wales in his grand-cut coat an' ponderous puggareed helmet, makin' him look for all the world like Achilles on the warpath standin' with a gun in his right hand an' his left foot planted firm on the dead body of a poor Bengal tiger that others shot while he was nice and snug in an embrasured howdyedo howdah high up on the back of an elephant tired of rajahin' about the jungle to give a couple of hours' excitement to men whose life's laid out for them like the way a table's laid out for high tea, an' it's high time for me now to be settin' myself to get shipshape to meet me fate for there's the bell of St George's soundin' seven an' if I was in the country I'd hear the lark, the ploughman's clock, an' herald of the morn.

She jumped out of bed, spread the bedclothes over the rails, and opened the window wide so that the air might flood the room, and she and her clothes might win the first freshness of the morning.

She dressed herself in an old skirt, blouse, and shoes, went into the kitchen, lighted the fire, planted a big oval pot filled with water on the fire; returned to the bedroom, and remade the bed. When the water in the big oval pot boiled, she brought from the little yard a galvanized bath, set it in the middle of the floor, poured the boiling water into it, cooled it, judging a suitable heat with the tips of her fingers. Then she stripped herself naked, stepped into the bath, and washed her body all over, pinching with pride the plumpness of her thighs and the firmness of her breasts, budding red at the tips. Her Nicholas was going to find a lot of stimulating charms in his Ella. Naked and dry, she hurried back to the bedroom, and dressed slowly, with constant self-admiration, putting on the white chemise, drawers, and petticoat, afterwards washing her teeth, rubbing them briskly with a brush sprinkled with camphorated chalk. The only one in the house who did it. She opened her mouth wide before a small looking-glass, and admired them, for they were even, white, strong, and really beautiful. Then returning to the kitchen, she emptied the soiled water from the bath, and placed the bath back on a nail in the wall beside the privy. She felt proud in her new clothes, and thought of the exciting time she'd have when Nicholas would be helping her to take them off, one be one, in readiness for the crowning of their connexion after holy church had incorporated the two in one. She would give her Nicholas a good time, and, in an hour or two, all she had would be his for ever an' ever, amen.

She filled the kettle, placed it in the heart of the blazing fire, and called up her mother.

The breakfast was a chill and bitter one, Johnny alone exhilarated, spooning an egg into him in honour of the great thing that was to happen soon in God's holy temple; while Ella and her mother sat sad, busy avoiding each other's eyes, sat silent and sad at the table.

—When I'm a big man, said Johnny, I'll be a bugler, like Nicholas, so I will, and blow Reveille when the day begins an' the Last Post when the day ends.

—Tom an' Michael, in their letters, say I'm doin' well, murmured Ella.

—I hope you'll never be a soldier, said Johnny's mother; and Johnny's joy was dimmed.

When she had nibbled a little toast and drunk a little tea, Ella went to her bedroom, washed her hands and mouth to get rid of any lingering crumbs, put on her coat and hat carefully, sat down on the bed, and cried a little.

Everything would be stretchin' out in front of me fine, she thought, pitifully, if it wasn't for the mind of my mother.

She was ready for any emergency, so she was, having with her something old and something new, something borrowed and something blue, and a lucky sixpence in her shoe – everything in apple-pie order, if it wasn't for the mind of her mother.

—Here's the cab for you, she heard her mother's voice cry from the kitchen.

Ella got up quickly, came into the kitchen, and watched her mother putting back the things that had been used at their breakfast.

—Goodbye, Mother, said Ella.

—Goodbye, said her mother shortly.

Something's up between them again, thought Johnny. One 'id imagine the mother 'id be proud her girl was goin' to marry a soldier. He saw Ella's lips quiver, and he felt a catch in his throat. He snatched up his cap from a chair, and went out into the street to watch the cab and to wave a fond farewell.

Ella stood watching her mother for a moment, her hand patting the hat on her head.

—Aren't you going to say something to me, before I go? she pleaded.

—You've made your bed, an' you'll have to lie on it, replied her mother.

Ella went swiftly out from her mother's presence, straight to the waiting cab. A side glance showed her figures standing at every door intently staring at what was happening outside of O'Casside's house. Far down the street, a ragged man, with head bent and eyes fixed on the ground, was singing querulously, The Anchor's Weighed. The driver held the door of the cab open for her, and Ella, tightening her lips to show all onlookers what she was made of, climbed into the cab, telling the cabman to drive to St Mary's Church, while Johnny waited to wave his cap in token of farewell whenever Ella waved a fond farewell to him from the window of the cab. The driver got on to his seat, caught up the reins, said Gee up, gee up, to the mare, and the cab began to move away to the sorrowful song of

> *A tear fell gently from her eye,*
> *When last we parted on the shore;*
> *My bosom heav'd with many a sigh,*
> *To think I ne'er might see her more.*

The song suddenly stopped, and the singer stooped to pick up a penny that had rattled on the pavement beside him. Then the singer started again, as the cab was passing by him, and Johnny waited, cap in hand, to wave a fond farewell to Ella.

> *The anchor's weighed, the anchor's weighed,*
> *Farewell, farewell, remember me,*

the singer sang, with his head bent and his eyes looking down at the ground.

But Ella's face did not appear at the window, nor did her well-kept hand wave a farewell to Johnny, though he watched, cap in hand, till the cab turned out of sight round the corner of the street.

And so the bride went forth to meet the bridegroom.

THE TIRED COW

JOHNNY STOOD in the deep of the doorway, pressing back as far as he could go, to shelter from the rain pelting from the heavens. He watched the slanting lines of rain falling on the hot street, turning the dust into a muddy confusion as rain and dust, forming a rapid stream, rushed along the gutters, gurgling over the bars of the gullies and disappearing, like a little waterfall, down into the sewers below.

It's too hot an' heavy to last, he thought, as he watched it hopping off the pavement, and glanced at the people in the houses opposite hurriedly closing their windows to prevent the rain from slipping into their front rooms.

How 'ud it be, thought Johnny, if God opened the windows of

heaven, an' let it rain, rain like hell, for forty days an' forty nights, like it did when the earth was filled with violence, an' it repented the Lord that He hath made man, causin' a flood till the waters covered the houses an' the highest tops of the highest mountains in the land? There'd be a quare scatterin' an' headlong rushin' about to get a perch on the highest places, to sit watchin' the water risin' an' risin' till it lapped your legs, and there was nothin' left to do but to close your eyes, say a hot prayer, slide in with a gentle slash splash, an' go to God; though you'd hardly expect to find a word of welcome on the mat in heaven, if God Himself had made up His mind you were better dead. But that could never happen now, for God had promised Noah, a just man and perfect in his generation, there'd never be anything like a flood any more; and as proof positive, set His bow in the cloud as a token of a covenant between Him and the earth, for Noah to see when, sick an' sore, he crept out of the ark to start all over again with what was left of himself an' family, with the beasts of the earth, all creeping things, and all the fowls of the air, male an' female, that he had carried with him all the time the flood remained over the surface of the earth.

There was the very rainbow, now, sparklin' fine, one end restin' on the roof of Mrs Mullally's house, and the other end leanin' on the top of one of the Dublin Mountains, with the centre touchin' the edge of the firmament; an', if only our eyes were a little brighter, we'd see millions an' millions of burnished angels standin' on it from one end to the other, havin' a long gawk at all that was goin' on in the earth that God made in the beginnin', an' that had to make a fresh start the time that Noah an' his wife, an' his sons, an' his sons' wives came outa the ark with the elephants, the lions, the horses, and the cows that musta given Noah the milk he needed when he was shut off from everything, till the dove came back with the olive branch stuck in her gob.

Johnny suddenly remembered that the day was Thursday, and all the cattle would be pouring down to the boats that carried them all to England. He stooped down, foraged out the key from under the weatherboard (where his mother had left it, in case he should want to go in), opened the door, and went in. He ran through the rooms till he found the ashplant that Archie had cut from a tree in Finglas when he was coming back home after having had a few drinks at The Jolly Topers. With the stick held tight in his hand, Johnny locked the door, replaced the key under the weatherboard, and hurried off down the street.

The rain was softly falling now, and the shining sun had made it golden. As he turned into drowsy Dorset Street, he could hear the cries of the drovers, pitched high or pitched low, as he ran along till he came to the corner of the North Circular Road, the broad highway from the cattle-market to the boats where the cattle were shipped to England to feed the big bellies of the English, as Archie said, while the poor ignorant Irish got the leavin's. Here he loved to stand to watch the passing beasts, holding his stick ready, shooing back any one of them that tried to turn aside from the straight road, running forward, when the animal turned with a low circular move of its horned head and a frightened look in its big eyes, to give it a parting swipe on the rump as hard as he could with the ashplant.

Here they were, in their hundreds, streaming along, holding up the traffic as they slowly crossed the road, a mist of steam hanging over them as the hot sun dried the falling rain that glistened on their hides. The drovers followed behind, giving vent to occasional ritualistic cries of hi-yup hi-hee-yup, encouraging the beasts on their way to the steamier pens of the cattle-boats. The drovers had taken it that the day would be a fine one, so none wore a coat or even a sack slung around his shoulders. Their clothes were soaking wet; water trickled down their faces from dripping hats and hair, and a scowl of discomfort marred every rough and ready face as they hi-yup hi-hee-yupped after the animals. Sometimes a cow would suddenly separate itself from the drove, and stretch out its thick neck to cool its steaming nostrils and take a drink from the rain-water that gurgled along the gutters; but an angry drover would quickly pounce out, bring his stick with a bang on the cow's flank, making her jerk her head up and scurry back to the drove, boring her way forward through the other animals from the swiftly falling stick. Then a herd of pigs came moving slowly by, grunting continuously, carrying their snouts along close to the ground, the drovers prodding them viciously behind the ears, if they halted in the march onwards. The pigs were Johnny's favourites, for their backsides were more like backsides than the backsides of the cattle and sheep, and the thwack of a stick as it fell on a pig's flank, and the sharp squeal he gave when the blow fell, were far more exciting than the silent start a cow or a sheep gave whenever a blow fell on them.

Johnny was in his element, rushing here and rushing there, hi-hee-yupping the cattle on in his own way, and getting in an odd shrewd knock with his ashplant on a cow or a sheep, before the animal was quick enough to dodge out of the way of the blow.

A cow turned left to try to meander down Dorset Street, but the bold Johnny and his ashplant stood in the way. The cow tried dodging, but Johnny, side-stepping left and side-stepping right, was always in front, with left arm extended, and right waving the ashplant, while he hee-hi-hee-yupped, eh, he hee-yupped right in the animal's face. The cow lowered her head and lowed. Johnny took a few steps backward.

—Eh, there, kidger, shouted a drover from the end of the herd, don't let the bastard dodge yeh! Let him have it over the snout; go on – right over the snout. He won't puck yeh. Go on – fair over the snout!

Johnny balanced himself on his toes, and brought the ashplant down on the steaming nose of the cow. She backed hastily away, turned swiftly round and hurried back into the midst of the drove, shaking her snout.

—Good kidger, good kidger, called out the drover happily; that larrup put the fear of God into her, hi-hee hi-yup, he sang as he followed the herd, Johnny stepping into the road beside him, eager to make the pride of driving the cow back into the right way last as long as possible; while the rain, made golden by the shining sun, continued to fall softly.

Suddenly the drover let an oath out of him as a tired cow ambled over to the side-walk, folded herself up, and lay down, with her forelegs tucked in under her, right on the path where everyone walked, carin' for nothin', an' just starin' straight in front of her, with her tightly-filled udders pressed hard against the wet pavement.

While a second drover held the rest of the herd bunched up close to the side-walk so that other cattle could pass, the drover nearer to Johnny ran over to the tired cow, and began to hammer her with his stick.

—Yeh whore's get, he shouted, slashin' away at her; get up on yer hind legs, an' waltz along to where you're goin' – he-hee-yup hi-hee-yup!

But his yellin' an' cursin' an' slashin' couldn't get a stir outa her that lay on the path where everyone walked, just starin' out in front of herself, lookin' as if she saw nothin', an' never movin', no matter how hard an' heavy the blows an' curses the drover gave.

—Eh, you there, he called to Johnny, come over here, an' give a fella a hand to get her movin'; for if she's once allowed to settle down, she'll stay well set for the night.

Johnny hurried over to where the cow was lying.

—Now, said the drover, when I twist her tail, let the bitch's ghost have it as hard as you can with the stick.

The drover gathered th' animal's tail in his hand, and twisted it round his arm, twisted it so tight that he seemed to be pullin' it outa the cow's body. A drover passing with another herd paused and ran over, and he and Johnny hammered the cow with their sticks, and the other twisted and twisted her tail till the sweat was runnin' down all their faces. The cow gave a quiver and raised herself jerkily on to her hind legs, still keeping her forelegs tucked under her.

A little crowd that had gathered, led by a gunner of the Royal Field Artillery, shooed and shouted to encourage the cow away from her need of a rest; the drover increased the tension of the twist in her tail, and Johnny and the other drover quickened the strokes of the sticks. Hee-hi heee-yuphi-hee-yup, they all cried together, but the cow slowly bent her hindquarters again, and sank down to the ground, never movin', starin' out in front of herself, an' lookin' as if she saw an' felt nothin', while the rain, made golden by the shinin' sun, still kept fallin' softly.

—All me efforts gone for nothin' – curse o' Jasus on it! said the drover, wiping the sweat from the tantalized look on his face.

His fellow-drover who was guarding the rest of the cattle waved his stick impatiently.

—Come on, for God's sake, he shouted. We can't stay here till she makes up her mind to get up an' walk. The kidger'll keep an eye on her for us.

—Keep an eye on her, sonny, said the other drover to Johnny, for fear she'd shift her quarters. We'll be back as soon as ever we've planted the others in the pens at the North Wall. And he went off to join his comrade, leaving Johnny to watch the cow starin' straight out in front of her as if she saw nothin', while the rain, made golden by the shinin' sun, still kept softly fallin'.

Johnny stood in the deep of a doorway, cautiously keeping his eye on the cow. Beyond an occasional twitch of her tail, she gave no sign of life. Every beast in the forest is God's, he thought, an' the cattle upon a thousand hills. But a sthray cow lyin' on a rain-wet street is not enough to make God bother His head to give a thought about it.

Time crept on, and soon he saw crowds of children coming home from school. Some stopped to look at the quiet cow, but

Johnny warned them off, tellin' them to go on off home, an' not be disturbin' th' poor animal. The sun went down, the rain still kept fallin' softly, but it was no longer golden; and Johnny shivered. He waited an' waited for the drover, but the twilight came instead, and the vivid red colour of the cow darkened. He'd wait no longer. His mother'd be home, and she'd wondher where he was. He came out from the doorway, looked around to make sure that the drover was nowhere in sight; then he stole away towards home. At the end of the road he looked back, and, in the purple of the twilight, he saw the dark mass of the cow still lyin' on the path where everybody walked, starin' straight in front of her as if she saw nothin', while the rain still kept fallin' on her softly; but the sun had stopped her shinin', and the rain was no longer golden.

THE STREET SINGS

GOLDEN AND JOYOUS were the days for Johnny when he was free from pain; when he could lift the bandage from his eye, and find the light that hurt him hurt no longer; that the shining sun was as good today as it was when the Lord first made it; glorifying the dusty streets, and putting a new robe, like the wedding garment of the redeemed, on the dingy-fronted houses. Now he could jump into the sunlight, laugh, sing, shout, dance, and make merry in his heart, with no eye to see what he was doing, save only the eye of God, far away behind the blue sky in the daytime, and farther away still behind the golden stars of the night-time.

The pain was gone, and life was good and brave and honest and wholesome and true. No sitting down, cramped in every arm and leg at school. No whining out, now, of numbers and of words; no reading that gave no hope, or put no new thing in front for him to see; no maps that made the living world a thing of shreds an' patches; no longing for the day to hasten its slow march forward; no wearying talk of God and His davyjack, the giant-killer; – nothing but the blue sky with its white clouds by day, and the black sky with its silver stars by night; no thought but his own – and God's warning against joy a long way off from him.

Sitting on a window-sill, he could watch the women scouring

their doorsteps; or, possibly, one with a little more money, painting it a bright red or a fair blue; or, in old skirts and blouses, cleaning their windows with rags and paraffin, sometimes exchanging gossip from opposite sides of the street, both busy at the windows, and never once turning to look at one another.

He loved to see the bakers' carts trotting into the street, Johnston, Mooney, and O'Brien's cart at one end, and Boland's at the other, one coloured green and the other coloured a reddish brown. The carts were big and box-like, filled with double rows of shallow trays on which rested row after row of steaming loaves, tuppence or tuppence-farthing each. Underneath a deep deep drawer, going the whole length of the cart, filled with lovely white an' brown squares, soda squares, currant squares, and crown loaves, covered with their shining golden crust, ruggedly tapering at the top, like the upper part of a king's crown. He loved, too, to watch the milk-carts come jingling into the street, filled with shining churns, having big brass taps sticking out through holes in the tailboard, all polished up to the nines; though, as Johnny's mother often said, if they were as particular with the insides as they were with the outsides, the milk'd be safer to dhrink. From these big churns the milkman filled a can with a long snout on which rattled the half-pint and pint measures used to dish out the milk as it was required to the women waiting at the doors with jugs and mugs in their hands, to buy just enough milk that would temper the bitterness of the tea they so often made for themselves, their husbands, and their children. Whenever he was fit, Johnny used to help the milkman, running around with the long-snouted can, filling half-pints and pints of milk into outstretched jugs; the women constantly grumbling that Mr Divene always gave them a betther tilly, so he did; Johnny defending himself be saying that he had to be careful with other people's property, so he had; and then, when the work was done, with the milkman sitting on the seat, he'd stand up in the cart, gather the reins in his hands, sing out a gee-gee-up, suit his balance cutely to the jig-jog of the cart, and drive the jennet back to the dairy.

Sometimes with other kids he'd stand stiff staring hard and listening curiously to a German band, foreigners – fleecing their pennies from the poor, so Archie said – wearing their blue uniforms braided with red or green, blowing their best into their big brass bugles; while the big drummer kept time, one two, one one, one two, to the tune of a song about a German soldier on his way with his regiment to the war:

They marched along down the village street,
Their banners floating gay;
The children cheered to the tramping feet,
As they marched to the war away;
But one of them turned around
To look back once again,
Although his lips gave forth no sound,
His heart sang this refrain:

Oh, love, dear love, be true,
My heart is only thine;
When the war is o'er, we'll part no more
From Ehren on the Rhine.
Oh, love, dear love, be true,
My heart is only thine;
When the war is o'er, we'll part no more
From Ehren on the Rhine!

On special nights, Johnny would hurry off to the back gate of the grocery store; would watch and wait for his opportunity to run over to the boxes that were piled against the wall, and swiftly pilfer all the lovely coloured sheets and slips of paper that had lined or bordered the boxes, gathering, like lightning, the blue, black, crimson, yellow, and green treasures to make crimson chevrons for his sleeves or yellow epaulettes for his shoulders; a green sash to go across his breast; blue belt round his waist; and many coloured strips waving gaily from his cap. Then, armed with a home-made wooden sword, he turned himself into a warrior, a conqueror of many, bent on battle, free from terror, ready to strike at the first enemy that came near, as he strode along streaming with coloured orders presented to him by Her Majesty Queen Victoria. Whenever a chance came, he would share his treasures with a group of Catholic boys, just home from school, decorating them with minor-coloured strips, changing them into soldiers, sergeants, with an ensign carrying a many-hued paper flag, and a drummer bearing on his hip a tin, veiled in strips of yellow and blue, rallying away for dear life, while the boys sang at the top of their voices,

We are ready for to fight,
We are the rovers;
We are all brave Parnell's men,
We are his gallant soldiers!

a song Johnny didn't like, for he was afraid that, in some way or another, it had a connexion with the Fenians; though his mother had told him his father had said that Parnell was a great Protestant, a great Irishman, and a grand man; and it was a good thing there was someone, anyway, fit to hinder the English from walking over the Irish people. When all the battles had been won; every country conquered; the Army safely home again; the decorations carefully removed, collected, and put away again, till the Army was needed again, it was grand to stand in the sunny street to wonder and argue about what would be the next best thing to do.

—Let's have a go at Duck on the Grawnshee, Touhy would say, an' I'm first.

—That me neck! Kelly would cry. Let's have Fox in the Den – a far betther game.

—Ball in the Decker, would be O'Halloran's choice; the daddy of them all, he'd add, an' I'm first.

—Count me out, if it's goin' to be Ball in the Decker, said Touhy.

—An' me, if it's goin' to be Duck on the Grawnshee, grumbled Kelly.

—Let Casside choose, then, said O'Halloran; an' for the sake o' the game, 've'll fall in with whatever he chooses. Hands over your hearts, an' promise yeh'll abide be whatever he says.

The Catholic boys got a thrill in playing with a Protestant. All the things promised by the Church to them were far away from him. They stared with interest at the look of fear and wonder that came into his face whenever he saw them crossing themselves, or heard them muttering a Hail Mary to the chime of the Angelus. And Johnny, though he liked them, thought them strange and to be pitied; for it is written, idolators shall not inherit the kingdom of God; and these comrades of his worshipped images, said prayers for the dead, which is contrary to the plain word of Scripture wherein it is written, God is not the God of the dead, but of the livin'; and again, Blessed are the dead who die in the Lord; showin' as plain as a pikestaff that if you are good, and die, you go straight up; and, if you're bad, and die, you go straight down; so that when you're once dead, prayers availeth nothin'. Then, too, they had a mortal dread of the Protestant Bible, the plain word of God, easy understood, even be kidgers; if you only have faith, and don't forget to ask God to open your eyes, you'll see all you want to see, an' hear all you want to hear, and understand all you want to understand of the truth as it is in Christ Jesus. Then they thought it a great sin to miss what they called Mass on Sundays an' holy days of obligation; and they had a curious custom of sprinkling themselves with holy water to keep the devil at a safe distance. Still, they laughed the same way as he laughed; and played the same way as he played; and shared what could be bought for a penny, whenever they had a penny to spend. So here he was in the midst of his Catholic comrades, singing and shouting and playing and making merry in his heart; with no eye to see, save only the eye of God that never closed, now far away behind the bright blue sky; and farther away at night, hidden behind the shine of the silver stars.

—Let's have Ball in the Decker, first, said Johnny, an' afterwards, Duck on the Grawnshee; an' I'll be last in both for the sake of the game.

Then they all laid their caps in a row at an angle against the wall of a house. They took turns, Touhy first and Johnny last, trying to roll a ball into one of the caps, the player doing his best to avoid rolling it into his own. When the ball rolled into a cap, the owner ran over to his cap, the rest scattering in flight, caught the ball up, and flung it at a boy nearest and easiest to hit. If he missed, a pebble was put in his cap, but if he hit a boy, then a pebble was put in the cap of the boy the ball had struck. The game went on till a boy had six pebbles or more (the number being decided at the beginning of the game). Then the boy with the six pebbles in his cap had to stand by the wall, and stretch out his arm, and press the back of his hand firm against the bricks. Then each boy, with a hard half-solid ball, had six shots at the outstretched hand; each aiming at hitting it as hard as he could, and enjoying the start of pain appearing on a boy's face whenever the hard ball crashed into the palm of his hand. Each boy had to go through the ordeal, the number of blows being the same as the number of pebbles in his cap. Johnny liked the ordeal; his hands were small and firm and hard, and the impact of the ball stung his hand far less than it stung the softer and larger hands of his comrades. So the game went on till they were tired, and many eyes were blinking back the tears from the smart of hands that were red, and stung fiercely.

Then followed Duck on the Grawnshee, in which a marble was placed in a slight depression, making it look like a squatting duck. Round the resting marble, a chalk circle was drawn. The boy who owned the duck on the grawnshee stood, with one foot within the chalk circle, watching the other boys who shot their marbles from the kerb, trying to knock the duck off the grawn-shee. If a boy failed to knock it off, he had to gather up his marble again without letting himself be touched by the boy who was doing the duck on the grawnshee; if he was touched by the duck, with a foot in the circle, after lifting or touching his marble, then the touched boy became the duck, and the other joined the rest who were trying to knock the duck from the grawnshee. When the marbles thrown had stopped so near the duck that the outstretch-ed hand of the boy who guarded the grawnshee could easily touch any who ventured to pick up a marble, the owners had to stand still, and depend on one who was a good shot to send the duck flying from the grawnshee, for when the duck was off the grawnshee the touch lost its magic, and the boys could seize their marbles and run off without danger, till the owner of the duck had replaced it on the grawnshee. So Johnny shot his marble at the duck on the grawnshee, or stood, watchful and alert, with one foot in the ring, ready to touch any boy within reach who made to get his marble lying motionless on the ground near the grawnshee; shouting, laughing as he did so, for hunger was forgot-ten, time had stopped, and his joy was full.

Often in the evening when the stars were still pale in the sky, the boys would see the girls skipping at the other end of the street, as many as ten or fifteen of them jumping gracefully over a regularly turning rope. The boys would slink up nearer and nearer to the skipping girls; the girls would occasionally glance dis-dainfully at the boys, but in their hearts they wished them to come closer. With a defiant shout, weakened with the tone of a shy shame in it, a boy, bolder than the rest, would jump in merrily; the rest would follow him, and joyous faces of boys and girls would shine out of thin dusty clouds raised out of the road by the beating of the skippers' feet dancing in the way of peace.

Tired of skipping, someone would suggest a ring; and boys and girls, their shyness gone, would join hands in a great ring, a girl, pretending to be weeping with her hands over her eyes, standing in the centre. Older people, the men smoking, the women knitting or gossiping, would stand at the doors, and watch the circling ring, singing as it circled,

Poor Jennie is aweeping, aweeping, aweeping,
Poor Jennie's aweeping on a bright Summer day.
Pray tell us what you're weeping for, aweeping for, aweeping for,
Pray tell us what you're weeping for on a bright Summer day.

I'm weeping for my lover, my lover, my lover,
I'm weeping for my lover on a bright Summer day,

the girl in the centre of the ring would answer.

Or the ring would stand still with arms held high while a player would dart in and out of the ring under the upraised arms as the circle of boys and girls sang in a metre livelier than the first tune,

> *In and out the window, in and out the window, in and out*
> *the window,*
> *As you have done before.*
> *Stand and face your lover, stand and face your lover,*
> *stand and face your lover,*
> *As you have done before.*

Shy, grey-eyed Jennie Clitheroe, with her curly head hanging, stood before Johnny. He wished she hadn't picked on him, for a lot in the ring knew he was gone on her, and had seen his un-covered eye often seeking her out as she sat on the seat opposite in the Sunday school; and his face went scarlet as he heard the titters of the ring.

> *Chase him all round Dublin, chase him all round Dublin,*
> *chase him all round Dublin,*
> *As you have done before.*

Johnny made off round the circle of players, dodging in and out under the upraised arms, with Jennie hotfoot after him. For a while he kept well in front, then slowed down so that she could catch him, but dodging her at the last moment so that she had to fling an arm round him. Pretending to struggle, he managed to give her girlish body a sudden and affectionate pressure, releasing her at once when the ring shouted Oh, Johnny, fie for shame!

So, in a cute and gentle way, this play and these songs touched the time when the girl would long to let him kiss her with the kisses of his mouth and his banner over her would be love.

Or, best of all, when the boys had come back from school; when they had done their home lessons, and had come out into the street to get what fun they could: some of them, with suitable sticks, would start a game of hurley; others would rush away, to return with old legs of chairs, ashplants with crooked ends, walking-sticks, or a rib of a big box, pared at one end to give a grip. Opposing sides would be chosen, and the real game would start – one group striking the ball up, the other group striking the ball down the street – pushing and cursing when the game went against them; and shouting and cheering when a goal was scored. And Johnny, with his long hair growing into his eyes; his bandage thrust like a wad into his pocket; his face flushed and wet with sweat, rushed here, rushed there, swinging Archie's ashplant, cursing, shouting, cheering with the best of them, pucking the ball viciously when it came his way, slashing at any shin that came too near the ball, his own legs trickling with blood from blows received from others, feeling no pain; for alive with energy, hunger was forgotten, time had stopped, and his voice rang loud in the chorus of the song of the street.

THE PROTESTANT KID THINKS OF
THE REFORMATION

ONE FINE day, when Johnny's eyes were feeling better, he waved a joyous goodbye to two youngsters who lived a few doors down, and who were now on their way to school, well braced in their little satchels carrying books and lunch.

When they had disappeared round the end of the street, he took some marbles and a butt of chalk from his pocket; with the chalk, he marked a ring near the wall of the house, right under the window, placing a row of three marbles in the centre. He then went on to the road, took a sharp step forward which brought him to the edge of the kerb, and shot a marble from his right hand, aiming at the three other marbles in the centre of the ring. The first effort failed; the second knocked two marbles out of the ring; and the third, carefully aimed, sent the last one flying.

—Gettin' surer in me shot, every day, so I am, he thought.

Suddenly, a shadow like the shadow of a monster crow fell on the space between him and the marbles in the ring, and Johnny knew that the Reverend Mr Hunter was standing just beside him.

Johnny had checked himself from letting the marble in his hand fly at the three in the ring, and now stood, silent, at the edge of the kerb, waiting to hear the voice and the word that was in the beginning; and the word that was with God; and the word was God.

—I'm very glad to see, said the voice and the word, that your eyes are very much better so that you can pass away the time pleasantly playing marbles. But playing marbles isn't everything we have to do, you know. Little boys have other things to do in the world besides playing marbles. Now and again, of course, now and again; well and good; but not always, oh, not always. A little soldier of Christ has to learn many things, besides the way to play marbles; and you are a little soldier of Christ, aren't you?

—Yessir.

—And can you tell me when you were made a little soldier of Christ, Johnny?

—At baptism, sir.

—Quite right, Johnny; quite right, my boy. Had you not attended Sunday school, you wouldn't have known that; and it's so nice to be able to answer questions asked by grown-up people, isn't it?

—Yessir, replied Johnny, feeling a little proud of himself. Hunter wasn't such a bad fella, after all.

Much nicer, very much nicer, went on the clergyman, than playing marbles, isn't it?

Johnny tensed himself. So that was it. Oul' Hunter was trying to catch him unawares. Trying to make out he was in the wrong. Oh, it wasn't fair, it wasn't fair.

—Much nicer than just playing marbles, isn't it, John?

—Don't know, sir, I'd rather be playing marbles.

—But marble-playing is just idleness, John; and hardness came into the voice of Hunter. Don't you remember what the Bible says about idleness?

—No, sir.

—It says, John, the idle soul shall suffer hunger. Think of that, suffer hunger! That's what God says through the mouth of the wisest man who ever lived. The idle soul shall suffer hunger. So you see, we all have to be very much on our guard against idleness. And the voice and the word and the man went into the house, all business.

Johnny gathered up his marbles, replaced them in his pocket, and stood leaning against the window-sill.

It was terrible the way you had to be careful of everything you said. Hunter the runter the rix stix stunter, hunter the runter the rix stix stunter, he kept on murmuring.

He peeped in at the window, and saw his mother rise to her feet from washing out the floor, to greet the rix stix stunter. Keeping close to the window, he heard what was said between them.

He heard Hunter opening the ball with, Really, Mrs Casside, your boy must be sent to school. It is plain that his eyes are much better, and it is very distressing to think of him spending his time playing marbles, playing marbles, day after day. In a few years, he will have to take his place in life, and it is necessary that he should be made into a firm Protestant young man in this dark and sorrowful Roman land. You know that we are hemmed in on every side by popery; and so each of us must do all he can to preserve the privileges so hardly won by the Protestant reformation.

—Black balls, hunter, murmured Johnny, hunter the runter the rix stix stunter.

—Yessir, he heard his mother say, I'll do my best to send him next week.

—Oh, not next week, said Hunter peevishly – today. Now is the accepted time, now is the day of salvation. Come, get him in, and bring him down. You can finish what you're doing when you return. Less than half an hour will do it all.

—Pig balls hunter, murmured Johnny viciously, hunter the runter the rix stix stunter.

So, with his hands and face washed and a clean collar round his neck, Johnny was lugged off to school beside his mother, with the Reverend Hunter walking a little in front.

What past-gone long-gone dog-done thing had bred this dragging of him along at the backside of this soft-hatted stiff-collared chancer to be fitted in to the life of a Protestant day school? Maybe because Moses had stopped to have a gawk at the burning bush; or that the Israelites were able to make mincemeat of the Amalekites; or that the followers of Christ were first called Christians at Antioch; or, maybe, it was really because of

The Protestant Reformation

In the sixteenth century the simple and pure gospel handed down by the apostles was, without doubt, in its last gasp and ready to go bang at any minute, which, had it happened, would have deprived us of the great peace, security, and freedom that Christians enjoy at the present day. The pope, cardinals, bishops, and priests, far from following after goodness and orderly conversation, were rushing round everywhere on palfreys, jennets, mules, and chargers, looking for thrills, and jack-acting in festive season and sad season, as if they, and they only, had a special permit to shake a lot of merriment out of life. Black friars, white friars, purple-hooded monks, brown-caped priests, crimson-cassocked cardinals, and mitred abbots were eating the people out of house and home, and there wasn't a sign to be seen anywhere that heaven was any the better for the taxing and tithing that went on without let or hindrance everywhere. Rags, bones, and bottles, framed in precious stones, were carried about in holy processions, and were honoured and venerated by the mutt-massed people. The holy college of cardinals was turning out saints by steam, and there were so many of them that if a man wanted to say Pray for me to each one of them, he would have to keep going hard for ten hours a day, without a break for breakfast, dinner, or tea, and even then, according to an unquestionable ecclesiastical authority, it would take him three hundred and sixty-five thousand years to get near the end of the litany, so that there was small chance of God getting a look-in in the way of hearing Himself talked about, and praised by His people.

It was commonly reported by those who were close up to the inner circle, that, if a monk was to be kept from straddling a judy, he had to be shut up in a stone coffin, and let out only under the supervision of a hundred halberdiers while he was having a snack in the first, second, and third watches of the day, but as this guardianship of the ladies was too costly and too troublesome, the monks had it all their own way, and there wasn't a lassie in the whole wide world who didn't know a codpiece from the real thing, even when her eyes were shut and her mind wandering. And if any man made as much as a murmur, he was hit on the head with an excommunication that sent him falling headlong down to hell, without the slightest chance throughout all eternity of ever touching the bottom, with the tortures getting worse every foot he fell, and the power to feel them getting stronger every second it took to fall an inch further, while, all the time, the poor tumbling soul was flushed with the remembrance that some monk was working overtime in an enjoyment that should have been his alone.

So the poor people were worn out trying to think of a change that would bring them a little less of the next world and a little more of this, and they secretly cried to God, and their prayers

must have been heard, for during this time, or thereabout, an
Augustine monk stuck in the monastery of Wittenberg began to
turn over the leaves of the Book of Books, the Bible, that was
anchored to a big-bellied desk with a heavy chain so that the
Book of Books couldn't be stolen by those unable to read or
write. And this monk, who was called Luther, read and read by
sunlight, moonlight, starlight, and candlelight, till he was nearly
blind, and he was greatly astonished at what he read therein, for
it wasn't a bit like anything he had read himself, or had heard
read by anyone else, it was all so good, so bad, so reading on and
reading ever, he prayed when he was puzzled, and reviewed in
his mind all that had been written, and all that had been preached
aforetime about the heavens and hell, the earth and all that was
under the earth, the sea and all that in it is, till he got to know
just where he was standing, and found out that there were differences here and differences there which wouldn't bear investi-
gation, and had a dangerous tendency to deceive and corrupt
innocent, simple, and stupid people who were anxious to
serve God in spirit and in truth to the best of their ability, so long
as they could get bread from heaven in a less laborious way and
at a reasonable price.

So Luther thumped his breast, saying as he thumped it hard
and heavy, am I right or am I wrong? And a voice so still and
small, that Luther could hardly hear it, answered first out of the
darkness, and then a voice answered out of the light, so loud and
shrill that it nearly burst the drum of his ear, each voice sounding
together though they spoke at different times, saying, Get busy,
man, and teach the truth of the gospel, for out of the teaching and
the truth will come swarms of fighting men, beating of drums and
blowing of bugles, big guns and little guns, and great ships of
war, so that red men, yellow men, and black men will become, in
course of time, the white man's lawful god-fearing and most
obedient batmen.

And Luther rose up like a giant refreshed, and after heart-
searching and mind-searching and soul-searching, he saw clearly
that the one thing the Church thought of was the laying-up of a
lot for a rainy day, which was repugnant to the plain words of
holy scripture, thereby causing an undue delay to the great
multitude of souls that waddled and squirmed and shuffled along
on the road to Mandalay where the gates of heaven lay.

So Luther told the simple people that they'd simply got to give
up obeying rules and regulations, and use their own judgement

about whatsoever things were true, whatsoever things were honest, whatsoever things were just, whatsoever things were lovely, whatsoever things were of good report, and to decide themselves as to what things to believe, what things to say, and what things to do, using the Bible, and only the Bible, as the general store of knowledge of what was and is and is to come.

But the popes and priests opened into a full stride of opposition, and they argued with him and fought him and persecuted him and tried in every way to double-cross and crucify him, but Luther stood firm to the shock in his smock like a rock and mocked them with many words, and laughed in their raging faces, telling them that they'd have to get up early in the morning, if they wanted him to sit still and sing dumb. So Luther kept thundering out the truth as it came straight from God, and the princes and many rich merchants who lived only for the truth as it is in Christ Jesus and was in Luther, and who scorned to do a wrong thing to their neighbour, in business or out of business, rallied and tallied and dallied and sallied round the doughty reformer, and cheered him up, and told him that the Lord was a very present help in time of trouble, so that Luther believed and spit on his hands and said, Let them all come, and he was made strong and hefty in his going in and going out and in his arguments from that very hour.

Then Luther decided to let things rip, and went at it, hammer and tongs, and made short work of the traffic of indulgences, a gilt-edged superstition that let anyone do anything from pitch-and-toss to manslaughter, so long as a suitable fee was dropped in the back pocket in the pants of a priest. And the big princes and little princes, margraves and meregraves, landgraves and landgrieves, and merchants in gold and silver and silks, and merchants in ebony and ivory and coffee and tea, drew their swords, and cheered Luther on, shouting, Go on, Martin, old boy, in the name o' God, and give them socks and cut the bowels out of them, and show them we know the Lord is our God who is gracious and merciful, and high above all nations, and prove to them that souls that are pure and simple have only to skim a few texts from the Bible to know all things, and to know how to deal justly with men present and men past and men to come, and your name will be a banner and a shout and a buckler to generations of popery-purged protestants as long as the sun shall move and the earth stand still.

Then Luther got excited, and showed, by miles and miles of documentary evidence, that the most secret sayings which puzzled archangels could be easily understood of the veriest babes and sucklings, so long as they really wanted to know what was the truth and what wasn't the truth, as it was written aforetime by the holy apostles and prophets.

But the Devil, getting anxious about his status, stirred up the hearts of the pope, cardinals, abbots, and abbesses to anger, and they made bloody war on all who were determined to follow the commandments of God in a pure and simple way, and many fierce battles were fought between the followers of God on the one hand, and the followers of Satan on the other, so that thousands on both sides were slain in an effort to keep the Christian church from perishing.

But Luther, at peace with God and himself, went on purifying and surifying and curifying and furifying the Christian faith so that the frightened red-hatted cardinals, looking out of high windows, saw the people happily going by, and saw the people looking up to see all heaven opened up to them, and the cardinals were sore afraid in their hearts. When they saw this busy traffic of true worship going on, night and day, without let or hindrance, and heard the people singing heart-to-heart honest-to-God hymns, they hastened to hide behind the curtains, and wist not what to do.

And the truth, the whole truth, and nothing but the truth, so help me God, spread like lightning, and came with a great flush and rush and gush to such as those who had nothing else to do but look for it, so that the people in millions queued up to read the Bible, with their kids, and while the parents read the Book of Books, the kids went swing-swong on the chains that bound the Bibles to the desks, so that the lives of the people began to bubble-bible up and bible-bubble over with beauty and a singular blessedness, for all their hearts were filled with peace.

And it came to pass that the anger of those who possessed not the truth was kindled against those who had it, and a great dispute arose about the word, whence it came and where it stayed and whither it went, so that each fell upon the other in a fierce fight that has lasted down to this very day. And such as were taken captive by those who had not the truth, had their right hands cut off and their noses sliced up, and were burned at the stake with their heads up; but those who had the truth showed mercy unto their captives, for they cut off their left hands only, sliced down their noses, and burned them at the stake with their heads down, so that they died more quickly.

So the reformation came wholly to England and partly to Ireland, bringing with it the Bible and a burning love of truth, love, peace, righteousness, joy, and fair dealing along straight paths and round corners. And England went from strength to strength and from power to power, having the finest army in the world, and the greatest navy in the world, and the biggest budgets in the world, and the wisest statesmen in the world, and she set out and conquered many races, taming the wild ones with love and great tact, so that red men and black men and yellow men came and ate quietly out of her hand and all these things were done that it might be fulfilled, which was spoken by the prophets about those wondrous ones who never lost their love for or steadfast faith in the Book of Books, the Bible.

A wave or two of the truth as it was in Luther splashed over Ireland, and so in process of time, The Reverend Hunter was born in Protestant circumstances that made him a sky-pilot, and Johnny was born a Protestant in circumstances that placed him in the position of being lugged along at the backside of this soft-hatted stiff-collared egg-headed oul' henchman of heaven, to be added to his swarm of urchins cowering and groping about in the rag-and-bone education provided by the church and state for the children of those who hadn't the wherewithal to do anything better.

Hunter, Johnny, and his mother came to the gate of the school.

—In you go, said Hunter, and, if you try hard enough to be a good boy, you'll succeed, and God will bless you.

Off the spiritual pirate toddled, and Johnny and his mother faced forward to the gloom of the doorway leading to the inner gloom of the school.

THE DREAM SCHOOL

IN THE dark porch, Johnny pulled back as hard as he could from the clasping hand of his mother, and whimpered, Doctor said I must do nothing but eat well and stay in the open air.

—You might as well be here, said his mother, as to be at home, boring your eyes out looking at the pictures in the books your

poor father left behind him. Besides your father would be unhappy in heaven, thinking of his little boy growing up to be
nothing but a dunce.

She opened the heavy door that was like the heavy door of a
prison, drew Johnny inside, and he found himself fast in the middle
of fear. They went up to the desk where the Principal sat cor-
recting the exercises of the seniors. He was a man of sixty years
of age, with colourless eyes that looked furtively at everyone and
everything. He had a pink bald head surrounded by a tufty halo
of white hair, and his face was partly covered with mutton-
chop whiskers a little less white than the pallor of his face,
brought about, Johnny was told afterwards, by too much quiet
whiskey drinking. He was a native Irish speaker from Conne-
mara, and his name was Slogan. He looked up with a quick
furtive glance at Johnny and his mother.

—Ah, he said, welcome to the bright little new scholar the
rector told me about, as he touched the boy on the head with his
thin, pale, bony, bubbly-veined hand. Don't be afraid, little boy,
he went on, pulling Johnny nearer to him till his pale eyes stared
into the timid eye of the boy. He snatched up a snaky-looking
cane from the desk, and held it out in front of Johnny's one good
eye. There now, he added, see it for yourself – it's not such a
terrible thing, is it?

—Johnny's a delicate boy, murmured the mother, and must be
treated gently on account of his poor eyes.

—We correct our boys only when it is necessary, said the master
with a tight-lipped grin. He got up from the desk, and catching
the mother's arm, he turned her towards the door. Off you go
home, my good woman, and give God thanks that your boy is
where he can share in what will be for his good.

The master led him over to a class that was droning out tables,
and sat him down on a bench between two boys, telling him to be
good, keep his eye on the teacher, and repeat with the boys what
the teacher was saying.

Four 'n one are five, four 'n two are six, four 'n three are seven,
four 'n four are eight, went on the singsong chorus, while Johnny's
one eye glanced dreamily at the green, brown, yellow, and purple
countries on a map of the world, with the British Possessions
coloured a vivid red, and all surrounded with the pale-blue waters
of the world, as all the children of the whole wide world murmured four 'n five are nine, four 'n six are ten, four 'n seven are
eleven in the purple, red, green, and yellow lands that he saw all

round him as he walked along murmuring four 'n eight are twelve, four 'n nine are thirteen – going along a great white road – a road white as the driven snow – that was banked on each side of him with daffodils as big as breakfast-cups nodding and nodding at him as he went along the snow-white road, and stretching their blooms to let in big black bees with crimson bands around their bellies, and big red bees with big black bands around their bellies, and purple butterflies with satiny black dots on the tips of their front wings and golden-satiny dots on the tips of their back wings, having crimson feelers sliding all over the bells of the yellow daffodils, and green butterflies with zigzag shining deep blue decorations on their wings that were bigger than any man's hand, and had their tips bordered with bronze, and bigger butterflies still, with front wings white having green stars on them and hind wings green with white stars on them, flew with all the others in and out and through the lovely sway of the gay and golden daffodils.

The sky above was a far deeper blue than the blue on the wing of the blue-dotted butterfly, while through the deep blue of the sky sailed white clouds so low down that some of them shone with the reflected gold from the blossoms of the daffodils. Many beautiful trees lined the road that Johnny walked on, and from some came the smell of thyme and from others the smell of cinnamon. Some of the trees bent down with the weight of blossoms, and numbers were heavy with plums as big as apples, and cherries bigger than the biggest of plums that hung in hundreds on their branches, so that he ate his fill as he walked along the white road.

Then after turning a bend he came upon a huge high gate of bronze, and on one wing of the huge high gate of bronze were figures, in beaten silver, of boys beating drums of gold, and on the other wing of the huge high gate of bronze were figures, in beaten gold, of boys blowing trumpets of silver, and over the heads of the figures of boys blowing trumpets and beating drums was the word SCHOOL. Johnny halted and wondered, and as he wondered, the gates slowly opened as the figures in beaten silver beat on their drums of gold, and the figures of beaten gold blew on their trumpets of silver.

When the gates were fully opened two boys like birds came running out with short-handled sharp-pointed spears in their hands; and they bowed down low before him, saying: Hail to the child of God and to the inheritor of the Kingdom of Heaven.

Enter, that wisdom, who sitteth on the seat of the mighty, may prepare the way before thy little mind to understand all the majesty and mystery of life that now is, and of the life that is to come.

And the two boys that were like birds, with the spears in their hands, led him gently through the open gate. And when they felt that he was trembling they said to him, Let not your heart be troubled, little boy. Then they stretched out their spears in front of his eyes, and he saw that the points of the spears were made of a sweet chocolate covered cunningly with the thinnest of silver tissue. And they walked through a lovely avenue of laurestililium covered with great trumpet-shaped flowers that were a delicate white in the morning, a ruddy gold at midday, and a deep dark crimson when the sun went down; then, through a narrower avenue of crocuaxenillium, to a tiny glade filled with the greenest of grass and newest and freshest of blossoms where, on a bank of primroses, sat a grey-bearded old josser, who asked Johnny his name and where he lived, then wrote it all down with a gold pen, having for its nib a gleaming emerald, on a great big white blackboard trimmed with jewels. Then Johnny was led away to a bath, hidden in blooming hawthorn, in which the water was lovely and hot and fully perfumed. When he had been bathed, he was rubbed smoothly with soft sweet-smelling oils till his flesh became as the flesh of a little child; and then dressed in silks as gentle as newly-risen, dewy-grown meadow grass. Then he was declared to be fit and free to wander about or play with the big or little kids who swarmed everywhere over hill, meadow, and dale.

On every little hill was a tower, and on top of every tower was a watcher to see if any child had grown tired so that he could be made to sit down and rest in beds of moss; or if a kid was anyway hungry the watcher ordered him a slice of currant bread and jam, and each watcher had a needle ready threaded to act should a seam burst or a button fly among the frolicking children. The paths all about the place were paved with tiles of vivid colours – red, green, lemon, ultramarine, orange, and black – fashioned in divers ways. Johnny found, when he made friends with some of the kids, that very few spoke English because it was hard to learn; so they mostly spoke in Latin saying *quo vadis* when they were coming, and when they were going replying *veenie vaynay vicinity vo*. Away in the distance spreading out for miles and miles to the right and to the left were orange groves and lemon groves, and the oranges were as sweet as the sweetest sugar and the lemons had the taste of honey with a faraway sense of bitterness in them. Pear, apple, plum, and cherry trees abounded, and were so cleverly trained that the highest fruit was well within reach of the tiniest kid that was prowling about, and was steady enough to stand on the tips of his toes. Beech trees, from which swings swung, were everywhere, and, in beds of huge red strawberries, tiny babies were resting on moss in nests of bulrushes. All the kids who were running, jumping, swinging, playing tag, and those little ones lying in their bulrush-nests who happened to be awake, unified their voices as one man and sang the song, We're happy all the day long here. With canes in their hands, cheery-faced women wandered about keeping a wary eye on the kids. The guides told Johnny in Latin that these women were specially employed to lash out with the canes at any kid who missed for a single second the joy that was to be got out of the things the place provided, and so made it sure that no kid could forget for a moment that he was a member of Christ, a child of God, and an inheritor of the Kingdom of Heaven.

Hidden away in a forest of blossoms were rows of low tiny-seated privies, and between them strutted up and down hundreds of clucking, gorgeous-coloured peacocks, and over the privies were bending boughs of lovely-scented shrubs, and in the midst of these lovely-scented shrubs were multitudes of tiny birds – red, blue, purple, green, and yellow – which immediately commenced to sing in chorus and kept it up the whole time any of the kids happened to be seated on one of the privies doing his duty to himself and to mankind in general.

The sun shone for ever gently, and nothing fell from the blue sky, save little showers of pollen now and again falling from the legs of passing butterflies and bees. Rabbits with black bodies and white heads and rabbits with black heads and white bodies came out in the evening from thick clumps of purple and white heather, whose every bell was as big as a thimble, and played with the children till the moon came out.

A trumpet blew a soft call, and they all sat down to a meal of fruit and snow-white bread, cooked in china ovens, hid away in little hills, and covered with heaps of wild honey gathered the first thing in the fresh morning from the hives that the bees packed in the hollows of the bigger trees. And when the night really fell, and they were jaded enjoying themselves, they all gently lay down to sleep in beds of musk and mignonette, with an orange moon in a purple sky staring them in the face, and each corner of the heavens gay with young and jostling stars. And Johnny slept sound.

Suddenly something crawled through the musk and mignonette, and his hand was torn by a bitter pain. He shot himself up and gave vent to a loud cry. He heard the sound of laughter all around him. He shoved the bandage from his good eye, and saw the whitish eyes of the schoolmaster staring down at him. Is this the place for sleep? he asked, while Johnny stuck the burning hand into his mouth so that the moisture might lessen the sting. Is this the place for sleep? the master asked again. Yes or no, boy? No, sir, murmured Johnny.

—Hold out the left hand, said the master, and we'll put a sting into it that'll balance the pain in the right so that both together'll keep you awake for a couple of seconds.

Johnny held out his hand, and the cane came down like lightning across his palm, sending a rending pain through his brain that made him quiver. He thrust the left hand beneath the socket of his right arm, and pressed it tight to stem the pain. He bent his head in an effort to hide the tears that broke out of his eyes.

—That little flip of the palm has made tears come, said the master. He's not much of a hero, boys, is he? And the school answered the question with a titter.

Put your hands behind your back, boy, said the master. Put them behind your back, raise your head, and look at your teacher, he roared.

Johnny, with a quick glance at the reddening weals dividing both palms into two parts, put them behind his back, and gazed mournfully at the teacher.

Three-times-one are three, three-times-two are six, three-times-three are nine, three-times-four are twelve, hummed the class.

A big-limbed, broad-shouldered boy of nearly fourteen, with a bush of tawny red hair and a face like a bulldog well able to smile, who was named Georgie Middleton, had silently watched, with a snarl on his lips, everything that had passed, and was now glaring at Slogan. He was the one boy in the school whom Slogan was afraid to flog.

Slogan lingered for some minutes listening to the class droning out the lesson. Then he turned away and began to resume the teaching of his own class.

—It was a God-damned shame to hit a half-dead kid like that, said Middleton loudly as Slogan passed him by.

PAIN PARADES AGAIN

A HOT STINGING pain, growing keener, then fading away, then growing keener again, flooding into an agonized throb of the brain, told Johnny that the old ulcer that had nearly healed had given place to a new one, and that he was, once again, in for many hours of agony.

This is the school, this is the result of going to school, he thought. When his eyes had got better, he couldn't resist the temptation of straining them to see what the teacher was writing on the blackboard, nor could he keep from peering into the books used in the class to see the pictures, or to try to follow what the teacher was talking about. And this was the result of it all – many nights of twisting about in bed and every minute of it streaked with pain.

The curse o' God on every school that was ever built and every teacher that was ever born! The way they maddened him, the way they talked about it. Hoity-toity haughty holy holy Hunter, with his God, is behind all pain, and He will help every brave and patient little one to bear it: and sly an' sleeky Slogan chimin' in after holy Hunter with his, It would be a very bad thing for children if they could go through their young years entirely free from pain; that if they could, there'd be no standin' them, and that, although they didn't quite know what it was, there was a purpose of some kind or another behind everything that anybody suffered: and oul' haughty hoity-toity holy Hunter goin' one better be sayin' that God sent sufferin's to try us and that if we bore them as we should bear them, uncomplainin', we'd come out of them like refined gold that had stood the test of fire, and would surely shine in the sight of all the angels of heaven, who wouldn't know how to feel pain even if they tried, and who'd have a fine laugh if they could only get a chance of seein' haughty hoity-toity holy Hunter and sly and sleeky Slogan squirmin' about on their bellies with the pain that's shootin' through me eyeballs now!

He called and called out to his mother as he tossed about in the bed, and when she heard the call, she came quickly to his side.

—It's at me again, it's at me again, Mother, he said; it's at me again, and turning on his belly, he tried to thrust his head down

deep into the hard and lumpy bolster that gave his head a little
lift from the level.

—Maybe you're only imaginin' it, she said softly.

—Imaginin' it, he echoed. I tell you I'm not imaginin' it, he
shouted. Shows all you care about it, he added.

—We'll go to the hospital, and the drops will make you all
right once more.

She soaked rags in cold water, and tied them round his temples,
waited till they grew hot with the heat of the pain, took them off,
and soaked them in cold water again, and bound them round his
temples.

—You'll have to try to go to sleep, Johnny, she said, in a
strained voice, for I have to be up at five to get Archie's breakfast
before he goes to work.

—That's all you care, he moaned, that's all you care about the
pain.

On she kept, removing, soaking, binding, till he lay quiet in a
troubled sleep, then she sank down beside him, dozed off, ready
to hear when a sleepy moan would tell her that he had wakened,
and that the pain was sharp again.

The morning's light crept in through the window, shone into
her barely-closed eyes; and she woke, stiff, anxious, and tired.
She strained her eyes towards the old alarm clock, and saw that
it was moving towards five in the morning. Stiff and tired, she
got up from the bed where Johnny lay stretched, lighted the fire,
put the kettle on, and sat down to wait for it to boil. When the
kettle began to sing she woke up Archie, then when it boiled, she
made the tea, poured out a cup for herself, and drank it in thought-
ful sips.

It looked as if her last kid would go blind. Curious, the doctors
wouldn't tell her what it was was wrong. If she'd a couple o'
guineas to give them, they'd tell her quick enough. Hurry into
the hospital, let the drops trickle into his eyes, and then hurry
out again: that was the ritual. Though what good it would do
her or him to know what was wrong, God only knew.

She looked at the picture of Queen Victoria, with the little
crown on her grey head and the white veil falling over her neck
and down her bare shoulders. Enough jewels in her little crown
to keep them all for the rest of their lives, with a little left over
for the poor. Crown o' jewels, crown o' thorns, an' her own boy
with a crown of soakin'-wet rags to deaden the pain in his
temples.

Give your boy the best of nourishment. Broth, porridge, milk, butter, an' eggs, and a few flowers, I suppose, if there was anything left over. Well, it was easy for the doctors to order things when they hadn't to pay for them.

She made Archie's breakfast, and he came out, full of sleep, quickly swallowed his tea and toast, and hurried off to the *Daily Express*, owned by a Mr Maunsel, flourishing then as the paper of the well-to-do and all the clergy in Ireland, where he worked in the Publishing Office from six till seven for ten shillings a week. At eight she got Johnny's breakfast ready, by cutting some slices of bread and by adding some hot water to the stewing tea. She laid two cups and saucers on the table, a sugar-bowl, half-filled with caster sugar, a cream-jug containing a ha'porth of milk, which was very precious, for it had to sanctify all the cups of tea taken by the three of them for the day. When all this was done, she looked over at the tangled figure on the bed, at the thin worn face nearly hidden by the damp cloths round the head, sighed and murmured, well, it could have been worse – he might have been born blind, and then there would have been no hope.

She went over to the bed, and gently shook the sleeping boy's shoulder. He stretched and muttered, all right, get up in a minute.

—Hospital, Johnny, this morning, hospital, she said, shaking him a little less gently. If we're not there be half past nine, we'll be there all day. The kettle's boilin' ready for your eyes. Come sit up at once, it's the best thing to do – makes it worse to linger.

She brought a basin half filled with steaming water to the bedside, and helped him to bathe his eyes till the lids were softened, and he could open the one that was called good. She bound the bandage over the bad one, then he dressed, sat down, and ate his breakfast. His mother heaped slack on the fire, and damped it down. She washed up the soiled breakfast things, and put Johnny's cap on his head. From a drawer she took out the ticket which admitted him as a patient to the hospital. She looked at the date, and found that the ticket had expired two days ago, and she knew that she had no sixpence just then to get it renewed. Perhaps they wouldn't notice it, though often enough the porter glanced at tickets to make sure that all paying patients were keeping their fees up to date. She'd have to chance it.

They hurried down to the end of the street, and caught a tram that brought them near to the hospital, for a penny, Johnny burying his head on his breast whenever the sun peeped out from behind grey clouds that piled themselves together in the sky. They soon found themselves sitting on the polished pitch-pine bench in the out-patients' waiting-room. Every five or ten minutes, a bell tinkled in the room where the surgeons worked, a patient near the door rose and entered for examination and treatment, while the others moved up to make room for those that had just arrived. At last, Johnny and his mother found themselves at the door waiting for the bell to tell them that the surgeon was ready to see them. She removed the bandage from his head so that he would be ready for immediate examination, for the doctors didn't like to have their time wasted. The little bell tinkled, and they went in, this time to a handsome-looking young man who had become the Resident Surgeon. The young surgeon got the nurse to bring him the details of the case, filed for reference in the hospital records. He looked at the details, then glanced at Johnny and his mother. Johnny gritted his teeth when the surgeon lifted his head to look at his eyes, for the light flowing in through the enormous windows stabbed its way into them.

—Um, murmured the young surgeon, another of them. The left eye's become a lot worse the last few days, hasn't it? he asked. And you haven't been here, now, for some weeks.

—His eyes seemed to be nearly all right, sir, and I thought he needn't come any more.

—It is for us to say whether he is to continue to come or not. For the future he is to attend the hospital till the doctor tells you that the visits may cease.

—He has to go to school, the mother murmured.

—Good God, woman, said the doctor, the boy can't go to school with his eyes in this condition. The doctor's eyes glanced at her worn-out clothes. The boy doesn't get a lot of food, does he?

—Not a lot, sir.

—Well, then, said the doctor emphatically, if he can't get the food he needs, he is to get all the air he can. Air, air, air, keep him out in the air from morning till night.

—He doesn't do anything at school, sir; just sits and listens. The rector wants him to go, and says it won't do him any harm.

—That's for me to say, and not the rector, snapped the doctor. What's your rector's name?

—The Reverend T. R. S. Hunter, sir.

The surgeon wrote rapidly on a sheet of hospital notepaper. Give this to your rector, he said, and he read out what he had written on the sheet of hospital notepaper. To the Reverend

T. R. S. Hunter. I understand that you press my patient, John Casside, to go to school. The boy's eyes are too bad to be troubled with school. He must remain in the air as much as possible, in the park, in the streets – anywhere. These are my strict orders, and you must not interfere in any way with the carrying of them out by the boy's mother. R. Joyce: Surgeon. Give him that, said the doctor, holding out the letter to Johnny's mother.

She made no effort to take it from him, and murmured, Oh, I daren't give the rector that, sir.

—Why daren't you? he asked.

—He would be annoyed, and it might do harm to the boy, later on in life.

The doctor remained silent for a few moments, then he slowly tore up the letter, and dropped the pieces into a waste-paper basket beside his desk.

—I wonder what the rector will do for the boy if he goes blind – give him a letter of admission to the Blind Asylum, I suppose. He handed her the prescription, and added, Get these things at the dispensary, and bring the boy to me on Wednesday, school or no school; and he tinkled the bell to show that he was ready for another patient.

After getting the remedies prescribed, they left the hospital, got on a tram, and reached home again.

Neither had mentioned one word about school; but Johnny rejoiced silently in his heart that for a long time, maybe for ever, maybe for years and maybe for ever, there would be no more of the misery of sitting still and stiff and sleepy in the droning out of the song of the spelling and the sums.

So he swallowed his spoonful of Parrish's Food cheerily, though no kind of a dinner had gone before, and said jauntily that he believed that the new young doctor would grow up to be a very clever doctor indeed; then he stretched himself on the horsehair-covered sofa for a rest before he went out to the street; while his mother, armoured in sacking to keep the damp out, scrubbed out the floor of the room. She was singing as she scrubbed, and Johnny saw her big black eyes sparkle as she sang:

> *She was lovely an' fair as a rose of the summer,*
> *But it was not her beauty, alone, that won me,*
> *Ah, no, it was truth in her eyes, ever beaming,*
> *That made me love Mary, the rose of Tralee!*

This was a damn sight better than the song of the spelling and the sums. And Johnny lifted his voice, and sang with her:

> *She was lovely an' fair as a rose of the summer,*
> *But it was not her beauty, alone, that won me,*
> *Ah, no, it was truth in her eyes, ever beaming,*
> *That made me love Mary, the rose of Tralee!*

—Lift your voice, Ma, let it go, chanted Johnny, let the house hear.

The two of them suddenly stopped singing, and listened. A knock with the knuckles had come on the door. The knock came again. She swiftly removed the sacking, and flung it under the sofa, went to the door, opened it, and God Almighty, it was the rector.

—I've called about Johnny, he said. Mr Slogan tells me he hasn't been at school for the last few days. That's a pity, Mrs Casside, a great pity.

—His eyes got bad again, said the mother, nervously fiddling with the leaves of a geranium growing in a pot near the window. The doctor gave me strict injunctions that I wasn't to let him go to school.

—Doctors differ and patients die, said the rector sarcastically. If we all carried out the doctors' strict injunctions, none of us would hardly move from the fire. What will the doctor do for him in after years when he has to make his way in life, unable to read or write?

—He has to go to the hospital three days a week now, said his mother, and on those days we can never manage to get back before twelve.

—Well, he can come to school as soon as he returns from the hospital. I will get Mr Slogan to mark him present on these mornings, on the understanding that he will attend later on, so that you have really no excuse for keeping him at home. Now, like a good woman, put his cap on, and I will leave him at the school.

Johnny's mother, after some hesitation, got the boy's cap, and silently fixed it on his head.

—You'll be very glad later on, Johnny, said the clergyman, that your pastor insisted that you should go to school, so come along, now. If your eyes pain you a lot, Mr Slogan will let you home a little earlier than the other boys.

—They're painin' me now, grumbled Johnny, and me mother heard what the doctor said.

—You mustn't argue with your mother, said the clergyman reprovingly, for she knows much better what is good for you than you do.

Johnny went slowly out, holding Hunter's hand. At the school, Hunter raised the latch of the door, opened it, and gently pushed the boy into the school-room.

—In you go, now, he said, and be a good boy. Then he softly closed the door and went his way.

Johnny hesitated for a few moments, listening to the murmur of the boys droning over their lessons. Then he went quietly on to join in the song of the spelling and the sums.

A CHILD OF GOD

JOHNNY'S LEFT EYE, ever the weaker, got better in a month or so, and he could go about the world again in a cockeyed way still wearing a heavy bandage over it.

—Now that he goes to day school, there is no real reason for keeping him from Sunday school or church, said the Reverend Mr Hunter, stroking his long black beard that was piped here and there with silver. We mustn't let him grow up into a pagan. The sooner he gets to know something about the things that belong unto his peace, the better, Mrs Casside. He can sit quietly, and listen to his teacher, or join in the singing of the hymns.

He put his pudgy hand on the boy's head, and patted the bandage.

—You must do what God wants you to do, John, he said, if you wish God to cure your sore eyes, or help you to bear the pain that He sends upon us all at times. Remember the little gold crown, John, that God is keeping safe for little boys who bear pain patiently, and readily do His will. You'd like to come to Sunday school and church, to be with the other boys praying to God and singing His praises, wouldn't you? And the pudgy hand patted the bandage again.

The bandaged head bent slowly down on the breast of the boy, but he did not answer.

—Of course he'd love to go, said his mother.

—Oh, let the boy speak for himself, Mrs Casside. Wouldn't you like to come to Sunday school and church, John?

The three of them stood still waiting.

—Say yes to the Reverend Mr Hunter, said his mother.

—Please, please, Mrs Casside, let the boy answer for himself. Wouldn't you like to come to Sunday school and church? he asked for the third and last time.

—I don't want to go to Sunday school or church, murmured the boy.

—You shouldn't say that, Johnny, said his mother. You know you love church and Sunday school.

—Why don't you like to come to Sunday school and church? asked the man and minister. Come now, answer, John, and remember, God is listening to you.

The boy lifted his head, and looked with the unbandaged eye at the cold common face of the man, half-hidden by the black beard and the round, soft, broad-brimmed minister's hat the man was wearing.

—The doctor said I was to use me eyes as little as possible, and I don't like Sunday school or church.

—Now, now, said the man and minister, neither church nor Sunday school can hurt your eyes, and you can hardly expect God to help the doctor make your eyes well again, unless you use the Sabbath Day to keep it holy; to worship God and give Him thanks and put your whole trust in Him. My own boy and girls love the Lord's day to come so that they may go to Sunday school and church.

—Ay, said the boy suddenly, because their father's a clergyman, and they can't escape.

—He'll be at Sunday school and church on Sunday, said the woman quickly, for whatever happens, he must be kept up to his religion.

—It will help, at least, to keep him off the streets, said the man and the minister. Now let us kneel down together, before I go, and offer up a little prayer to our heavenly Father.

The woman knelt down, leaning her elbows on the seat of a chair; the boy knelt down beside her; and the minister kneeling down too, faced the opposite way, and said in a cold and common manner: Oh God, our heavenly Father, giver of all good things, give Thy blessing unto this woman and unto this boy, that she may bring him up in the knowledge and fear of the Lord;

that he, in full fear of Thee, may learn in all humility to submit himself in lowly reverence to all his betters, governors, teachers, spiritual pastors, and masters, and so grow more worthy to call upon Thee for blessing and mercy. Through Jesus Christ, our Lord.

The woman murmured Amen, and the three of them got up from their knees to face the world once more.

—Goodnight, Mrs Casside, said the man and minister; I'm sure John'll be a good boy, and give no trouble to his mother. And off toddled this black-whiskered, snug-souled gollywog gospel-cook who brightened up the will of God with his own.

On the Sunday morning, dull with a heavy drizzle of rain, Johnny's grumble that the doctor said he wasn't to go to school was met by his mother telling him that in years to come, when he was looking for a job, he might be glad of the minister's recommendation – clergymen had such a pull everywhere these days. So the boy was made ready, with his bandage washed the night before, his shabby little sailor-suit well brushed to make it look braver; broken-soled boots made to gleam with the rubbing in and polishing up of Cooney's cake blacking, his mother thrusting in cut-out cardboard soles, full of a faint faith that these would serve to keep the wet out from his feet till he came home again; and, finally, on his head was placed the faded velvet sailor-cap with frayed floating ribbons, and the gold-lettered inscription, HMS Condor, giving the cap a grandeur that was a little too much for it.

—Now remember, said his mother, giving him the finishing touches, that if the minister speaks to you, you are to be very polite and take off your cap when he's talking to you.

—The doctor did say, Ma, that I wasn't to go to school.

—The doctor hasn't to keep you, and doesn't know that I have to keep the minister on my hands, so whenever he asks you again do you like to go to Sunday school and church, be sure to say, yessir.

—Ma, said the boy suddenly, doesn't God know everything a boy's thinking?

—Yes, Johnny, and even everything he thinks before he thinks it.

—And He hates boys who tell lies, doesn't he, Ma?

—He doesn't love boys who tell lies.

—Well, said the boy with resolution, if I'd 'a said I liked going

to Sunday school and church, when I didn', it 'ud been a lie, an'
God 'ud 'a known it.

—You young scut, she said, giving him a slight shake, if you
thry to make fun of your mother, I'll give you a welt that you
won't be the better of for a week.

—I wasn' tryin' to make fun of you, he said.

—Hold your tongue, she answered testily; you'll have to be a
lot older before you can understand these things. And for the
future, every Sunday morning, rain or shine, off you go to Sunday
school 'n church, and the sooner you fit yourself into that fact,
the better.

With Prayer Book in pocket and Bible in hand, he went off in
the drizzling rain down Dorset Street, full of a feeling he didn't
know was rage, soothing his way along with a murmur of all the
curses he could think of.

A hundred yards on his way, he felt the first soft plashing
dampness sending the message that his mother's cardboard
soles had yielded to the wet pavement, and soon at each step he
took, his boots gave vent to that sucking, plashing sound telling
of cold and saturated feet, that would go on teasing him throughout the time of hearing the Bible read and of the singing of praises
to God. Keep him out in the air as much as possible, and keep
his feet warm and dry, said the doctor; dry 'n warm, keep his feet
dry 'n warm, said the doctor. Oh God, give me a new pair of
boots, a new pair of boots. Oh God, give me a new pair of boots,
he murmured as he hurried along.

—Oh God, give me a new pair of boots, jeered a voice beside
him, and there was Harry Tait saunthering beside him, havin'
heard, too, everything he'd been mutterin'.

—Why don't you get your ma to buy you a new pair of boots?
asked Harry. I wouldn't go to Sunday school with boots like them
on me, so I wouldn't, not for nuts.

—Me others is gettin' soled an' heeled, lied Johnny, for he
wasn't goin' to let Tait know that what he'd on was all he had;
and they haven't been sent back yet, he added, as they turned into
a narrow lane that led to the chapel yard of St Saviour's Catholic
Church. They lingered to look at a number of people filling bottles
from a huge butt on a stand at the southern site of the chapel.

—Fillin' their bottles with holy wather, that the priests tell
them'll keep them from harm 'n broken legs 'n bein' run over, 'n
dhrives away the devil squealin', who has horns out of his head
'n flames shootin' out of his mouth that's biggerin the Gap o'

Dunloe, 'n nails on his fingers able to tear a man's belly open at one rip.

—Us Protestants don't believe in holy wather, said Johnny proudly.

—Me mother always tells me to run whenever I'm passin' a Roman Catholic chapel, said Tait, in case anyone of them 'ud put an eye on a Protestant boy with a Bible in his hand, or a Jesuit 'ud dangle an image in front of his face.

—I'm not a bit afraid of them, said Johnny, standing deliberately to look through the arched entrances at the people hurrying into chapel, dipping their fingers into stone fonts at the entrance of the porch, and blessing themselves as they went in or came out.

—I'm not afraid neither, said Tait, only me ma says that if ever they get the power again, they'll light big big fires in the middle of all the wide streets, 'n burn, bones 'n all, all the Protestants they can lay hands on, till there isn't sign or light of one of them left.

—I know a Roman Catholic woman, said Johnny, when she meets me always asks me how is me eyes, and one day when it was rainin' she gave me a fistful of liquorice balls.

—Me ma wouldn't let me take liquorice balls from a Roman Catholic, so she wouldn't; 'n I wouldn't play with them, for they worship images 'n pray to people no bettern ourselves; 'n they hate the Bible, 'n are always goin' about watchin' to snap it out of the hands of little Protestant boys 'n girls, to tear it into ribbons as soon as they get safe round a corner.

Johnny felt the damp from the drizzling rain seeping through his threadbare trousers, and he began to walk as quick as he could towards the street where his school lay, murmuring silently to himself, Oh God, let the rain stop; please, God, let the rain stop.

—See, Tait said, as they moved on, the Bible-marker me sister made for me; scarlet, with grand gold letters on it spellin', Immanuel, that me ma says means God with us. You've none, only th' oul' text-cards the teacher gives out, 'n I give away.

—Mother's nearly finished one for me, if you want to know, replied Johnny, that'll be as good as yours, bet you.

—Copier, copier, sneered Tait.

—No, I'm not a copier, for it's green, see now.

Tait lurched viciously against him, causing one of Johnny's feet to splash into the gurgling waters of the kennel.

—You're a liar, he said, for your mother's makin' none, for

cause I heard me ma sayin' you were gettin' poorer 'n poorer since
your oul' fella died, 'n soon yous 'ud not get goin' to Sunday
school or church, the way you'd be without boots on your feet
or a stitch on your back. You're afraid to put out your tongue
for fear there'd be a black mark on it, so I knew you were a liar,
see now.

Tait's a head over me, thought Johnny, 'n I have a bad eye 'n
the other's too sore to look long at anything, so it's the best o'
me play to keep quiet 'n say nothin'.

—You're a liar, an' that's a big big sin, specially about anything that has something to do with the Bible, and again Tait
lurched violently against him.

—I want to go to Sunday school, so let me alone, an' don't be
pushin' me.

—I'll push you if I like, said Tait savagely, so I will. Yah, if I
had your scabby eyes, I wouldn't go out at all.

Red with shame, Johnny suddenly dodged round Tait and
rushed furiously down Lower Dominick Street towards the house
where Sunday school was held, and as he raced along, he could
hear the mocking shouts of Tait following him. Scabby eyes,
scabby eyes, scabby eyes!

Panting, he pushed open the heavy door at Number Twenty-
five, across which was screwed a heavy brass plate telling everyone that this house was St Mary's National School for Boys and
Girls. Crossing the wide hall, mounting the wide front staircase
to the first floor, he went into the front drawing-room where the
junior members of the school gathered, and sat down, with his
heart beating, near the window on one of the benches forming
three sides of a square. On the end uncovered by a bench, on a
chair sat, full and heavy, the teacher, Miss Valentine. While
waiting for others in her class to come and for the school to open,
she talked to various boys and girls, asking them questions about
their fathers and mothers, their sisters and brothers, but she took
no notice of Johnny; oh, she never noticed Johnny, no, she never
noticed Johnny.

The walls of the room were a pinkish buff splashed with ink-
stains (for on weekdays the room was a secular school). On the
walls were many maps and a chart that told you all the things, and
showed you all the things a Cow gave to Man.

Then three other boys came in, Miss Valentine shaking hands
with each as he passed her; but she never noticed Johnny, oh
no, she never noticed Johnny.

On the floor where his feet rested, a little pool gathered from the water that oozed out of his saturated boots. His damp trousers began to feel cold and uncomfortable where he sat on them, and he fidgeted about so that the wet part of his pants might be lifted from his legs to keep the wet from soaking into his skin. He looked long and long at the fire at the other end of the room, and longed to be nearer to it, nearer my God to thee, nearer to thee.

Tait came in, and moved airily towards the class, shaping, as the boys often said he was, because his oul' fella had a shop, with his warm topcoat, polished boots, nicely parted hair, and a face like the face of a well-fed goose. He tried to slip into his place in the class, but Miss Valentine quick as lightning beamed on him, put her arm round his neck, and kissed him on the cheek; kiss me, kiss me mother, kiss me quick. Red in the gills, Tait sat down and glared at us, 'cause we grinned at her havin' kissed him. Two or three minutes more, and in came the Reverend Mr Hunter who went up to a little table near the fire, warmed his hands for a few moments, and then turning to us all, said, Let us pray. There was a hurried sound of many moving as all knelt down on the floor to listen to the wary hairy airy fairy dairy prayery of the bearded shepherd the leopard the rix stix steppard. He prayed that all our eyes might open to see wonderful things coming out of God's law; that we might increase in that true religion only to be found in the Bible; and that these children here present might ask only for those things which it would please God to give them. Lots of things I liked, lots of things I wanted, lots of things I longed for, little drops of water, little grains of sand made the mighty ocean and the mighty land.

When me eyes are well again I'll land one on Tait that he won't forget in a hurry. I'll crooken his jaw for him; they'll have to shut up the shop while they're plasterin' up the crack in his kisser, a crack that'll be big enough to climb in and look out again, thrust 'n parry like the South Wales Borderers in the battle of Isandlwana at the towerin' Zulus teemin' in on top of them, fightin' till the last man fell, with Melville an' Coghill cuttin' their way through the blacks, thick as bees around them, gallopin', gallopin', gallopin' away with the colours tied round their middles, sweatin' with the ceaseless slash-slash of their swords, reddenin' the black back 'n breasts of the Zulus, with their blood fallin', fallin' 'n slidin' down dead under the gallopin' horses, mad with fright, 'n furious to save the colours tied round the middles of the

men fightin' for England's honour, through Jesus Christ our
Lord, amen.

Oul' whiskers finishes his prayers 'n we all get up from our
knees 'n slump our bottoms down on the seats again facin' our
teacher 'n waitin' for her to begin.

Over Hunter comes to our class, 'n lookin' at me, says, Glad
to see, John, that your mother sent you to us, 'n hurries off to
his own class held in a room below.

Then the band played 'n Miss Valentine commenced to make us
chew chunks outa the Bible 'n the Prayer Book. The seventh,
eighth, ninth, an' tenth verses of the sixth chapter of the second
epistle of St Paul to the Corinthians. You say the seventh verse,
Sammy Good. The eighth verse, Benjamin, go on, By honour and
dishonour, by evil report and good report. Go on, you now, Ecret,
please. As poor, yet making many rich; having nothing, yet
possessing all things. Good boy; now, you, Casside, say this
after me, By the word of truth, by the power of God, by the
armour of righteousness on the right hand and on the left, as
deceivers, and yet true; as unknown, and yet well known; as
dying, and, behold, we live; as chastened, and not killed; as
sorrowful, yet always rejoicing; as having nothing, yet possessing
all things, as – when you're speaking, Casside, don't keep your
teeth so close together, but open your mouth a little more. Massey
you, as poor, yet making away as fast as he can goes Melville to
save Queen's 'n regimental colours, gallopin', gallopin' for all he's
worth, lettin' fly with his revolver till the last round's gone, with
assegais flyin' over him like swallows sailin' south, an' Casside,
what are you moonin' for there, you're not payin' the slightest
attention, or mindin' to keep your hands still, and look at your
teacher, 'n listen to what Benjamin's saying, as there are also not
three incomprehensibles nor three uncreated, but one incompre-
hensible, and one uncreated; for you, Casside, tell us where's
that taken from; the psalms, no, not the psalms, not near the
psalms, nothing to do with the psalms; if you were listening you'd
know the Athanasian Creed, as also there are not three incomprehensibles nor three uncreated, but one uncreated and one in-
comprehensible; going on to the catechism tells us that we are
to keep the sabbath day holy, for in six days the Lord made heaven
and earth, the sea and all that in them is, and rested on the
seventh day; we mustn't play marbles or spin tops or fly kites or
anything, but lying on the grass in the Phoenix Park, me an' me
ma came on her, with a fella in a green corner, kissin' 'n kissin'

her, while me ma was whippin' me by as fast as she could, tellin'
me not to drag me feet, for Miss Valentine's legs were out-
standin' again' the green of the grass 'n the black dress driven up
be the gaiety of the commotion of his hand comin' closer 'n
closer to closin' the school.

Johnny slid off the seat on to his feet, bent his head and clasped
his hands together, while the Reverend Mr Hunter closed the
mornin's work with the blessing of God the Father, God the Son,
and God the Holy Ghost, evermore, world without end, amen.
Then he came over to Johnny's class and sent a smile soaring
around.

—Would you mind bringing little Casside to church, he said to
Miss Valentine, for fear he'd meet with any accident on his way
there?

—Oh no, I don't mind in the very least, responded Miss Valentine, not in the very least, for he's a dear little boy, sir, and a dimple
twinkled in her cheek.

—Hurry along as quick as you can, said Hunter, for it's
pouring out of the heavens, and off he went, leaving the sign of
a good growl on Miss Valentine's kisser.

—Pouring outa the heavens, she muttered, and I'm left to
pull this half-blind kidger after my heels. Look here, she said,
gripping Johnny's arm, you'll have to step it out, or I'll be soaked
through before we get halfway there, and I've no intention to be
laid up on your beautiful account.

She buttoned her ulster tightly round her body, as she looked
sourly out at the rain that was pelting down heavens hard, filling
Johnny with fright as he thought how wet he'd be before he
reached the shelter of the church-porch in Mary Street. Miss
Valentine opened her umbrella with a hasty snap, caught the boy's
hand in hers, and hurried him out, saying, C'm along, now, and
no nonsense.

He was pulled along at a half-gallop, his spine jolting whenever
he stepped from pavement to street or from street to pavement,
for he couldn't see when he came to the edge of a path, and
sometimes nearly fell on his face when he struck his toe against
a kerb, usually followed by an angry comment from Miss Valentine to keep, at least, his good eye open, and not pull her down
flat on the mucky pavement.

—The ends of my skirt'll be ruined, she grumbled, for I can't
hold it up, keep my umbrella straight, and attend to you all at
the same time. It's a positive shame that your mother insists on

sending you to school and church, and your eyes the way they are!

The wind blew against their backs as they scuttled along, and Johnny, hot and panting with the haste, felt cool trickles of water running down his legs where the beating rain had entered through the arse of his trousers.

They ran in by the gate, trotted over a narrow concrete path between grass beds, dived into the porch where members of the congregation were taking off wet coats, gabardine ulsters, and folding up streaming umbrellas, till the floor of the poor porch was a pool and the mat at the entrance to the nave a sodden mass of fibre; while the sexton in the middle of the porch was pulling a long rope, sinking his body when he pulled and rising when he let the rope go slack, shaking the bell in the belfry into a monotonous ding-dong ding-dong ding-ding-ding-dong, as the men, women, and children passed from the dim porch into the dimmer body of the church.

—Give your feet a good wipe on the mat, warned Miss Valentine, so that you won't soil the carpet in the aisle, as she went off to her place in the choir, to help in singing loud praises to God.

Johnny rubbed and rubbed his feet on the sodden mat, trying to get some of the water from his boots that were more sodden than the mat under them; and taking off his saturated cap, with drops of rain from his hair trickling down his cheeks, he went into the church and crept quietly into a pew on the north aisle, sitting down on the edge of the seat so that his rain-soaked trousers would press the less on his legs.

Then the bell gave a last little tinkle, and latecomers hurried in, and, after bending their heads down for a second or two in silent prayer to show everybody they had made no mistake and were in the right place, settled themselves in their seats and waited for the service to begin. Massey, passing by, caught sight of Johnny, and at once turned aside, sidled into the pew, and perched himself on the seat beside him.

Oul' Hunter, and his curate, a tall thin man, came out of the vestry and moved slowly over to their places in the chancel, one to the right, the other to the left, to the piping of a tune on the organ. Both knelt in silent prayer a little longer than any member of the congregation, because, of course, they were parsons. Then the tall thin curate began murmuring in a thin tired voice, while all the congregation stood up on their hind legs, O Lord correct me, but with judgement, not in Thine anger, lest Thou bring me to nothing. Dearly beloved brethren, the scriptures moveth us in sundry places to acknowledge and confess our manifold sins and wickedness.

—How would you like to have a swing outa Hunter's whiskers? asked Massey.

Johnny said hush, and giggled, screwed up his face seriously, for he was afraid that he would laugh out loud at the picture rushing into his mind of Hunter yellin' 'n yellin' while he was swingin' outa his whiskers, swing-swong swing-swong, now we're off to London Town, safe 'n sound in Hunter's whiskers, take your seats, take your seats, please, for I wish Massey hadn' come into my pew, 'cause he'll do somethin' to make me laugh, 'n Hunter'll tell me ma about it 'n turn her against me for days, 'n I hate the hard 'n cold look comin' into her eyes when Hunter howls a complaint against me; for even when I try to make up to her she'll shake her head 'n say No, Johnny, I'm black out with you for what you done in church; now we're kneelin' down to say the general confession, all together boys, one, two, three, 'n away, I beseech you, as many as are here present, to accompany me with a pure heart 'n humble voice to the throne of His heavenly grace, saying after me, that if it hadn' been rainin' we'd ha' gone to the zoo today, but, next Sunday, me 'n me da 'n ma are goin' first thing while you are streelin' off to Sunday school to cod with the monkeys that the rest of our life hereafter may be pure and holy so that at the last you have to be snappy on accounta if you weren't quick the buggers 'ud snap a bit outa your fingers 'n you have to be careful for the keeper's always knockin' about pryin' to see what you're up to, for me da says he knew a fella was pulled for squirtin' a chew of tobacco into a monkey's eye so that he squealed out, let us worship 'n fall down 'n kneel before the Lord our maker, an' the elephant's dangerous to thrick with, always eatin' spuds 'n carrots 'n cakes just like us to sit down while oul' Hunter's readin' the lessons in his white surplice an' the tall thin curate listenin' in his white surplice with a solemn puss on him waitin' his turn to read the second lesson, for the day I grow up to be a man I'll go to sea as a skipper of a three-masted schooner with mainsail 'n foresail 'n jibsail 'n topgallants 'n I'll run up 'n run down the ratlines same as you'd run up an' down stairs standin' steady in the crow's nest when she pitches fore 'n when she pitches aft, an' I believe in the holy Catholic church, the communion of saints, the forgiveness of sins and the life ever sailin' an' sailin' thousands 'n thousands of miles over blue seas 'n green seas and black seas 'n red seas, an' I'll live on islands where honey's flowin' down the trees with none to eat it 'n none to share it but meself an' there'll be birds like thrushes only red 'n bigger, 'n birds like gulls only blue 'n bigger, 'n there'll be no goin' to Sunday school or church in the mornin' or in the evenin' 'cause everyone'll be happy, for there's Hunter goin' to preach, settlin' his glasses on his nose 'n coughin' a little before startin' on his sermon, sayin' somethin' about becoming followers of the Lord having heard the word in much affliction he rambled on an' rumbled on an' gambled on an' ambled on an' scrambled on an' mummy-mummy-mumbled on an' yambled on an' yumbled on an' scrambled on an' scumbled on an' humbled on an' grumbled on an' stummy-stummy-stumbled on an' tumbled on an' fumbled on an' jumbled on an' drumbled on an' numbled on an' bummy-bummy-bumbled on, while here 'm I sittin' in the pew shiverin' cold as cold can be with me wet clothes clingin' to me back 'n stickin' to me legs.

At last the sermon ends, an' up we get on our pins to sing a hymn, fortified forth in Thy name, oh Lord, I go, my daily labour to pursue; Thee, only Thee, resolved to know, in all I think, or speak, or do, well, so I will, so help me God, to stand in me trousers without lettin' me legs touch them. Kneelin' down we get the blessin' an' then stream out down the aisles towards the door into the porch to see the rain pouring outa the heavens and peltin' off the pavement.

The congregation grumbling graciously, havin' received a blessing, button themselves into their macintoshes 'n coats before they dash out into the rain on their way home at tip-top speed. Johnny shivered, hesitated, and lingered in the porch watching the rain pourin' out of the heavens an' peltin' off the pavement, hopin' that it 'ud ease off a bit before he started to toddle home, toddling home, boys, toddling home. We give the pretty girls the wink, we drink an' laugh an' flirt an' drink, an' when the morn has dawned we think of toddling home, boys.

Tensed with the dread of the drenching the rain would give him, he closed his eyes and prayed silently, his heart full of faith in his heavenly Father: Please, O God, let the rain stop quick so that I won't get any wetter on me way home.

Again he murmured the words as slow as slow could be:

Please God Almighty, let the rain be stopped that I may go home without gettin' any wetter than I am now, amen.

He kept his eyes shut, even the one sheltered under the bandage, as tight as tight, for a long time, then opened them again, and saw the rain pouring out of the heavens and pelting off the pavement.

The sexton came out of the church, took off his black gown and hung it on a hook in the porch, put on a heavy topcoat, pressed a bowler hat down on his head, took a bunch of keys out of his pocket with a large one hanging from the middle, looked at Johnny and at the rain pouring out of the heavens and pelting off the pavement.

—Why haven't you set off home? Why are you lingerin' here? he asked.

—I was shelterin' from the rain till it stopped a little.

—Well, Johnny, me lad, you can't stay here. I have to lock up the church, and the rain won't ease off today, so you'd better dart off and get home as quick as you can. Besides, aren't you too much of a man to be afraid of a little drop of rain? If I was a young fella like you, I'd ask nothin' better than the excitement of dashin' home through the wind an' the rain.

Then he shut one half of the heavy oaken door, and opened up his umbrella. So Johnny looked brave, smiled at the sexton, hunched his shoulders, and ran out of the porch into the rain that was pouring out of the heavens and pelting off the pavement.

Then he ran and ran till he panted and panted; ran slower and slower; ran quicker and quicker, flushed and faint and frightened; feeling the rain slashing and slashing him, seeping and soaking through his thin clothes, flowing down his back and bottom, while his bandage hung heavy round his head; water mixed with sweat ran down into his good eye, smarting it, and making him blink so that he ran into a man hurrying home out of the rain, who struck at him and cursed, and stood and cursed after him, till the running boy was out of sight, as he ran on swiftly, sobbing softly, till he at last came into his own street, came up to his own house, and kicked desperately at his own door.

His mother opened the door to him. He slid in saying, I'm all wet, Mother, drenched through 'n through with the heavy rain.

She hustled him up to the fire, changed the soaked bandage for a dry handkerchief, stripped the steaming clothes from his fevered body, rubbed his shivering legs vigorously with an old bit of sheet till life came to him again, and warm security took the sorrow out of his sobbing.

—A nice state for you to be in after bein' gathered into the arms o' God, she said, as she dried his dreeping hair. A church that 'ud send a delicate half-starved child home to his mother in your state is round a corner 'n well outa the sight o' God; while Johnny stood naked before the fire, shivering and crying more merrily now that heat was here, and comfort and sympathy and safety.

—Every stitch on him sappin' wet, she went on, 'n here now I'll have to be wastin' the little coal I have left tryin' to get your clothes dry before the mornin' for you to wear goin' to the hospital to get your eyes looked after. Ah then, if oul' Hunter comes here before I forget the wettin' you got, I'll give him a piece of me mind about the thrue 'n everlastin' gospel of man mind thyself, for if you don't no one else will; 'n every one of them blind to the dhrenched condition of the kid stuck in the church there helpless, forgin' colds 'n coughs in his little chest; with his tiny ears trying to take in brassbound opinions issuin' out of a mouth stanced up high in a pulpit, pittin' the laws o' God against a child lowly sittin' in a big pew, fairly frozen with the cold 'n wet, an' he frightened facin' unundherstandable things shrouded in the veil 'n value of a white surplice, that, sold second-hand, would bring in enough to keep a woman 'n her kid for the length 'n breadth of a week, without the need of a thought for the want of whatever coin 'ud buy sufficient candle to light up the idea of a prayer in the last gleam of her mind to God before she plunged away into a night's sleep.

She put him to bed and gave him hot tea to drink, and covered him up, and tucked him in. He shivered and felt cold, and coughed and fell asleep and dreamed of a green ship with red sails and a yellow flag flying from a white mast sailing on a blue sea. He woke in the night, and felt cold and shivered and coughed, and couldn't, and gasped out, and found his breath gone. He got frightened and called his mother, and called and called till she got up in her shift, and rubbed his chest, gave him hot tea, and coaxed him to try to go to sleep again; but he shivered and coughed and cried.

In the freshness of the morning he was hot and dry-skinned, hoarse as hell, with a whistling breath that came with pain and went with pain and tightness. His eyelids were stuck together with the stuff that had oozed from his eyes during the night and piled up in a crust over his lids. His mother hurried up with her other son's breakfast, and got him off to his work. Then she hurried to the publican, J. P. Farrelly, JP, a poor-law guardian, who gave her a red ticket for the doctor; then she hurried to the dispensary where the porter told her that her sick boy alone in his bed 'ud have to take his chance, and hurry or no hurry, she'd have to take her turn with the rest of the people; and that neither he nor the doctor was at the hasty beck and call of those entitled to Poor-Law Dispensary relief.

So she waited, and moved and moved up after those in front of her, till at last she left the red ticket with the doctor demanding his attendance on one John Casside, aged eight years; then she hurried home to wait and wait for the doctor, who came in the evening, said the boy had a bad dose of bronchitis, gave her a prescription, and said if she hurried she'd just be in time to get it made up before the dispensary closed.

Fixing a bonnet on her head and throwing a shawl round her shoulders, she sallied out and ran steadfastly to the dispensary, reaching it in time to get the medicine; then she started back again, walking swift when her breath gave out, and racing when her breath came again, till she reached home with tired legs and an aching mind, to give her boy his medicine, bathe the sweat from his face and breast, settle his bed, and sit beside him till he slowly sank into a cough-disturbed slumber.

One evening some weeks later he sat by the fire, better, with an old blanket round him, and his teacher, Miss Valentine, bringing a bag of oranges, came to see him. She said how sorry they all were that Johnny hadn't been able to come to Sunday school or church; but they all hoped he would soon be back with them again and that the Reverend Mr Hunter sent Johnny his love, and they were all very fond of Johnny, he was such a good boy, and and they knew it wasn't his fault that he missed Sunday school and church for the last few weeks, and and and she brought Johnny a lovely scripture picture-card that was given to those who attended, and and and and she hoped it would bring Johnny's thoughts nearer to God.

So Johnny's mother said Miss Valentine was very kind, and made Johnny say Thank you; and Miss Valentine shook Johnny's hand as she went away, with Johnny's mother showing her down the stairs and opening the hall door for her.

When Johnny was alone, he moved the bandage higher up on his head, put the scripture picture-card against his good eye, peered a long time at it, and saw a big bunch of daffodils and a verse from the Bible. Spelling the words out slowly, he could not make them out, but they were these:

> And the light shineth in darkness; and the darkness comprehended it not.

BATTLE ROYAL

IT ALL began again when Johnny got over the attack of bronchitis – the wakening in the morning, feeling the hand of his mother shaking his shoulder, and calling on him to get up, get up; the washing of his eyes, heavily caked with discharge, bathing, bathing them in water as hot as he could bear it; then the careful insertion under the lids of his bad eye of a pellet of ointment called dominus by the hospital, because it was to be used at home, home, home, sweet home, and the fire out, full of atropine to distend the pupil, and so distend and weaken the ulcer on the cornea. Then the hot and hasty swallowing of tea and dry bread, the fixing of a sixpenny satchel over his shoulder, containing a lunch of two cuts of dry bread; and his mother's last warning to him to hasten himself a little, so as not to be late for roll-call, and have Slogan complaining to Hunter, and Hunter complaining to her; the slinking into school; the opening prayer; and then the song of the spelling and the song of the sums; the play hour arriving, the rush into the muddy yard, with its few patches, near the church, of grass and clover; the sitting down on one of the grass patches to eat the two cuts of bread as it was written, He gave them bread from heaven to eat; the watching of the others playing marbles, playing cards, smoking, flogging tops, or wondering what a group of bigger boys sometimes did between two distant buttresses of the church, catching some boy and knocking him down with a lot of loud laughter, while the boy on the ground cried out when the others fiddled with his trousers; then back to the school again when Slogan's bell rang a return to the song of the spelling and the sums.

One day at play hour, Johnny wandered over to a mangy patch of grass, sat down, and began to eat his lunch. For awhile he watched the thick smoke belching from the towering chimneys of the bottle-blowing factory, watched it spread and spread till all the sky in view was hidden by its yellow murk.

The golden gleam on an angel's wing, he thought, 'ud be well tarnished, if it passed even quick through smoke as heavy as that – he'd return to heaven looking like a chimney sweep.

Then he dimly watched a group of boys pegging-tops, tops with long, sharp steel spikes in them. They wound cords round grooves in the tops, then slung the tops with a quick jerk to the ground, holding one end of the cord in their hand so that the top spun rapidly as the cord unwound, which, with a clever thrower, made the top spin on its spike with a pleasant humming noise. The boys had made a ring with chalk on the ground, and in this ring a boy's top lay quiet on its side. Each thrower aimed at hitting the top of the ring with the spike of his own top, and, if he did, he got three blows at the boy's top with the spike of his own top; and, if he managed to split it, then his top was a conqueror of one. One boy had a top that was a conqueror of twenty others. As he looked and munched his lunch, a passing boy stopped beside him.

—What'r you doin'? he asked.

—Just sittin' here, an' eating lunch.

—You're in Foster's class, went on the boy. What's your name?

—Johnny Casside's me name.

—I've jam on me bread, said the boy. Have you any?

—No, Johnny replied, I'm tired of jam.

—Shapin', jeered the boy, tryin' to do the big. You're sayin' that because you've none.

He suddenly gave Johnny's hand a sharp slap, knocking the bread out of it on to the ground.

—See, he said, turning the bread over with the toe of his foot, it's dry, not even a scrape o' drippin' on it.

A boy, older than either, came up, glanced at Johnny, and caught the other boy by the arm.

—Come on, he said, dragging his friend away by the arm, come on, and don't talk to scabby eyes.

Johnny's eye strayed over to where a few big boys were smoking between two buttresses of the church, and he thought he saw the big-boned, tawny-headed Middleton beckoning to him. Not feeling sure, he puckered his brows together, narrowing his good eye so that he could see better and make sure that Middleton wanted him. Then he saw Middleton beckoning again, and heard him call out decisively, Eh, you there, come over here a minute, you with the bandage over your eye.

With his heart beating, Johnny got up from the grass patch, and ran over to Middleton, and stood nervously before him, while the group of boys nearby stood and stared curiously and scornfully at him. Johnny looked up at the big-mouthed, red-headed boy, who looked down at him with a wondering, but not unkindly, light in his grey eyes; while the rest stood around, big-fisted, cruel, rowdy, and cute, waiting for the big Middleton to question him.

—What's the matter with your eyes, sonny? he asked.

—Ulcers, Johnny answered.

—What's ulcers?

—Things that grow on your eyes, an' give you lots of pain.

—What sort of an old bitch must your mother be to let you come to school and your eyes the way they are?

—It's not me mother's fault, said Johnny defensively. Oul' Hunter makes her send me.

—Hunter'd dock the supply of parish coal they get, if he didn't go, sneered a stocky boy named Massey, who had yellow buck teeth and big patches on the knees of his trousers.

Georgie Middleton looked savagely at Massey, and said, I'm speakin' to him, and not you, so shut your damned mouth. There's more'n him gets parish coal.

—Massey gets it himself – I seen it goin' in, said another boy, eager to please Middleton.

—Any brothers an' sisters? asked Middleton of Johnny.

—Three, two away in the soldiers, an' one sister, said Johnny.

Massey giggled and murmured, Wonder if she's good-lookin' enough for a ride.

—He doesn't know the difference between a girl an' a boy, said a dirty-faced fellow named Ecret.

—Yes I do, answered Johnny stoutly, one wears trousers and the other doesn't.

Doesn't she? went on Ecret; just you lift up a girl's clothes, an' you'll see she wears them all right – white, with frills on the edges, an' wide at the ends so's a fella can get his hand well up.

—Ever had a look at your sister in her skin? asked Massey, grinning.

—Let's take down his trousers, an' see whether he's a boy or girl, called out bullet-headed, thick-armed Ecret, whose boots

were laced with twine, badly blackened over, as he laid a threatening hand on Johnny's shoulder.

Johnny struggled to free himself, but Ecret twisted his hand in
the shoulder of Johnny's coat, and held him tight. Johnny lashed
out with his foot, and just scraped Ecret's shin.

—You raspy little juicy-eyed sparrow, roared Ecret savagely,
for one pin I'd lay me hand hard across your snot!

—Let's see you doin' it then, said Middleton suddenly. You
who're so bloody quick with your hands, let's see you doin' it,
an' we'll see what'll happen.

There was a tense silence. Ecret grinned foolishly and gradually
loosened his hold of Johnny. It wouldn't be worth while dirtyin'
a fella's hand on him, he murmured.

—Go on, go on; don't draw back now, persisted Georgie
Middleton, while the others, scenting a row, gathered closer, and
listened with glistening eyes to hear what would be said between
the two big boys. One of them nudged Ecret, and whispered to
him, Go on, Fred, give the cheeky chiselur a crack across the
snot.

Ecret sniffed, and muttered uncomfortably, Oh, I don't want
to disfigure anything that Middleton chooses to make his pet.

—You're a liar, shouted Middleton savagely, he's no pet of
mine! I simply called him over to answer a few questions, and you
couldn't keep from butting in with your spitty prate.

Ecret moved nearer to Middleton, and glared at him resentfully.

—Who's a liar? he asked threateningly.

—You're a liar, insisted Middleton.

—How am I a liar?

—In saying he was a pet of mine.

—I didn' say he was a pet of yours.

—Yes, you did.

—I didn't; I said *if* he was a pet of yours – didn't I, boys? he
asked, turning towards those gathered round; didn't I use the
word *if* in what I said?

Massey moved forward with steps that dragged a little, stood
beside Ecret, stiffening his lurching shoulders, and glaring at
Middleton.

—I heard Ecret distinctly putting the *if* into what he said, an'
that's two agen one, he half-shouted triumphantly.

Middleton looked fixedly at Massey for a moment, then he went
close up to him, and thrusting his face close up to the other's, said

warningly, If you take my advice, Massey, you'll get your inter-ference to crawl away while I amn't lookin'.

—I'll not crawl away, nor run away neither, said Massey, with fear-tinged doggedness.

Middleton brought his head closer to the head of Massey, till their noses almost touched, his face flushed, his eyes gleaming, and his hand tremblingly clenched.

—Don't be tryin' to thrick yourself into a mighty mood, he said loudly, for when I say Ecret didn' use the word *if*, he didn't, see!

—An' I say I heard him usin' it, said Massey, as doggedly as before.

—You're a liar, he didn't! shouted Middleton, and with a sudden thrust forward he bumped his head sharply against the head of Massey, making him stagger back a few paces.

Johnny was hemmed in to the front by the circle of boys who had gathered to watch the dispute, and though cold and frightened, a glow of joy warmed him as he saw the head of Middleton bumping the head of Massey.

As Massey staggered back, Middleton followed him up, swiftly, and again bumped the head of Massey with his own, shouting as he did so, You're a liar an' a double liar, for he didn' use the word *if* from start to finish!

—Eh, there, eh, whose head are you bumpin? protested Massey, pale, tense, and quivering.

—Whose head am I bumpin'? mocked Middleton, knocking Massey's head harder than ever with his own; maybe you know, now, whose head I'm bumpin'!

Suddenly Ecret shoved Massey a little to one side, and stood, surly and snarling, before the excited Middleton.

—If the whole school's afraid of you, Middleton, we're not, he said, with bitterness; an' I say, with Massey, that I did put an *if* into what I said, and the head that bumps Massey's bumps mine!

Middleton hesitated to reply to this challenge, and glared redly at the two boys before him, weighing them up, their combined strength, power, courage, and skill in a rough-and tumble fight. His eyes wandered from one to the other as they stood defiantly there, breathing heavily, and waiting to see what he would do.

Middleton tried to quickly measure the amount of resolution behind their stand. Should he go on and frighten them, and, if they stood firm, would he be able to maul the two of them to-gether? It was risky, and his hesitation became apparent to those gathered around. Johnny's heart had gone as cold as the water bubbling from a spring in the dead of the night.

—I can't bump two heads together at the same time, he muttered lamely.

—No difficulty in it at all, if you want to do it, said Massey, a little more boldly: bump one, and you bump the two.

Middleton knew now that if he didn't go on, he would move back from his place as the big fellow of the school. He couldn't in his heart let himself lose his grip on this sense of power that stuffed his pride with sweetness. He saw that both of the boys who were glaring at him had noticed his hesitation, and were growing bolder. He knew that they thought he was beginning to be afraid.

—Bump Massey, and you bump me, said Ecret.

—Bump Ecret, and you bump me, said Massey.

Middleton clenched his hands and bared his teeth.

—If I wanted, he said, I'd bump the two of your heads to-gether, and I wouldn't want to take a week's holiday to get ready for it; but there was an undecided ring in the tone of his growling voice.

—Well, only let us know when you're ready to start, sneered Massey.

—An' we'll not let an'thin' get in your way, added Ecret.

A big boy chucked Middleton by the sleeve of his coat. One down, the other come on, he whispered. Take them that way, an' you'll knock the stuffin' outa them.

—I'll punch the two of you, said Middleton, taking the hint, one down, the other come on.

—You're lookin' for something soft, said Ecret, for the two of us together's hardly a right match for you, so take us together, or cry off; an' there's the coward's blow, and he gave Middleton a slight tap on the shoulder with his closed fist, as the bell carried by Slogan tinkled a warning that playtime had ended, and all were to return to the song of the spelling and the sums.

—I'll fight you both, one down, the other come on, said Middle-ton fiercely, baring his hard, stained teeth. That's fair, with the odds against me – isn't it, boys? he asked, turning generally to the crowd around.

—One down and the other come on, chorused a number of the boys. That's fair, an' gives the odds to them.

—There's the coward's blow back again, said Middleton, lightly striking with his closed fist, first the shoulder of Massey, and then the shoulder of Ecret.

—After school, then, on the way home, in Brady's Lane, said Ecret.

The bell was now tinkling impatiently, and all hurried back to school in a buzz of talk and a cloud of exciting wonder as to what would happen on the way home in Brady's Lane. Slogan several times glanced curiously at the boys as they hummed over their work, sensing that something was on the mat, but deliberately taking no notice of the hidden excitement shown in the tenseness of the boys. Johnny, for the first time, hoped that the hour ending school would take a long time to come. He could slip away on the way home, but he knew that he must stand by the boy who had stood up for him. There was no escape from having to watch these three fellows pounding each other's faces. He hoped that someone would come forward and make peace; or, that somehow, Slogan would hear of it, and prevent the fight. Too soon he saw the head boy of each class collecting the books, and knew that the school for that day was nearly done. The boys brought the books up to an assistant teacher who piled them back in the press, and shut and locked the door. He saw the boys returning to their places to sit down or stand up, waiting tensely for the word of dismissal. He saw the sun shining on the bald part of Slogan's head as he bent over a book, made a mark, shut it with a sharp movement, and put it aside. He saw him stand up, and give the signal for the parting prayer. There was a shuffling noise as the boys went down on their knees. Johnny heard Slogan tell some boy to fold his hands and close his eyes, and then the prayer came booming over the quiet school, asking that all done that day might sink deeply into the young innocent hearts gathered together, and bring forth fruit to the boys' good and the glory of God's holy name, Amen.

There was a loud shuffle of feet as the boys hurriedly rose from their knees, and streamed impatiently out of the school. As Johnny moved out in the crowd, he felt a hand catching his arm, and looking up, saw the flushed and anxious face of Middleton looking down at him.

—You'll hold my coat for me, sonny, he said, and watch me turning the faces of two bowseys into chunks of bleeding beef.

Johnny smiled wanly up at him and murmured, You knock hell outa the two of them, Georgie.

—You wait, he answered, you just wait.

A group of boys walked round Massey and Ecret, telling them how best Middleton was to be bayed, harried, and, finally, tired out, so that when it was plain that he had weakened enough, they could sail in and finish him off in their own good time.

—For Jasus' sake, don't let him get one home on either of you, or else you're done; fence him off, and fight cute; dodge round him just outa reach till he puffs, then dart in under his guard and give it to him fair on the solar plexus.

In Brady's Lane, a narrow gutway running between the backs of a row of little houses and a railway bank, all halted and got ready. The backyards of the houses, with the group favouring Massey and Ecret, stretched across the north end; and the railway bank, with the group favouring Middleton, stretched across the south end of the gutway, forming an oblong in which the fight was to take place. Middleton slowly and firmly removed his coat and handed it to Johnny, who slung it over his shoulder. Then Middleton unbuttoned his braces at the front, and tied them as a belt round his middle, rolled up the sleeves of his shirt, showing his grimy and knotty arms, and waited, venomous and nervous, for the fight to begin. Two big boys, one from Massey's group and one from Middleton's, took charge of the affair, to see that everything was done on the square, and to watch for fouls. Middleton's second took a step forward, and announced to the other group that Middleton was ready. Massey and Ecret were trying to settle with their second as to which of them should first tackle Middleton.

—Best for Ecret to go in first, argued Massey, 'cause he's lighter than me, an' can dodge round an' take the puff outa him.

—I say you're the best, retorted Ecret. You're heavier than me, an' if you can only manage to give him a few homers in the higher bit of his belly, I'll dance in then and put the tin hat on him.

—Eh, you there, said Middleton's second, settle who's to go in first, will you, and don't keep Middleton waitin' here till he's groggy with age.

—Here, if you can't agree, said the other second impatiently, toss for the one that's to go in first; tails for Ecret, heads for Massey; and he deftly spun a well-worn halfpenny in the air. The coin fell and showed a head. First turn for you, Massey, said the second. Massey peeled off his coat deliberately, rolled up his shirt sleeves, and rubbed his arms briskly, while Johnny prayed that the battle would go against the two boys, and that Georgie would prevail.

—Ready? asked the second.

Massey nodded.

—Ready? again asked the second, turning towards Middleton.

—Long ago, answered Middleton, with assumed carelessness.

—Go, then, shouted the second, and Johnny added softly, The arm of the Lord and of Middleton be strong in the battle today!

Middleton stood still, his right arm hanging slantwise over breast and belly, his left held crookedly out from the shoulder, watching, with gleaming eyes, the crouching movements of Massey, taking a step forward and quickly stepping back again, waiting for a good chance to spring in and strike, while Middleton stood still, watching, with gleaming eyes, every movement of Massey's.

A window in one of the houses opened, and a woman thrust out a head, covered with tousled withering hair, and looked down threateningly on the fighters.

—What are yous all up to down there? she bawled. Goin' to tear an' rip each other up, are yous? Get outa that lane, yez gang o' blaguards, and do your fightin' somewhere else!

But Middleton never took those gleaming eyes of his off the crouching movements of Massey.

—G'on, get outa that lane, roared the woman again, or I'll send a polisman down on top o' yous in double quick time! Amusin' yourselves manglin' each other. Is that the sort of gentle God-fearin' conduct yous are learnin' at school?

Massey suddenly jumped towards Middleton who made a swinging blow at the head of the jumping figure, but Massey sprang back in time, and Middleton swung around on his toes to face towards Massey again and stand still; watching, with his gleaming eyes, every stir made by the crouching, creeping Massey, while Ecret, too, stood still, and watched and gnawed his knuckles nervously.

—Looka that, looka that, said the woman from the window; if the poor boy hadda got that knock, he'd 'a had his head opened. Aha, here he is, here's the polisman comin' round the corner, now!

Middleton turned to give a swift apprehensive glance behind him, and, like lightning, Massey sprang in as his fist shot forward, and as Middleton turned his face to the front again, Massey's fist crashed on to his mouth. Then Massey sprang back out of reach, and all saw rich blood welling fast from Middleton's split lip as he grinned viciously, and silently and steadfastly watched once more.

—I'm goin' down to the street this very minute, shouted the woman at the window, to send the bobby at a gallop up to yous, an' I hope the jail'll house the whole o' yous be tomorrow mornin'! and she pulled in her head, and banged the window down.

Massey suddenly dodged nearer to Middleton, dodged back, and shot forward again, and the heavy, hard, soiled fist of Middleton went whirling over his head as he sprang back to safety.

—Careful, Massey, careful, me son, said a friend in the watching group; he very nearly got home an' heavy on you that time,

—Is this the policeman comin' round the corner? suddenly asked a boy from the group of Massey's backers.

Again Middleton turned a swift look behind him, and again Massey sprang forward; but Middleton, anticipating by instinct or cunning, swung round like a flash, shot out his fist with all the venom and power that was in him as Massey sprang forward, and all heard an agonized grunt and squeal as it cracked on Massey's jaw, who staggered back, frightened and sick, while Middleton, following him up, swung his left fist under Massey's ear, sending him crumpled up to the ground to crawl away into the crowd on his hands and knees, making a quiet moan.

Ecret, pale-faced and lip quivering, stood at the edge of his group of friends, hesitating, but they kept pushing him out towards Middleton, saying, Go on, in with you; don't leave him a second for a breather, make a dash for it, man!

But he had waited too long, for as he made a few reluctant steps forward, Middleton came towards him with a savage rush. Ecret put out his hands blindly to stem the rush; they were swept aside, and, in a flash, there appeared on Ecret's face a horrible bloody blob; agony shot into his eyes, and he reeled round; Middleton's clenched fist splashing into the blob and spreading it over the whole face till one of the blows tipped him headlong over the huddled body of his friend, Massey.

The group that had favoured Massey and Ecret shrank back against the wall of the houses, and watched Middleton standing in his shirt and trousers, with a snarling grin on his blood-dripping lips, looking down on the fallen boys.

—You're not goin' to give in as quick as all that, he said mockingly. Maybe now yous'll believe that when I say Ecret didn't use the word *if* in what he said, he didn't, see!

Two boys came over to Middleton, and took him gently and

proudly by the arm, beckoning Johnny to come over with the coat he was holding.

—Put on your coat, Georgie, one of them said. It's all over, an' all the two o' them want, now, is a chance to get well – a couple of girls' spits is all they were.

A glow of joy warmed Johnny as he ran over holding out the coat which Middleton put on slowly, with silent and sure pride, gloating as long as possible over the two kneeling boys, soaking their soiled handkerchiefs in the blood that flowed from their gashed faces.

Then Johnny and his friends gathered round Middleton, one of them putting a Woodbine in his mouth, lighting it while Middleton puffed slowly, holding it carelessly between his split lips, now staining the cigarette with red streaks. Then they all turned and walked high-headedly away, talking and laughing over all that had happened, leaving the two boys kneeling in the lane, soaking their handkerchiefs in the blood that flowed from their gashed faces.

VANDHERING VINDY VENDHOR

JOHNNY, Georgie Middleton, O'Halloran, Kelly, and a few others were hard at it playing hole and taw with marbles when the Jew passed by. A gadabout glazier, his back was deeply bent by the weight of a huge frame filled with sheet glass slung over his back, and kept in place by wide straps crossing his shoulders, helped by a wider one circling his waist. The Jew was short and stocky; bushy-headed, and a tiny black beard, tinged with grey, blossomed meagrely on his chin. A pair of deep black eyes stared out from a fat white face. Long locks of jet-black hair straggled down his forehead. The trousers of a shabby black suit were well frayed at the bottoms; his boots were well down at the heels; a new black bowler tightly clasped his head; his neck was rasped with a high and hard and shining white collar, set off by a gallant red, green, and yellow patterned tie. The Jew's arms were held out in front of his body to strengthen the resistance to the heavy weight on his back. His body was so much bent that the back of his head was sunk into the back of his neck to enable him to look to his front and to see any possible need for his services. The sweat was trickling down his cheeks, and glistening patches showed where it had soaked through his clothes near his armpits and the inner parts of his thighs. He walked with short steps because of the heavy pressure of the burden on his back. As he trudged along, he kept twisting his head as well as he could, now to the right, now to the left, ever on the alert for a possible job, chanting tirelessly as he marched along, Vindys to mend, to mend; vindys to mend! He kept his eyes well skinned for any window that might have been broken by a marble, a stone, a ball, or a drunken husband, as he went on chanting his Vindys to mend, to mend; vindys tot mend!

The sun was shining so brilliantly on the glass in the frame that O'Halloran said the Jew seemed to be carrying on his back the remnants of the pillar of fire that led his forefathers in the journey through the wilderness.

Every ten steps, he'd give the glass-filled frame a steady hoosh up on his back, never halting in his slow strut and never breaking the lilt of his Vindys to mend, to mend; any vindys to mend!

Suddenly the Jew hopped like a bird towards a broken window in a house fifty yards down on the other side of the street; and the boys, after gathering up their marbles, hurried down to see if Mrs Muldoon would give him the job of putting in a new one.

The Jew lingered a little before the broken window that had been replaced by a sheet of brown paper. He gradually came nearer, then with a finger poked a round hole in the paper, and, bending forward, peered into the room. Leaving the window, he came to the hall door, knocked gently, and stood patiently waiting for the door to open.

—I wouldn't care to have that weight o' glass pressin' on the top o' me arse for the length of a day, said O'Halloran, as the boys stood watching the antics of the Jew.

—One o' the lost sheep of the House of Israel, laughed Johnny.

—I never remember seein' a Jew as shabby-lookin' as that fella, murmured Middleton.

—Looka the sun shinin' on the glass, said Kelly, the shirt must be stickin' to his back.

—I betcha he hasn't got such a thing as a shirt, jeered O'Halloran; betcha again that the collar he has is only a dicky.

—An' I betcha, rejoined Kelly, that in less than a year he'll be rollin' about in a carriage an' pair.

—Damn cheek of them comin' here, said another boy, thinkin' we're not well able to mend our own bloody windows.

—Doesn't look as if we could, does it? questioned Middleton tersely. That one has been like that for the last six months.

—More, added Kelly.

—I wondher where does he come from? murmured Johnny.

—Jericho or Jerusalem, o' course, said Middleton. Where the hell d'ye think he come from? They're pourin' into every country outa Palestine in sthreams.

The Jew again knocked gently at the hall door, and stood patiently waiting for the door to open.

—He'll hardly find Mrs Muldoon ready to hand him out a welcome, said Kelly.

—Let's go over an' give him a hand with the knockin', said O'Halloran.

They went over to where the Jew was patiently waiting for the door to be opened, while his gentle and deep black eyes watched them suspiciously.

—Y'ought to knock a little harder, Mr Abraham, said Kelly; the woman of the house is a little hard o' hearin'.

—A lot harder, oh, a lot harder y'll have to knock, Mr Isaac, echoed Johnny gleefully.

—She'll hear it only if you knock the right way, Mr Jacob, said Georgie Middleton; like this – and catching up the knocker, he gave several terrific bangs that shook the door, and could be heard a mile away. Then he stepped back, and left the door to the Jew. The Jew stepped back too, as if he were afraid of something suddenly happening after the thundering knock at the door.

Before he had quite caught his balance, the door was whipped open and a lean, grey-haired, angry-faced woman, with a kid of two in her arms, stood glaring at him.

—Who th' hell's tryin' to knock down the door on the top of us! she yelled. What d'ye mean, she asked of the Jew, be shakin' the house down? That's no civilized way to knock at any decent person's door. The Lord Lieutenant himself couldn't dare give a loudher knock than that.

—They'll be goin' round shortly hittin' our doors with hammers, said Middleton.

—The vindy, said the Jew mildly, the vroken vindy; I put it een for negs to nodings.

—The vroken vindy, mimicked the angry woman, hoisting the child from one arm to the other; well, if you knock again as you knocked before, you'll have a vroken door to put in as well as a vroken vindy!

—I put it een for negs to nodings, pleaded the gentle Jew, the vindy.

—Ah, for God's sake, go to hell outa that, exclaimed the indignant woman. I've something betther to do than to be spendin' time an' money ornamentin' the house for the landlord. Carry the glory of your negs to nodings somewhere else, for the hand that put the vindy out can put the vindy in again. So saying, she hoisted the child on to the other arm, turned on her heel, and shut the door, leaving the Jew gawking at the closed door, and the boys gawking at the undecided Jew.

O'Halloran went over, and touched him on the shoulder.

—You put the vindy in, mate, he said confidentially. When the lady of the house sees it shining in its proper place, she'll pay. I know Mrs Muldoon to be a decent woman. Isn't she, boys? he asked, turning to the others.

—She's the heart of the roll! chorused the rest.

The Jew hesitated; looked at the window, at the boys, and back at the window again. His right hand hopefully fingered the buckles binding the straps holding the frame to his back.

—So help mine Godt, he said, I put the vindy in for negs to nodings, I svear.

—You go ahead, oul' son, said Middleton, and put in the vindy. Mrs Muldoon's a woman of her word, and won't see you sthranded, once the vindy's in – will she, boys? he asked of the others.

With one voice they all repeated that Mrs Muldoon was the heart of the roll.

—Come on, then, he added, an' give Jacob a hand to get rid of his weight.

They all crowded around the Jew, unbuckling the straps, and helping to lift the heavy frame from his back, carefully leaning it against the wall of the house. The Jew took off his shabby black coat, and began the job of putting in the window.

He took from a drawer in the lower end of the frame a hammer, chisel, pincers, and putty-knife. The boys watched him knocking out the jagged pieces of glass that still remained in the frame of the broken window. The clever white hands, a little too plump, worked swiftly, chiselling out the hard putty, and taking out the little nails that had held the old pane of glass in its place. When all had been cleaned and made ready for the new pane, the Jew took a diamond from a hip pocket, measured a sheet of glass with a square, and brought the diamond, in line with the square, along the surface of the glass with a swift, shrill, scratching sound. Replacing the diamond carefully in his hip pocket, he broke the measured piece of glass from the sheet with a clever pressing twist of his supple fingers. This pane he placed in the cleaned-out groove in the section of the window-frame, skilfully and carefully driving in the little nails to keep it steady in its place. Then rolling some putty between the palms of his hands, he deftly dabbed it along the margin of the new pane of glass, pressing it home with his fingers, and smoothing it off with his putty-knife.

A tired smile came into his tired face as he worked away.

—Ireesh boys, he said, as he pushed the putty home, are so clevair andt so kindt, better than all oder boys, I svear. I do a goot shob, he murmured, giving the finishing touches to the putty border, a goot shob for negs to nodings, negs to nodings. When the lady see de new vindy, she say goot shob, goot shob; danks.

He wiped the sweat from his face into the sleeve of his soiled shirt, replaced the tools and remains of the putty in the drawer of the frame, put on his coat, gathered the straps of the frame in his hands, bent down and gave a mighty hoist that carried the frame on to his back, buckled the straps once more, and, going over, knocked gently at the door.

—A goot shob for a goot kindt lady, he said, as he gently knocked at the door.

He heard a loud titter from the boys; and the tired smile fell away from his tired face as the door stayed shut, and no one came in answer to his gentle knock. He went on waiting patiently, the hot sun sparkling on the glass, heavily pressing on his bent back.

The boys slunk slowly away, tittering, and stood at the corner of a street higher up, watching the Jew waiting patiently at the door that never opened. The street was lonely. The curtains in all the houses had been pulled close together, or the blinds had been pulled down to keep the burning heat of the sun from the front rooms of the houses. No one was in the street; it was dead silent; nothing but the Jew standing pensively at the door, and the group of boys laughing and jeering at the quiet knocking, knocking at the door that never opened.

—Eh, you there, the Jew heard a voice crying out from the midst of the laughter and jeering, here's another vroken vindy, Abraham, so you may as well make a goot shob of it while your hand's in, and the lady of the house's sure to geev you negs to nodings for it!

A little flock of sparrows fluttered down from the roofs of the houses, and gathered around the feet of the waiting Jew. They had caught sight of the dried bits of putty lying on the ground, and hoped that some kindly power would turn them into crumbs of bread; so they hopped here and there, cocking an odd eye at the figure of the Jew, waiting and wondering before the tightly closed door. Suddenly they all flew off again to the roofs of the houses as a stone bounded off the pavement, striking the Jew on the calf, tearing the shabby trousers and making a little gash in the flesh of his leg. His head, sunk down in the back of the neck, turned quickly to look at the group of boys standing at the corner; but they were all innocently looking away in the opposite direction, and the sunken head turned back again to see if the door had opened.

Another stone shot off the pavement close to where the Jew was standing. He turned slowly to give a wistful look at the boys; turned his head back to look at the door, gave a long look at the mended window, started to walk away, hesitated, and half turned to go back to the door, hesitated again; then slowly set off down the deserted street, his body bent far down by the weight of the huge frame, filled with glass, that he carried on his back; his arms stretched out in front of him to stiffen the resistance to the weight; the back of his head sunk deep into the back of his neck so that he could see where he was going, still chanting peacefully as he trudged along, Vindy's to mend, to mend; any vindys to mend!

A loud cheer broke from the group of boys gathered at the corner, as they saw the Jew go.

CRIME AND PUNISHMENT

WITHOUT HIS usual cut of bread for lunch that day Johnny sat on a mangy clump of grass watching, with his good eye, Georgie Middleton and a group of cronies sitting between two church buttresses, playing cards, smoking fags, and arguing vigorously. He looked, came nearer; and Middleton lifted his head, and smiled.

—Come over here, and stand near me for luck, he said to Johnny.

Johnny came nearer, a little shyly, leaned a hand on Georgie's shoulder, and watched the play. They were playing twenty-fives for a penny a game and a ha'penny for the best trump out each deal. After every sixth game a boy took his turn for the following six games to stand aside and keep watch in case they should be suddenly surprised by oul' Slogan coming upon them unawares. Massey was now watching, and impatiently waiting for the six games to pass so that he could get back to the sport again. The cards were dealt, the tricks played and gathered, and Middleton won. Again the cards were dealt, given out, the tricks played and gathered, and again Middleton won.

—That's the third game for me, hand-runnin', said Middleton delightedly. Look alive, Ecret, and deal while the luck's my way.

—I'll deal, ejaculated Massey. That's the sixth game, now, and it's Ecret's turn to stand and keep nix.

—It's only the fifth, responded Ecret, there's another game to go yet.

—Sixth, I tell you, persisted Massey; didn't I count them carefully? So up with you off your hunkers, and take my place here.

—I tell you it's only the fifth game, growled Ecret, as he shuffled the cards.

—Sixth, sixth, sixth, repeated Massey impatiently, and he stretched over to take the pack of cards from Ecret's hands.

—No blasted bickerin', now, while I'm winnin', said Middleton testily.

—But fair's fair, grumbled Massey. I've watched here through the six games; and, accordin' to rules, it's Ecret's turn to take my place and keep nix for the crowd.

—Sit down then, snapped Middleton, eager to get another penny in the pool while he was winning; sit down, if you want a hand so badly, and Johnny, here, will keep nix for us all. He looked up at Johnny, and added, Make yourself useful, Johnny, be keepin' your good eye well peeled, an' if you see oul' Slogan turning the corner, give us the tip so that we'll all be talkin' about David watchin' Bathsheba havin' her bath, before he comes close.

Johnny became almost ill with fear that he wouldn't see Slogan quick enough, if he came round the corner. He hadn't the courage to say that his eye wasn't good enough; so he strained this one eye open, and stared fixedly at the corner round which Slogan would probably come, if he came at all. He prayed that he would not come, and that the bell would shortly be heard proclaiming that the time for cards was past, and that all must return to the song of the spelling and the sums.

—Somebody shy in the pool, said Middleton; only ninepence in it, so there's a wing missin' – who's shy?

—I am, said Massey, who was dealing the cards. When he had given them out, he added a penny to the pool. Ecret's lead, and spades is trumps, he added, peering expectantly into his hand.

They led and trumped and took their tricks; shuffled and cut and led and trumped and took their tricks, while Johnny stared and stared at the corner round which danger might come, and longed and longed for the warning bell to ring.

Suddenly there shot into his eyes a pain like the piercing of many needles, flooding into an agony that shocked his brain and flashed a glare of crimson light before him that made him clench his teeth and press his lids tight together till a stream of scalding evil tears forced their way between them, and ran hotly down his cheeks. Then he felt himself jerked back by the shoulders, and heard the sound of scrambling feet. When the pain subsided, he opened the good eye, and saw Slogan taking up the money in the pool, and gathering the cards, with a scowl on his face; while the group of boys looked on, embarrassed and silent. When Slogan had gathered up all the money and the cards, without speaking a word, he left them standing there, awkward and resentful.

Middleton turned savagely on Johnny.

—How the hell did you manage to let him sail down on the top of us like that? he snarled, but Johnny, burning with shame and shaking with sensitive fear, gave out no answer.

—Caught us all, like a lot of shaggy sheep, muttered Massey.

Middleton turned and struck Johnny sharply across the mouth with the back of his hand, making the boy's lip bleed, as he shouted, You half-blind, sappy-lidded, dead-in-the-head dummy, you couldn't keep your eyes skinned for a minute or two an' save the few bob we were bettin' from buyin' Bibles for the heathen buggers of Bengal!

—Caught us all, like a lot of shaggy sheep, muttered Massey.

Middleton gave Johnny a vicious shove that sent him reeling.

—Away, for Christ's sake outa me sight, you hand-gropin' pig's-eye-in-a-bottle, you!

The others laughed loud, crowded round Johnny, pushed and pinched him, as he turned and walked slowly away from them.

Turning the corner, he heard Slogan belling the end of the playhour; and, passing the master, he entered the schoolroom, sat down in his place, and screwed his good eye into a lesson book, while his heart thumped in his breast. The boys poured into the school, and his classmates sat down beside him, whispering excitedly about all that had happened.

Suddenly the hum of the school was hushed, for Slogan, standing at his desk at the upper end of the room, was ringing his bell, and all the boys, save Johnny, knew that when the bell was rung from that place some very important thing was about to be said by the master. All that were in the school heard the master's voice coming out of the stillness, with a dull tone of joy in it, like the quavering notes of a sickening bird.

—As I was walking about the playground today – prowling about, I think you all call it – I caught a number of our more respectable boys deep in a very sinful pastime, a pastime that we can safely associate only with papist corner-boys; to wit too-whoo videlicet, card-playing, and gambling like good ones in this game with the devil's prayer book, forgetful that they were Protestant boys baptised in the brine of the Boyne water giving them a great responsibility to behave blameless before God and man and Roman Catholics, who are always on the alert to exaggerate any little indiscretion that respectable Protestant boys may commit. In the first feeling of righteous indignation that came over me, I was going to make an example of every boy connected with this sin by giving each a sound and thorough whaling; but instead of that, I will leave it to their conscience to punish them more than a firm application of the cane could. But there is a certain boy mixed up with it whom no one would think, at the first go, could be connected with the card-gambling, and this boy must be punished; and I am going to punish this boy now, and punish him well. I am going to punish him in such a way that he will think twice before he indulges in the vice again. This brave little fellow, on whom I'm going to test the valour of my cane, was on the *qui vive* so that the card-school wouldn't be disturbed by the bold bad teacher, but this brave little boy didn't watch well enough. He fell asleep at his post, and in a few minutes he is going to feel very sorry that he didn't keep a better Spartan watch and ward. That little boy's mother is a widow, so he has no father to take care of him; and it is meet, right, and my bounden duty to do everything possible to make sure that no bad tendencies are allowed to creep into the nature of the widow's little son. And when I have reddened his backside with this cane, I'm sure he'll be a better and more careful little boy for a long time to come, and run a mile away from a card whenever he sees one. He swished the cane through the air, and grinningly asked the school, Who was he who said, spare the rod and spoil the child, boys?

—Solomon, sir, Solomon, sir, shouted a dozen of the boys.

—And in what part of the Bible do we read that counsel?

—Proverbs, chapter thirteen, verse twenty-four, shouted a dozen of the boys.

—And what are the exact words, boys?

There was a dead silence, and only one boy held up his hand.

—Well, Ecret, my boy, tell the dunces the exact words used by the wise man, Solomon, when he advises us to deal in a bright way with bold boys.

—He that spareth his rod hateth his son, sang out Ecret, with his head up.

—And wasn't Solomon inspired of God? asked Slogan.

—Yessir, responded the school.

—How do we prove that? questioned the master.

The school was silent.

—All Holy Scripture is inspired of God, said Slogan, and the Book of Proverbs is part of Holy Scripture, and chapter thirteen and verse twenty-four is part of the Book of Proverbs; *ergo*, the counsel in the verse, he that spareth his rod hateth his son, is holy and inspired of God without a possible doubt. So, boys, wouldn't it be very sinful of me to neglect or despise the teaching inspired of God, seeing that I stand *in loco parentis* to you all, and particularly to the widow's little son, brave little Johnny Casside?

—Yessir, Yessir, responded the whole school, all save only Georgie Middleton, for Johnny saw that his head hung down, and that he took no part in what was going on between the boys and their master.

—The ayes have it, said Slogan, nodding brightly towards the boys; so come along, Johnny, come along up here to me, my son, till I pay you the attention counselled of God, which will be painful, but which will, ultimately, add a lot to your moral and, I hope, spiritual progress.

—Slogan's callin' y'up, whispered a boy on Johnny's right;

wants to biff you for playin' cards durin' playhour, so he does. But Johnny cowered his head down to the desk, and made no offer to stir.

—Eh, there, said a boy to his left, nudging him in the side, d'ye hear? He's callin' you. Y'are to g'up to him – d'ye hear?

—Come along, boy, said Slogan, down to Johnny; come along, and get it over. But Johnny hung his head towards the desk, and made no offer to stir.

—He hesitates, said Slogan. Thus conscience doth make cowards of us all; and thus the native hue of resolution is sicklied o'er with the pale cast of thought. Come on, come up here.

—He's not makin' a single move to stir, sir, said the boy on Johnny's left.

—Come on, come up, come up, come on, chirruped the master. Remember what your godfathers and godmothers promised for you – to submit yourself lowly and reverently to all your governors, teachers, spiritual pastors, and masters; so up you come; and in later years you'll rejoice when you remember the caning a good master gave you. Then he looked down at Johnny, and went on in a voice of quiet and steady sternness: Are you going to come up quietly, boy, to take your medicine, or must I go down, and wallop you up to me?

Johnny slowly and fearfully climbed out of the desk, and taking as many steps as possible, came towards Slogan, his heart thumping hard, and the sweat breaking out all over his forehead. He felt that Slogan wanted to beat away on him the fear that made him afraid to lay a hand on the other and bigger boys; for he had heard Middleton, Massey, and Ecret say that if Slogan ever tried any thrick of caning them, they'd open his bald skull with a slate. He halted a little distance away from the master, just out of reach of the cane.

—A little nearer, a little nearer, boy, purred Slogan; you've got to get it, so make up your mind to take it like a little Spartan. Tell me, boy, what's a Spartan? He doesn't know what a Spartan is, grinned Slogan, turning towards the school. Well, Spartans lived a long time ago in Greece, and were famous for bearing pain without a murmur. In Sparta every little boy, whether good or bad, was continually caned to make him hardy. So just shut your mouth, close your eyes, take your caning calmly, and all the school will look upon you as a little Spartan. I see your britches are a little threadbare, but that will make it all the more exciting for you. Now all we want are two strong and willing boys to come up here and stand ready to hold you down, if you squirm too much, so that you can get the full benefit of a kindly, if stern, Christian castigation. Whom shall I choose for the honour? And Slogan looked slowly and lovingly at the tense figures sitting in bunched-up lines in the yellow wooden desks.

—Will I do, sir? called out Massey, popping up his hand to attract the master's attention.

—You, Massey, said the master, will do nicely for one. You're pretty strong; and, if the need arises. I'm sure you will do your duty. Now, just one more. The biggest boy in the school ought to have the honour of holding the bold boy down – you, Georgie, come along here, and help.

Middleton's face reddened as he bent his head down to the desk and muttered, I'd rather not, sir.

Slogan put a hand behind a less-deaf ear, bent forward sideways, and said, Eh?

Middleton, keeping his head bent, raised his voice and said doggedly, I'd rather not, sir. I want no hand in any boy's batterin'; an' besides, the kid's too delicate to touch.

Slogan went white to the gills.

—Middleton, he said, with quiet bitterness, you had better learn to give an opinion only when your master asks for one.

Middleton suddenly stood up, and a dirty, dog-like scowl lined his harsh face as he pressed his soiled hands on the top of the desk so hard that the knuckles whitened.

—The kid had nothing to do with it, he rasped out; it was me and the others. He didn' play, an' doesn't know how, an' he kep' nix because we made him.

A deep silence spread over the whole school.

—Georgie Middleton, said Slogan, in a dead level voice, glancing over the whole school with his shallow eyes, will be leaving us all in a month of two to go out and fight his way in the world, and I'm sure we all wish him the best of luck. He is to try for a job in a big store where the manager wishes to give a start to a boy who has just left school. Mr Middleton has asked our rector to give Georgie a character, and the rector has asked me for a general report of his conduct here. If Georgie wants to get on in the world with the help of a good start, I'd advise him to be careful to make his master think well of him. Am I right, Georgie Middleton? asked Slogan, now fixing his eyes on the head-bent boy.

Middleton fought his fear for a moment, then the whole school heard him murmur, Yessir, as he sank into his seat, shocked into the feeling that dangers flooded the way of an open courage.

—And don't you think, Georgie, that this boy here should be punished for his own sake? went on the master. There was a pause, and then the whole school heard the murmur of Yessir from the mouth of Middleton.

—Come along up here, then, said Slogan, and stand ready to help as soon as I need you. And Middleton, pale, and a little sick with shame, slouched up; and, sullen and bitterminded, stood near the radiant, iron-bowelled, ratty-hearted master, who put his hand out and patted Georgie's shoulder.

—You're a good boy, Georgie, he said, for you have had the manliness to acknowledge an error which many of us might very well hesitate to do; and there is more joy in heaven over one sinner that repenteth than over ninety and nine that need no repentance. And now, he went on, gripping Johnny by the collar of his coat, we start to cane a little conscience and a lot of caution into the soul of a wilful little boy.

Johnny shook when he felt the grip on his shoulder, and his stomach went a little sick with the foreknowledge of the pain that was to come upon him.

—Me mother said I wasn't to be touched because me eyes are bad, he said hurriedly and imploringly. Don't beat me, and I'll promise I'll never do the like again. Then he felt the searing sting of the cane across his thighs, and he screamed and tore at the master with his little hands, twisted his body and lashed out with his feet at the master's shins. Some of the kicks got home, the master gave a dog's yelp, and a burning glare of cruelty shot into his paly eyes.

—Here, Massey, and you, Middleton, he yelled, hold his arms stretched out over the desk till I knock the devil of resistance out of him!

The two boys caught hold of Johnny's arms and pulled him over the desk, leaving him at the mercy of the smiter, while the panting boy pleaded please, sir, don't. I didn't mean to watch for the card-playin', really I didn' – oh, you're cuttin' the skin off me!

But the bastard, sweating and puffing, with rigid snarling face and shining eyes, panted and sliced and cut and cut again and again. Johnny felt Massey twisting his arm, pretending that he was hard to hold. Slogan, at last easing off, gave a few more vicious strokes, then stopped to wipe his face in his handkerchief.

—Up on the chair with you, now, beside the desk, he said to the quivering boy, and let the school have a good look at you. A slice across the legs sent Johnny, with a suppressed cry, to leap quick on to the chair, chorused by a titter from the school at his haste to get there. Ashamed to rub the maddening sting in his backside and legs before the school, he balanced himself on the chair, with the eye-bandage that had loosened in the struggle, hanging round his neck, his eyes torturing him with the ache of the disease and the tears that had poured out of them, and his whole nature shaken with the confused wonder at what people were doing to him and what people were thinking of him; there he stood balancing on the chair, doing his best to check the sobs that tossed about the very beating of his heart.

Slogan looked at him for a minute, and then shook his head, and there was contempt in the shake.

—He wasn't much of a Spartan, after all, he said, turning to the school, with a grin, and the opinion I have of him now is less than the one I had before. Well, we'll have to be careful of him, for one sickly sheep infects the flock, and poisons all the rest. He glanced again at Johnny. We'll give him a minute or two to pull himself together and try to be a man, but if he goes on annoying the school with his baby blubbering, we'll have to cane him quiet – isn't that so?

—Yessir, chorused the school.

A bell rang for change of positions; those who had been seated in desks, formed into standing classes, and those who had been standing, sat themselves down in the desks. Johnny still shook a little with gentle crying till Slogan stood before him, angry, threatening, cane in hand.

—Finish the whinging, finish the whinging, boy, quick, or – and he shook the arm of Johnny. The boy tried to check the sobbing, tried to look calm, and sobbed again.

—Stop it at once. D'ye hear? Are you finished?

—Yessir, murmured Johnny.

—Finished, quite, quite finished, are you?

—Yessir.

—Well, let's hear no more of it. Not a squeak out of you, or the cane'll be twisting round your legs again.

With a steady effort of will, Johnny kept quiet, stood sullen on the chair, and waited and watched Slogan return to his desk, and bend over it to correct exercises. He looked at the thin stream of sunlight flowing in by the door, left open to give air to a room hot with the breath of children and teacher.

Then the bell rang again, and all that were standing filed into the desks. The Regulations of the Board of Education were turned with their face to the wall, and an oblong strip of millboard having written on it, Religious Education, was turned to face the school. Rapping on his desk with a heavy, glossy ebony ruler, Slogan silenced the murmur of the school. He put down the ruler on the desk beside him, and bent his hoary oul' head, saying softly, Let us pray.

There was a clatter of moving bodies as all got down on to their knees. Slogan knelt down, too, resting his hoary oul' head on his arms that rested on the seat of the chair from which he had risen to pray. The ebony ruler lay motionless on the desk beside him. O Lord, open Thou our eyes that we may behold wonderful things out of Thy law. The ebony ruler lay quiet on the desk beside him. Our Father which art in heaven. Hallowed be Thy Name. Johnny could see the pink baldy head of him, with its hoary edging, as Slogan bent down over the seat of the chair on which his arms rested.

Johnny suddenly slipped down from the chair he stood on, a flood of mighty rage swept through him; he whipped up the heavy ebony ruler, and with all the hate in all his heart, in all his mind, in all his soul, and in all his strength, and a swift upward swing of his arm, he brought the ebony ruler down on the pink, baldy, hoary oul' head of hoary oul' Slogan, feeling a desperate throb of joy when he heard the agonizing yell that Slogan let out of him when the ebony ruler fell.

Still gripping the ebony ruler, he made for the open door and the sun. He saw Georgie Middleton grip Ecret's shoulder as Ecret made a movement to rise and stop his flight. He saw, as he flew past, the hand of Massey stretched out to hinder, and he heard the blasting curse of Massey in his ears as the ebony ruler came down on the outstretched hand. Away out through the door he dashed, across the road, down the narrow mucky Brady's Lane, shinned speedily up the rough-cut stone wall of the railway embankment, dropping the ruler as he climbed, heard in a clitter-clatter way the rush of an oncoming train, cleft by a sudden frightened, piercing whistle, plunged over the rails, checked for a second or two by the rush of the wind carried by the train, as it went thundering by, saw dimly as in a mist a white-faced driver's mouth opening and shutting frantically; but pulling violently out of the intaking wind of the passing train, he sliddered down the other side of the embankment, ripping his trousers and tearing a rent in his leg with the jagged end of a jutting stone; rushed up the street opposite, turned down the next on the left, pushed open the hall-door of the house, burst into the room, and fell, exhausted and fainting, at his frightened mother's feet.

When he came to himself, his mother was bathing his body with water soothing and warm. The sting in his legs had ceased, for his mother had softened them with vaseline. He stretched his hand out, and gripped his mother's bodice.

—Don't let oul' Hunter or oul' Slogan come near me, Ma, he pleaded.

—They won't be let within an ace of you, she answered; but why did you come dashing in, and why did they beat you till your poor legs were covered with bunches of weals?

—Oul' Slogan bet an' bet me because he said I watched an' kep' nix for boys playin' cards behind the buttresses of the church at playtime. I couldn't get out of it for they were biggern me; an' besides, me eyes 'ud be in the way of me seein' how to use me mits in a fight; 'n I didn't want to, but they made me, 'n oul' Slogan came on top of us; 'n because all the boys were biggern me, he bet 'n bet me till he was tired.

His mother softly fixed the bandage round his bad eye, snuggled him gently under the bedclothes, bent down and kissed him.

—Rest and sleep sound, she said, and forget all about it till the morning.

And he lay down safe with her who would watch over him, and wended his way into a deep sleep.

THE LORD LOVETH JUDGEMENT

MRS CASSIDE sat down near the fire on a butter-box that had been covered with a strip of old red cloth. As she sat by the fire on the butter-box that had been covered with an old red cloth, she saw with a sigh that the straw in the mattress on Johnny's bed was coming loose quick and fast. The stitching of a hundred and one nights was failing to keep it together, and so she sighed. She saw the kettle, tarred from the smoke of the fire, tottering on the hob, its leaking bottom patched with little discs o' cork and tin, sold in the hardware shops for six a penny on a cardboard sheet; the frying-pan and saucepans that were, thank God, still holding out; the cupboard standing big-bellied in the corner, safely guarding the little stock of delft. She saw, and shivered, that a number of the springs were beginning to show through the covering on the horse-hair sofa, now leaning a little faintly against the wall of the room under the window; the narrow strip of cotton twill that was doing all it could in its service as a sheet to keep Johnny's bare legs from the pricks of the straws sticking out of the mattress; the lean blanket and the coats struggling to keep him warm; the kitchen chairs, still sturdy; the steel fender, polished with emery paper till it shone like silver, battling the ashes back to their proper place; the pictures of Nelson Bound for Trafalgar Bay and Queen Victoria gradually growing old amid the fading roses on the wallpaper; the two-leaved mahogany table, bought by her husband from a Fenian forced to fly the country; the big box, coaxed from the grocer for sixpence, where the coal was kept, crossed by a plank carrying the bucket holding the fresh water, a bucket that had to be used, too, for the carrying down of the water spoiled by use; and on the window ledge the two geraniums, one white, the other red, and the purple-cloaked fuchsia blossoming blithely amid the wrack of the common things around them. She saw and shivered as she sat on the butter-box that had been covered with the strip of old red cloth.

The hours went by, and the boy slept sound. Archie came home from his work, took his tea, read the paper; asked why Johnny was in bed, was told that he wasn't well, and said that the kid was always sick; and then went out to have his fling in his own way after his day's work.

Then the darkness came, and the stars stared out of the darkness as she sat by the fire on the butter-box covered by the old red cloth.

If God be with us, she thought to herself, who can be against us? A great many can be against us, came in an added thought, and some of them are strong. She got up and lighted a duplex kerosene lamp that stood on the two-leaved mahogany table. If God be for us, who can be against us? Below in the hall she heard a commotion out of which her name was called. She went out to the lobby, and peered over the banisters into the gloom below.

—Who wants me; who's callin' me? she called down.

—It's the Protestan' minister; he wants to see you; been lookin' for you; somethin' about Johnny; the Protestan' minister, said lively and sad, young and old voices up to her out of the gloom. The regular beat of her heart changed to a troubled throb. She

wished she hadn't spoken. She wished she hadn't shown herself.
Wished she hadn't come out of the room. She wished she hadn't
lighted the lamp. Wished she had stayed sitting still by the fire on
the butter-box covered with the old red cloth, leaving whatever
trouble had come to her alone in the gloom of the hall. Johnny
must have done something very bad for them to flog him the way
they did.

—Is that Mrs Casside up there? The voice of the minister came
up, like the voice of a harpy, up from the gloom of the hall.

—Yessir, this is Mrs Casside talkin' down to you from the
lobby. Won't you come up, sir, please?

—Please bring out a light of some kind, my good woman,
that I may be able to see my way.

She returned to the room to fetch a lamp and a light to his
path, the rough path that led the minister in the way to her room,
so that he might bring forth light to the thing in her son's heart,
quiet now in a dear deep sleep making darkness and light alike
to him; unaware of the enemy at the gates about to enter where
light is as darkness; seeking to set sorrow where joy should stand
up, stand up for Jesus shall reign where'er the sun doth his succes-
sive journeys run, His kingdom stretch from shore to shore, till
moons shall wax and wane no more, cursed be he that perverteth
the judgement of the stranger, the fatherless, and widow.

With the lamp in her hand, she went out to the lobby, and held
it as low as she could over the banisters, to light the minister's
way up the narrow stairs to the room. She saw the faces of those
who lived in the house and the house next door watching the
Protestant minister carefully climb the stairs to the lobby where
the mother waited for him; watching him till he passed out of their
sight into the home of the widow and her sons. The minister
stood blinking in the semi-darkness as Mrs Casside tremulously
put the lamp back carefully in its place on the little mahogany
table. She placed one of the sturdy kitchen chairs beside the
minister, and he sat down stiffly. She sat down straight-backed
on another, waiting for him to speak, with her hands clasped
tightly together in her lap.

—I have left very important work, very important, to come
here, he said, as he gave a glance around the smoky room, to
have a talk to you about John. He paused for a moment, then
went on. He ran away from school today, Mrs Casside – do you
know why?

—Yessir. He told me all about it. The big boys made him keep watch while they gambled with cards, and Mr Slogan came up and caught them. Though he didn' lay a hand on any of the others, he laid heavy hands on Johnny; and then the poor boy ran away.

Just like these hopeless people, thought the minister, always making excuses for their children. Severity is the only possible kindness.

—John didn't tell you, he said, out loud, that his master, Mr Slogan, is, at the moment, ill in bed; that he had to be helped home after John had given him a savage and violent blow on the top of his poor head with an ebony ruler. Did he tell you all about that, Mrs Casside? Then there is a bad, a very bad bruise on one of Mr Slogan's shins from a vicious, a very vicious kick given by your son, John. Did he tell you all about that, too, Mrs Casside?

Facing him, the woman sat silent and stiff and still.

—Now, went on the minister, we don't want your little boy to grow up to be a criminal; but if he is to grow up to be readily able to do his duty in that state of life unto which it has pleased God to call him, these dangerous inclinations must be checked, and checked, if necessary, with a very rough hand. Now, don't you agree with me, Mrs Casside?

Facing him, the woman sat silent and stiff and still.

—If your boy won't willingly do it, then he must be made, must be made, Mrs Casside, to order himself lowly and reverently to all his betters, went on the smooth, soft, cold voice. If this sort of conduct goes on unregarded in the way of suitable punishment, he will be encouraged to do again and again the things that will utterly unfit him to be a sober and decent member of society. The attack upon poor Mr Slogan was the act of a right young blaguard. The boy has richly earned a severe caning, and he is going to get it; and then go down on his knees to his master, and humbly beg his pardon before the whole school.

Facing him, the woman, sitting silent and stiff and still, shivered.

—When Johnny wakes in the morning, I'll speak to him about what he did to Mr Slogan, the woman said.

—The morning, the morning, said the minister testily; wake the little rascal up now, and tell him that I will meet him at the school the first thing in the morning; and that immediately after prayers, a severe caning will make an example of him before the whole school; and, that when he has been suitably punished, he will go down on his knees, and beg his master's pardon for his blaguardly conduct; so that, in future, he will never dare to raise a hand against anyone whom God has set in authority over him.

Facing him, the mouth of the woman sitting stiff and still quivered and spoke softly, very softly.

—The boy may be awake tonight with his eyes, sir, the quivering mouth said, and to do what you ask would be to torture him above what he might be able to bear.

—I tell you, said the minister impatiently, that you will ruin your little boy, if you go on coddling him in this way.

The mouth of the stiff still woman quivered again, and the mouth spoke softly.

—He has had dry bread and tea for a good many meals, since his father died, said the quivering mouth; clothes that shiver when a breeze blows; boots that just about hide the bareness of his feet; and hours of eye pain rock him restlessly at night – neither I nor God, sir, coddle the boy.

The minister stood up from the chair.

—Each of us must learn to bear with the tribulations which God may see fit to inflict upon us, and which may work out an exceeding weight of glory. But what you have to remember at the moment, Mrs Casside, is that God is angry, very angry, with your boy. If he isn't punished one way, he'll be punished in another, and, very possibly, in a more severe way. He must be made to take his just punishment, lest worse befall him. I beg of you to be firm, Mrs Casside.

He moved softly towards the door while the woman rose from the chair, crossed the room, and sat stiff, still, and silent, with her hands clasped in her lap, on the butter-box covered with the old red cloth, facing the minister, facing him fair, as she sat on the butter-box covered with the old red cloth.

—So, the minister went on, please be at the school with John the first thing in the morning. I will be there to take charge of the boy, and I can assure you that the punishment will be given under my own personal supervision; and, after it is all over, I feel sure we shall have a better pupil, and you will have a better son.

The soft mouth of the stiff and still figure, sitting on the butter-box covered with the old red cloth, hardened.

—Tomorrow, the soft mouth that had hardened said, tomorrow, sir, is one of the days when I bring the boy to the hospital.

The hard mouth of the minister twitched with irritation.

—There is to be no putting-off of the punishment, Mrs Casside, the hard mouth said; remember that. The caning must be given while the blaguardly act is fresh in the mind of the boy.

The soft quivering mouth of the woman sitting on the butter-box covered with the old red cloth hardened to the hardness round the mouth of the minister.

—Tomorrow morning, the soft mouth that had hardened said, the boy will be where God, through the doctors, may give ease to his eyes. The harsh hand that fell on him today shall not fall on him tomorrow, or the next day, and its dark shadow shall he never see again. Tell that to Slogan from the boy's mother.

—Mrs Casside, Mrs Casside, said the hard mouth of the minister, tightening.

—Goodnight, said the soft voice that had hardened. As you go, leave the door open so that the light from the lamp may show you some of the way down.

And the minister slowly put his soft hat on his head, and went his way.

Then the stiff and still and silent woman went over to the bed where the boy lay, and his sleep was sound; and she bent over and kissed him.

THE DREAM REVIEW

JOHNNY WOKE and tried to open his eyes but the thick red lids were tightly stuck together with the matter that had oozed from them during all the still hours of the night. Rubbing hard and roughly, he tried to force some of the yellow crust away, but the inflamed lids held together fast. He tore at the crust with his fingernails till the hardened matter burst and he could open his eyes a little. He peered out in front of him, but the room was full of darkness and he couldn't see. He closed them again, and slid his hand over the top of the bed feeling for his trousers. In its movement his hand touched the bandage that had fallen from his head during the night. He tied it loosely round his forehead covering the left eye completely, and the right eye partly, with its folds. Again he slid his hand over the top of the bed in search of his trousers, but failed to find them. Sitting up and bending sideways, while the framework of the bed creaked and the old rusty laths rattled, he stretched out of the bed and ran his hand cunningly along the splintery floor. Touching a garment, he lifted it, and feeling the seat and fork and buttons, knew it was his trousers, and laid it beside him on the bed.

The morning must be well into the day now, for a long time ago, when he was only half awake, he had heard the postman bawling out the names on the letters that he had brought to the people of the house. He moved over to a warmer spot in the bed. Suddenly he heard the sound of children cheering, and putting the bandage away from his ears, he sat up, leaning on his elbow, and listened.

He heard the voice of his mother talking to some oul' wan at the door below. He slid out of bed, felt his way over to the door of the room, and opened it a little so that he might hear what the two women were saying.

—I couldn't think of lettin' him go, said the voice of his mother, 'n his eyes the way they are.

—Poor little chiselur, said the voice of the other oul' wan, poor little chiselur.

—I put a bit of cloth over the window, went on his mother, to keep th' light of the mornin' from wakin' him before they'd gone to the review, for Queen's birthday 'n all as it is, I couldn't let him go with Archie, 'n his eyes the way they are.

—Poor little chiselur, murmured the other voice, poor little chiselur.

—Looka the kids o' the school collectin' to march to Nelson's Pillar to take the thram to the Park Gate, where they'll get off an' walk to where the Royal Standard's flyin' square-quarthered with the Irish Harp, the Scottish Lion, 'n the English Leopards, waitin' for the gallopin' arrival of the Lord Lieutenant to start things goin', with hats off, attention, 'n presented arms to the playin' of the National Anthem. Johnny was lookin' forward to seein' the stiff consequential step of the grenadiers in the march-past, 'n the gorgeous sthrut of the kilted highlanders, 'n the common 'n dignified go-by of the infanthry o' the line, the proud throt of the artillery horses, right o' the line 'n pride of the army, pullin' the guns, an' the gallant cavalry glintin' as they go by in a dancin' walk to the crisp tappin' of the kettle-drums: — but I couldn't think of lettin' him go an' his eyes the way they are.

—Poor little chiselur, said the voice of the other oul' wan, poor little chiselur.

Johnny closed the door softly, groped his way over to the window, touched the cloth that covered it, gripped it, tore it down, and flung it on the floor. The light from a May sky flooded the room. Pushing the bandage from his eye, he looked out through the window at the gathering of children headed by Slogan the schoolmaster and Hunter the minister, moving off on their way to witness the review. Each child wore a red-white-and-blue rosette and oul' Slogan carried a small Union Jack.

The light streaming into the long-darkened eye of the boy shot pain down to the roots of the socket; but he clenched his teeth and stared down on the street, saw Hunter lift a hand, and the gathering moved off in line, three abreast, cheering strongly as they strutted along, and singing joyously,

> '*The Twenty-Fourth of May, the Queen's birthday,*
> *We'll let it rain tomorrow, but it mustn't rain today!*'

Then Johnny darted a look at the sky, and saw that the sky was a bright grey, but not blue, and that the sun shone faintly.

He went over to the bed again, cautiously turned down the rotting clothes, crept in, drew the clothes up over him, and lay still for many minutes. Then he clasped his hands, intermingling his fingers tightly together, and lifted them higher over his head, stretching till the sockets of his arms cracked; murmuring in mild madness, O God, let the rain come, let the rain come quick, heavy 'n quick, comin' down on the streets, in the fields, 'n in the parks on the people 'n the children goin' anywhere, the whole day through, without ceasin' a second, to fall on everything, right out to a long way off from where I'm lyin' now. Let the faint clouds that are in the sky grow strong, deepen, and sthretch till they cover the spaces where there's none; 'n God, let the wind come too, a sharp wind 'n a bitther, to make the rain fall worse 'n harder, till it thrickles over the skin so that the joy sought afther be people 'n children may be hidden from them, bringin' a fear 'n a shiverin' 'n a heavy longin' to all that they were not where they may be, because of the bitther wind 'n the sharp rain fallin', right out to a long way off from where I'm lyin' now!

He thickened the folds of his bandage and covered his eyes again so that the light in the room became a deep darkness. He stayed still, breathing softly, creeping close to sleep, connecting his thoughts with a world of marching troops; the clatter of guns rollin' over the stony sthreet; the jingle of cavalry swords hangin' by the hips of the riders, breastplated, or braided 'n belted; 'n

the infanthry heavy 'n the infanthry light thrudgin' along, less
gloriously covered, but spick 'n span as the best of the others;
cross-belted an' pouched; knapsacks hoisted high to the tops of
their backs; rifles at the slope, 'n helmets 'n busbies sthrapped
tight to the chin; steppin' out with a left-right, left-right, I had
a good job but I left it; left-right, left-right; never missin' a beat,
risin' up, swingin' back, comin' down all together: the feet of the
young men poundin' out of the pavin'-setts a song of the nation's
pride 'n power.

He could see the tightenin' up of the bodies of onlookers
watchin' from the paths 'n windows as the regiment swung past
with the officers' band playin'

> First we mopped the floor with him,
> Dhragged him up an' down the stairs;
> Then we had another go, undher tables, over chairs,
> Such a sight you never saw; before he'd time to say his prayers,
> Rags an' bones were all we left of the man who sthruck O'Hara!

folleyin' the regimental band of fifes an' dhrums, waitin' for their
chance to play when the other band stopped, the fifes an' dhrums
marchin' hard on the heels of the bearded pioneers, with axe an'
pick an' shovel on their shouldhers.

It was a grand thing for the Colonel on horseback, an' he
leadin' nine hundhred an' ninety-nine men, each armed with
rifle, bayonet, 'n a hundred rounds of blank, the whole crush
folleyin' him as one man, so that if he only gave the word, a left-
turn at the double over the wall into the river, boys, they'd all
turn left as one man, rest a hand on the parapet 'n vault plump
into the river without askin' why, on accounta they daren't dis-
obey any ordher of the officer commandin'; for theirs to do 'n
die without to want a reason why is the beginnin' an' end of a
soldier's life.

Johnny heard the onlookers murmurin' that he was the youngest
colonel goin', with the Afghan 'n Burman medals lyin' snug on his
crimson sash, on accounta havin' ridden with the troops from
Kabul to Kandahar, 'n had followed in the wake of Colonel
Burnaby, givin' the first welt to Theebaw afther a hot, heavy, 'n
forced march of fifteen hours through a tree-darkened 'n thropical
jungle.

They had come right up to a fortified stockade of the rebellious
Burmans; had been given the ordher for the bugles to sound the

charge; 'n in the middle o' yells, squeals, flyin' spears, glitther o' knives an' yataghans, beatin' o' gongs, bangin' o' bells, 'n blowin' o' bugles, the bayonets worked their way forward 'n slashed with red the bronzed breasts of the Burmans.

Johnny shot his hand down under the clothes on to his belly, and his first finger fell firmly on a nipping flea, 'n he rolled it tightly over his flesh, crushing it till it cracked, 'n then flicked it with his finger 'n thumb till it fell mangled on to the palliasse of the bed, formin' another little bitin' bastard gone where the good niggers go.

When what was left of the panic-stricken lepped over the stockade, flyin' hell for leather, to get away into the jungle, the Lancers in white dhrill and big sun helmets came floodin' out into the clearin' round the stockade, an' shoved their lances into the bellies 'n backs of the screamin' Burmans, yellin' Dew ay mong draw, British muscle behind British steel, diggin' the bowels outa them, 'n dungin' the jungle with them; showin' what they get for mockin' n' jeerin' at British rule 'n British justice; seconded be a British cheer that made the animals wandherin' in the jungle cock their ears to listen 'n wondher at the few dark figures left to crawl away 'n hide in the thick 'n hot grass, mutterin' to their terrible 'n merciless gods of wood an' stone for help, before they stiffened out in the great stretch that was to last them for ever 'n ever.

Johnny suddenly tensed his whole body 'n tightened his mouth fiercely as a spasm of pain shooting through his eyes set his brain on fire for several minutes. Relaxing as the pain passed slowly away, he shifted the bandage so that the part dampened by the gush of water from his eyes lay off his forehead. Then he began to doze and dream again.

He saw the Colonel feeling the glossy neck of his charger, carrying' him proudly at the head of the Fermanaghs, marchin' left-right, left-right, I had a good job but I left it.

Suddenly, on the other side of the river he heard the skirl of the bagpipes, with the dark bass dhrone never ceasin' to nurse the tune of the tenors; an' the flow of the shawls, the wag of the bonnets, and the swing of the yellow-sthriped kilts showed the gay Grahams footin' it out to la-la-la, hielan' laddie, hielan' laddie, busy blowin' the guts outa themselves, an' thryin' to get all the notice that was knockin' about on the earth. Lettin' themselves go to get to the gate of the park before his regiment, they were; but he'd soon show them to the differ, if the motto of the

Fermanaghs, *Sinneraria est magnificat sancteeorum*, Latin for great sinners are as great as great saints, meant anything off the common.

But the kilts let the hielan' laddies lash out with their legs in a walk that couldn't be betthered, so the Colonel gee-geed up his horse, gave the ordher of At the double; but the Grahams broke into a throt at the same time that sent them a little ahead of the Fermanaghs.

The Colonel raised himself in his stirrups and dhrew his sword.

—Come on, men, he shouted, an' show these hielan' bousies that the Fermanagh Fusiliers'll not enther any park arsin' afther any crush greedy for glory. So come on, me boys of Ormond Quay an' Stoneybatther. For your counthry an' your Colonel, gather to the gate of the park with a speed that'll make the others appear to be goin' backwards!

All the people cheered an' cheered, as the Fermanaghs surged forward at a gallop, heads sthrainin' to the front, shouldhers gathered together, breath comin' in heavy pants, grippin' their rifles tight at the thrail, sweatin' fast an' furious as they ran full-tilt for the park gate, with the Grahams dhroppin' their playin' of hielan' laddie to dash headlong for the gate, too, with the people on the paths shoutin' an' hissin' an' booin', an' runnin' out in front of the hielan' laddies to bar their way, gettin' a grip of the swingin' kilts, an' holdin' on like grim death so that the hielan' laddies had to halt in their stride 'n thry to prevent the excited crowd from tearing the kilts offa them; but many failed to hold on, 'n, except for bonnets 'n cross-belted cartridge pouches, were left runnin' about lookin' as they looked when they first came into the world, only a bit bigger.

Many made a beeline for the shops on the side-walks to cover their nakedness, settin' the women, who were lowerin' lemonade, screamin' in high ordher, an' sendin' them flying' out to the sthreet, in fear, to see the whole crush o' the Grahams mucked up an' messed about 'n put to confusion, made worse be the officers soarin' in their saddles an' roarin' to their men to fall in, an' form fours, an' number off, an' get into column o' companies, to march on in the way they were goin'; their shouts shockin' into obedience those who had raced into the shops on the side-walks, causin' them to rush out again, thryin' to cover themselves suitably with their bonnets an' pouches; an' lookin' wildly at their officers for information and advice; scandalisin' the world-wide decency of the English army before the rovin' eyes of the Dublin people; while the policemen that were knockin' about called out for all to behave like sensible men 'n women, an' act like ladies an' gentlemen who have the knack of lookin' at only what they're told to see; while the Fermanagh Fusiliers were pourin' into the park in a lather of sweat, an' smilin' that the race had been won, without fear or favour from anyone, leavin' the Grahams in such a state of disability, on accounta the loss of their kilts, that hundhreds of them had to be rushed back to barracks in closed-up cabs to keep tongues from talkin' about the strange things suddenly seen in the city of Dublin.

When ordher was restored, 'n the Grahams seen that nothin' further was to be gained, they came marchin' into the park playin' the Cock o' the North, and sidled up alongside the Fermanagh boys rattlin' out the Rocky Road to Dublin in rare style.

Suddenly an aid-dee-cong dhressed up in green buckskin breeches, blue coat, blossomin' with gold braid, an' wearin' a cocked hat with a red-'n-black plume stretchin' out of it, like a sthream o' smoke 'n flame, came gallopin' up on a white horse, an' stuck himself between the two colonels, demandin' to know, without any shilly-shallyin', why all the commotion had been caused, an' remindin' them that they wore the uniform of Her Majesty the Queen, which ought to weigh with them towards keepin' away from anything that 'ud show up Her Majesty's throops in front of the Irish people, who were always on the keeveev to ferret out anything likely to cast a slur on the great thradition of the English army that stood for so much that was necessary to keep the world safe an' clean; an' if there was any more of this buggerin' about with the good name of the throops he'd let the Lord Lieutenant know all the details, an' have the officers responsible up on the carpet to show the reason why the Irish were allowed to sthrip important units of the armed forces, leavin' them ignorant as to what course to take under the circumstances of them bein' naked nearly from the waist down.

Then up spoke the Colonel of the Grahams, tellin' the red-an'-black-plumed get that we lived undher a constitutional monarchy, an' were all free to think our own thoughts an' carry on accordin' to the dictates of our conscience cryin' out against showin' reverence to a tandragee elegant-speakin', cock-hatted, aid-dee-cong bowsey, hot an' half-baked from a military nursing-home.

Here the Fermanagh Colonel gave his horse a jab o' the spur, an' got between the bargin' boyos; stickin' his bake in undher the cocked hat of the aid-dee-cong, looking him straight in the eye an' sayin', sotto-voice, Here, let's have the matther out with restraint; for we would all be betther employed in attendin' to our duties than to be arguin' the toss with a fella who runs home the minute he gets the chance to tell his oul' wan everything; who's ready at the wind o' the word to come bargin' into the barracks to make a show of the whole regiment; so take a friend's advice an' buzz off before a puck in the royal snot unsettles you for the rest of the day, an' don't be shovin' your conk in where it isn't needed or wanted or valued; so push off while the sun's shinin', with your little arse nestin' safe in the saddle, on your horse back to where you came from, snug undher the flappin' of the royal banner; an', with that, the drum-major of the Fermanaghs suddenly let fly with his staff an' gave a larrup to the hind-quarters of the horse, sendin' the cock-hatted spitabout careerin' out of sight.

Then the Fermanagh boys an' the Grahams wheeled to the left, an' marched shouldher to shouldher down narrow leafy lanes, the blue sky over them diapered with great, spreading, gently-waving masses of red an' white hawthorn, makin' the soldiers bend low to save their busbies an' bonnets from bein' swept off by the thorn-sprinkled blossoms. On, then, an' out of the narrow, shady, leafy lanes to the fifteen acres, green an' level, an' slowly risin' into little mounds high enough to let regiments disappear when they'd done all they had to do for the moment; an' low enough to let them come into sight again suddenly when the time came for to show themselves to the civilians, ravenous for the march-past and the sham battle; big enough to easy hold the Army of cavalry an' infanthry an' Medical Corps, with their white canvas-covered wagons havin' a big red cross on each side, so that any enemy would recognise at once that they were only there to splice up and tinker up the wounded; an' artillery, field an' horse, and the Army Service Corps, with their wagons, mostly pulled be mules, facin' towards the spot where the Viceroy 'ud first show himself.

Now he comes glidin' out in his victoria, dhrawn be four nut-brown horses, at a quiet an' respectable throt, with his lady puffed an' prim an' parasolled beside him; an' all the massed bands at the same identical tick o' the clock burst into God save the Queen; while the artillery, horse an' field, fired a royal salute o' twenty-one guns, half hidden be a thick shrubbery of hazel an' black-thorn bushes; big globes of thick white smoke, a little thin at the edges, rose from behind the bushes like balls o' wool, folleyed be big bangs that made the civilians thrill as they felt the ground shake an' quiver undher their feet, feelin' how safe they were in havin' such a multitude of armed men to frighten all foreigners; while the soldiers standin' in line gave a foo-dee-joy, be firing away, one afther another, so that the rattle o' musketry roamed from one end of the line to the other an' back again three times; the soldiers at the command of their officers wavin' their shakos an' helmets an' busbies an' bonnets an' bearskins on the points of their bayonets; at the same time givin' a three-times-three cheer for Her Majesty the Queen an' her heirs an' successors for ever an' ever.

Then the Viceroy, dressed in a black clawhammer coat, white waistcoat, cream buckskin breeches, brown topboots, an' a little black bowler hat, with a rosebud in his buttonhole, swung himself on to the back of a white horse sprinkled with black spots, an' set off, afther sayin' fare-ye-well for awhile to the grand ladies, folleyed be a sub-sovereign's escort of blue-tuniced, gold-breast-plated, silver-helmeted, red-plumed horse guards, an' a covey of equerries in green coats with silver-braided epaulettes, an' red coats with gold-braided epaulettes, an' green coats with bronze-braided epaulettes; with red stripes down green trousers, an' white stripes down blue trousers, an' green stripes down black trousers; trottin' quick between the ranks of the avenued soldiers, eyes front, standin' stock-still like wooden soldiers set down on a table be a boy; with the officers rooted in their proper places to the right or to the left or in front of their particular companies, as if all were undher a spell; while the inspection went on, passin' by field artillery in their blue uniforms, piped with yellow; an' horse artillery in uniforms of blue, with their coat so heavy with yellow braid that the men had to bend back to keep themselves from fallin' forward, with red flaps hangin' from their busbies, an' a yellow cord hangin' from the red flap down to the thick yellow cord on their shoulders, then coilin' undher the arm to be looped over the chest, an' at last danglin' down in two knot-like tassels on their chests. Flowin' round, the Viceroy went on to pass through the lines of the red-coated infantry, with their blue facin's, an' buff facin's, an' white facin's, an' green facin's; the Viceroy throwin' an eye here an' an eye there to make sure that every chin-sthrap went undher the chin in the right place, an' that the belts holdin' haversack an' knapsack an' pouches crossed in the dead centre of the breast; an' the water-bottle hung fair an' square on the left hip; an' the pipeclayed belts showed no detri-mental stains; an' that all the brass buttons an' badges sparkled with the dint o' polishin', reflectin' the upright cleanliness of the British soldiers standin' with their rifles at the slope, rememberin' that it wasn't theirs to reason why but only just to do an' die; with the colonel of each regiment meetin' the boyo at the right o' the line an' throttin' beside him till the last man of the regiment was reached, an' the Viceroy jogged on to inspect another regiment; folleyed by his equerries sittin' stiff on their saddles, their eyes fixed on the Viceroy's arse in front of them, movin' on to see that everything was in apple-pie ordher for their Queen an' counthry.

A few Fenian faces in the crowd among the Irish, gathered where the less respectable people were lookin' at the goin's-on, done a little booin'; but were soon collared by the police, an' cuffed out of the vicinity; though, of course, there was no real objection to the poor so long as they conducted themselves decently an' in ordher.

The Viceroy throtted through the line of the blue-tuniced, yellow-braided, white-plumed Prince Albert's Own Hussars, right in front o' the Queen's Lancers, lovely in their black-breasted red coats, long black plumes fallin' down over their square-topped helmets; through heavy dhragoons with red-plumed brass helmets; an' light dhragoons with black-plumed silver helmets; then cantherin' by the highlan' regiments, proud of their bagpipes, goin' strong, with their yellow an' green tartan; an' green an' white an black tartan; an' red an' yellow an' blue tartan; lookin' as brave in their finery as any contingent in the whole British army; havin' their officers standin' like pillars before them, with their glitterin' jewelled dirks stuck in their stockin's.

At last he came to cock an eye over the Fermanagh Fusiliers, stickin' out their chests like good ones, meetin' the Colonel with a lazy lift o' the hand who came to a swift salute with the back edge o' his sword touchin' the tip of his nose; an', fallin' in, folleyed half a length behind His Excellency, noddin' his approval of the splendid shape the Fermanaghs were busy puttin' up, silent an' stiff as standin' dead men; till, nearin' the end of the rear line, he stood up in his stirrups an' clapped the Colonel on the back, sayin', It's thrillin' to see such a fine body of Irishmen waitin' the chance to lay down their lives for their Queen an' counthry; an' be God, the tattle that goes on about Irish disloyalty is nothin' but effan lies if you ask me. So keep this goin', Colonel, an' I'll put in a good word for you to oul' Vicky, an' depend on it, you'll have the Ordher o' St Patrick bloomin' on your breast before the year's out, or me name's not Jack Robinson.

With that, he galloped off to the grand-stand, smothered in scarlet an' gold, to take the salute of the march-past of the cavalry goin' by at a walk an' a throt an' a gallop; the horse artillery folleyin' fast at their heels; an' then the infanthry swingin' along at a quick-march of thousands on thousands of legs shootin' forward an' backward at the same moment, showin' the civilians the way to walk, with the rifle regiments carryin' their rifles at the thrail; but none of them comin' within a mile of the steppin' out as one man of the Fermanagh Fusiliers, with the well-dhressed Irish on one side an' the ragamuffin Irish on the other, cheerin' like hell as they sailed by to the strains of Farewell But Whene'er You Remember The Hour.

The sham battle came on, and off the Army went into hidlins; with the cavalry, artillery an' mosta the infanthry goin' one way, an' the Fermanagh Fusiliers an' Grahams goin' another, to meet in combat as soon as the artillery paved the way for it be limberin' up an' openin' fire on a scrawl of both regiments left where they were sure to be seen, so as to goad the artillery to concentrate to their hearts' content on them; the rest of the Grahams and Fermanaghs manoeuvred round on their bellies an' caught the artillery in the rear, cheerin' in on them with a rush at the point of the bayonet an' a shout of Faug a balagh, takin' all their guns an' spikin' them before they could realize what was afther happenin'; dhrivin' them helther-skelther among the opposin' infanthry, causin' a panic an' a quick rethreat. But the cavalry, formin' up, came on at a gallopin' charge, leavin' the Fermanaghs and Grahams only a second to jump into a square an' meet them at the bayonet's point; while the inner ranks fired volley afther volley into the cursin' cavalry, pokin' with their lances an' slashin' with their sabres, but failin' to make any little laneway in the square formed be the volley-firin' fusiliers an' highlanders; till the frightened horses couldn't stand it any longer, an' turned tail, to rush off back on the poor devils comin' on, so that there was a terrible muck-up, an' in a minute they were all makin' full speed from where the volleys never stopped for a single second, mowin' down horses an' men in a shockin' rout.

The Colonel o' the Grahams, seein' the ways things were goin', jumped on top of his horse, drew his sword, an' shoutin', Now or never, now an' for ever, led them in a cheerin' charge afther the flyin' cavalry, seekin' shelther wherever they thought they could find it, fleein' hotfoot among the civilians; an' leavin' the whole fifteen acres litthered with sabres an' rifles an' busbies an' helmets an' colours an' guidons an' lances, while the bould Fermanaghs spread themselves out like a fan an' chased the flyin' enemy well beyond the bordhers of the civilian onlookers. The Prince Albert's Own Hussars, called the Cherry-pickers, because of their crimson trousers, flew panic-stricken, as fast as their horses could go, straight to where the Viceroy an' his butties were standin', gapin', on their grand-stand, an' there was a wild screamin' an' scattherin' of the silken an' satin clad ladies as the red-trousered hussars tore by; hundhreds fainted with fright an' thousands burst their stays an' split their drawers asundher, trying to get out o' the bed quick, when you get a backyard call, for fear of accidents; waitin' only to slip on your pants, handy on the floor beside the bed, an' out an' down the two flights o' stairs of ten steps each; holdin' fast be the banisters, if you don't want to be listenin' anxious for the bell of 'n ambulance; goin' down the hall with the hands well out to keep any collision away; then out into the yard, straight on over the flags, like ice undher your bare feet, feelin' with your fingers yourself safe at last into the harbour, with the oul' mit searchin' out the right place to sit down on; your throne soggin' wet as usual, for the other lowsers in the house never give a thought to anybody else who may have a likin' for a dhry 'n decent method of meetin' nature; bravely hummin' their way through life, up to their ankles in their own slush; unfit to feel the need of anything outside of what they have to do themselves; an' always forgettin' the inlook an' outlook of others who are strivin' to do unto others as others should do unto them, which is only fair if you think it out.

A dash'll have to be made for the house as soon as me trouser's buttoned, for there's the rain slashin' off the roof; an' I can't stop here till it eases. Off I go now up the path into the house again, 'n up the stairs, into the room outa the cold an' the rain; with a swift wipe of the feet in the trousers an' a plunge into the warm bed, to listen to the rain fallin' on the flags, an' dullin' with rust all the glitter 'n pride 'n glare of plume 'n pennon 'n bugle 'n breastplate saggin' under the fallin' rain, fallin' swift on every-one right out to a long way off from where I'm lyin' now.

LIFE IS MORE THAN MEAT

JOHNNY DIDN'T bother much about food or raiment. There wasn't much of either to be had, so he took what was given, and forgot to thank God.

Looking back, he could remember two suits that had come fresh to his body: one, a blue sailor suit, with gold anchor and gold stripes on the sleeve, topped with a blue velvet cap, having HMS Condor in gold letters round the band; and a soft tweed suit, fitted after many trials, and finally accepted from a Jew for two shillings down, and a shilling a week after, till the full price was paid. He had it on now, patched and stitched till it was tired; coaxed with care to stay together a little longer. Each touch a warning that a tear was near, with his mother nightly nursing tweedy wounds, closing them up with deft and crinkled and patient fingers. Although all its early simple pomp was gone, it hung on hard to life, a shade from the sun in the summer, a shivering shelter from the seeping rain, the biting frost, and the cold blowing blasts of the winter.

Food was rare, though there was almost always a hunk of bread to be had, but it often tasted like dust and ashes in his mouth: dust to dust and ashes to ashes. After a few years of meagre fare, anyway, his belly ceased to put up a fight, and took patiently the bread and tea and Parrish's Syrup that trickled into it; getting a start of surprise when a potato came along; and battling hastily to create a welcome whenever meat or fish came tumbling in.

How good it was for John the Baptist always to have within his reach loads of locusts and wild honey. Going about his business, and never having to bother as to where the night would fall on him. When his hat was on, his house was thatched. And the Israelites, too – look at them! Quails flutthering outa the sky, croaking out, Catch me, catch me, so that nothing had to be done but wring their necks and roast them. (Though in all fairness, and to give God His due, He sometimes flooded the bay with fish, causing poor Dublin streets to ring with the cry of, Dublin Bay herrin's, tuppence a dozen; tuppence a dozen, the Dublin Bay herrin's; which meant a daily feast of hot or cold baked herrings for a week or more for all.) And the manna, too, dropped down from heaven for their special benefit, though it didn't keep them from grousing. Well, there was no manna dropping down on the streets of Dublin for poor boys to gather; only dung and dirt that the traffic pulverized into dust, choking the throats and cutting the eyes outa the passers-by whenever the stronger breezes blew.

Once a week, after Archie had given to the house what he had put aside to give it, Johnny and his mother set out to buy in the week's supply of tea and sugar. This meant a long journey to Lipton's in Dame Street. Before, they used to get these things in the London and Newcastle Tea Company who gave brass and bronze checks to their customers, according to the amount of tea bought, which were used, when enough had been gathered together, to buy chinaware and ironmongery. But Lipton had come, and other stores had to take a back seat.

So Johnny, furnished with a sailor's kit-bag, having large eyelet holes through which a cord ran so that the mouth could be closed, set out with his mother on a far journey for the corn and wine in Lipton's, on a cold and rainy evening.

How he hated the journey, and how tired the walking made him, for there was nothing stirring, nothing in the walk to make his feet light or lift them in a dancing step; often his mother had to tell him not to drag his feet, but to walk like an ordinary human being. Then, without knowing, he'd hang on his mother's arm till she'd cry out, oh, don't be dhraggin' outa me like that; can't you walk on the legs that God has given you? He'd take his arm away, and journey on through the wilderness of streets, shuffling his feet, and lagging a little behind.

What wouldn't he give, now, for a good topcoat, an' he goin' along Dorset Street, facin' the spittin' rain an' the penethratin' wind, whippin' in his face an' stabbin' him right through his coat an' trousers, an' tatthered shirt, making him feel numb an' sick as he dragged himself along afther his mother, protectin' himself as well as he could be holdin' the kit-bag spread out like a buckler in front of his breast.

He kept his eye on his mother ploddin' along in front of him, carryin' a basket an' an oilcan, dhressed in her faded an' thin black skirt an' cape, her shabby little bonnet tied firmly undher her chin, the jet beads in it gleamin' out of it as bright as ever; an' she steppin' it out, hell-bent for Lipton's, ignorin' all the shops that lined the way, stuffed out with all sorts of fine an' fat goods that God never meant her to have.

There were fruiterers who had piled out on the path heaps of apples an' pears from England, dates from Tunis an' Thripoli, figs from Turkey, and oranges from Spain, transported outa the sun by bullock or mule, in thrain an' boat to the wind-swept streets o' Dublin; all callin' out to be eaten; but Johnny and his mother passed heedlessly by, on their way to Samarcand and Lipton's.

Farther on, they'd pass through an avenue formed be tiers on tiers of cabbages an' cauliflowers, bushels of turnips, bins of spuds, hanks of onions, an' bunches of carrots, ready to be plucked, weighed, scooped out, or handed over to anyone who needed them; but Johnny and his mother passed heedless by, turning neither to right nor left to view the kindly fruits of the earth.

Then they'd pass through an alley of butchers' benches piled high with cutlets, chops, beef for boiling, and beef for roasting; with the butchers in their blue and white overalls, bawling, buy away, buy away, new shop open; but Johnny and his mother went by unheeding, heading straight to where they had set themselves to go.

On from Dorset Street into Bolton Street, where his mother popped into a chandler's shop, and filled the can with half a gallon of oil, and her basket with quarter a stone of washing-soda, a bar of yellow soap, two candles, a penny box of Colman's starch, and some bundles of firewood, bought to fulfil what was spoken by the prophet, saying, Wash ye, make ye clean; to keep the hearth aglow; and to be a light to them that sit in darkness.

As they passed through the gauntlet of shelves and shelves of cheese, bacon, eggs, and piles of bread, made fresh from the sweet-smelling wheat, grand and golden, enough to feed five thousand, hallowed bread, bread to comfort the heart of man, bread from the earth, bread from God, on sale by the bakers, Johnny suddenly saw his mother step to the left, and hurry on, as a drunken man came staggering along the path. The man lurched in towards the shop, knocked against a tray of pigs' feet, and sent them flying all over the place.

Good God, man, what are you afther doin'! shouted the shop-boy, as he rushed over to gather them up, a crowd gathering to laugh at what had happened. Like lightning, Johnny slid a lump of bacon into the folds of his kit-bag, and snatched up an egg as he passed by, running like hell to catch up with his mother who was a little ahead. Catching his mother's arm, he cried that he was cold, and ran her trotting along till they turned down into the dark and gloomy King's Inn Street, and he was safe and thrilled, but trembling.

Through Liffey Street they went, a street of old furniture shops, all shuttered close now, the street deserted, save for an odd straggler trudging over the straw and sodden paper that littered path and road; up the quay, across Essex Bridge, both of them bending to battle the breeze that swept up the Liffey, down Capel Street, into Dame Street, and, at last, into the warm, brightly-lighted, busy, big shop of Lipton's.

Johnny paused for a moment to look at himself in the huge mirrors panelling the walls, just inside the great door, showing him and his mother as lean, skinny-looking gazebos entering the shop.

—They'll show us up as fat as fools, goin' out, said his mother, laughing.

The shop was crowded, full of white-coated counter-jumpers handin' out tea an' sugar an' margarine as swift as hands could lay hold on them; with men in brown overalls trotting along pushing mountains of tea an' sugar in packages on little throlleys, moving silently and cunningly through the crowded shop, to fill up the vacancies on the shelves.

They waited their turn to get their seven pounds of sugar, a pound of tea for one an' six, an' a two-pound pot of Lipton's special plum an' apple jam; Johnny packing them in the kit-bag, while his mother slowly and feelingly put back sixpence change into the pocket of her skirt, strengthened with added lining to keep such treasures safe.

—Well, that'll have to provide us with whatever else we may need for the rest of the week, she murmured, lettin' the sixpence go at last when she felt it settle in the bottom of her pocket.

Johnny swung the kit-bag over his shoulder, an' he an' his ma manoeuvred to the door through the people thronging the shop; pausing to see themselves in the mirrors, looking like fat pigs, bulging cheeks, great round bellies, an' enormous bodies, showing how great the stuff was that Lipton's sold; then the pair of them plunged once more into the dark night, the spitting rain, and the biting breeze; Johnny feeling all these trials less when he remembered the egg in his pocket and the bacon in the bag.

Out in the street, moving forward in the kennel, was an old grey-bearded man, with a creaking voice, singing dolefully to the busy street. The collar of his coat was pulled up, as high as it could go, and his neck and chin were sunk down in it as low as they could go to shelther them from the wind and the rain; but when high notes came, the head had to be lifted to get anywhere near them, so the thin neck rose out of its cosy nest, to sink back again when the high notes were over, and the low notes came back. Quite a number of people paused in their hurry, searched in purse or pocket to hand out a penny; and Johnny felt envious that money could be so easy earned be the cracked singin' of

> *Let us pause in life's pleasures, an' .count its many fears,*
> *While we all sup sorrow with the poor;*
> *Here's a song that shall linger for ever in our ears,*
> *Oh, hard times, come again no more.*
>
> *'Tis the song, the sigh of the weary,*
> *Hard times, hard times, come again no more;*
> *Many days have you lingered around my cabin door,*
> *Oh, hard times, come again no more!*

—Since we haven't anything to give him, it isn't fair to listen, said his mother, pulling the arm of the pausing Johnny.

When they got home again, Johnny spilled the sugar, tea, and jam out on the table. Then he put the lump of bacon and the egg right where his mother could see them when she turned round after taking off her wet things.

When she turned, she stared.

—How, in the name o' God, did those things ever creep into the kit-bag? she asked.

—I fecked them, said Johnny gleefully. When the dhrunken man fell an' scatthered things, I fecked them as I passed.

—A nice thing if you'd been caught feckin' them, she said, in a frightened voice. Never, never do the like again. D'ye know, had you been nabbed, it 'ud have meant five years or more in a re-formatory for you? Never do it again, Johnny. Remember what you've been taught: Take no thought for your life, what ye shall eat; nor yet for your body, what ye shall put on; for the life is more than meat, an' the body than raiment; and your heavenly Father knoweth that ye have need of all these things; so keep your hands from pickin' an' stealin', for the future; and she carefully placed the bacon and the egg in the press.

Johnny sat silent by the fire, drying his damp trousers. After a few minutes he saw his mother putting on her bonnet and cape.

—Where'r you goin' now, Ma? he asked.

—I'm goin' out to get a couple o' nice heads of cabbage, with the sixpence I've left, to go with the bacon tomorrow, she said.

JOHNNY HAD been confined to the house all day, save when he had been sent for a message; looking right and left down the street before he started; and then darting to the shop to get what was wanted, and back again to the safety of his home, as fast as his legs could carry him, for there was war between him and his Catholic comrades. For the last few days whenever they had clapped eyes on him they had booed him, called him a swadler, or sent stones flying at his heels. They lay around corners to pounce on him, shake him up, push him about, knock anything he had in his hand out of it, and tried to land a kick on his arse when he broke from them and ran. Only in the company of Middleton or Ecret, when he was in the street, did he feel safe. Today coming home with a glass of beer (after his mother had said We'll be extravagant for once in our lives, and had kept back a shilling out of the rent), he had met Kelly coming along, picking and eating bits out of a loaf he held under his arm. Kelly kept his eyes fixed in front of him, pretending not to see Johnny; but just when Johnny was passing, he suddenly shot out a foot, tripping him; but Johnny managed to save himself from a bad fall, and only a little of the beer was spilled on the path.

Johnny ran over in a rage, and smote Kelly hard in the snot, sending him flying home with blood flowing out of his nose.

—Keep away from them for a few days, Johnny, advised his mother, when he told her what had happened, till the whole thing's over. They just all go daft when we show the slightest sign of doin' a devoir to the throne. They'll soon forget all about it; and, anyhow, you shouldn't be flauntin' your loyal rosette in front of their faces.

—It's jealous they all are, said Johnny, looking down at the red, white, and blue badge shining in the lapel of his coat. They're boycottin' me because their ma's won't bring them to see the illuminations I'm goin' to see with you, tonight.

For all parts of the city of Dublin where the real respectable people lived, and where the real respectable people worked, were celebrating in honour of something to do with the Majesty of Victoria, Queen of Great Britain and Ireland and Empress of India; to show their love and manifest their loyalty to her in millions of lights and multitudes of flags, banners, bannerettes, pennons, guidons, standards, gonfalons, and divers other symbols displayed on decorated posts linked together by lovely coloured festoons; pictures of the Queen and Members of the Royal Family, placed cunningly in suitable spots where all could see them without inconvenience or discomfort.

All this was done that her subjects might be reminded and stimulated to offer deep prayers quietly in their hearts, as they promenaded round looking at these gay diversions, to the Lord our heavenly Father, high and mighty, King of kings, Lord of lords, and only Ruler of princes, beseeching Him to behold with His favour our most gracious Sovereign Lady, Queen Victoria, so that she might always incline to His will, and walk in His way; and be strengthened so that she might vanquish and overcome all her enemies; shoving as quick as they could into the middle of the prayer a petition that it might please God, too, to endue the Lords of the Council and all the Nobility with grace, wisdom, and understanding; and to give the Magistrates grace to execute judgement and to maintain truth.

And it was the bounden duty of the wealthy and respectable who had security and comfort in the sufferance of the Lords and the Nobility, to rejoice and be glad over the happy and prosperous life lived in the Realm of England and in her dominions; showing the Realm's glory and their own jubilation by hanging out all things they could lay their hands on, of a comely shape and a happy hue, from windows, walls, towers, turrets, battlements, steeples, spires, balconies, balustrades, pinnacles, belfries, gables, and all other prominent places fit to be adorned, as outward and visible signs of their certain faith of a happy life and a holy death under the rule and during the reign of Her Most Gracious Majesty.

The Sunday-school scholars were having a tea-party and a magic-lantern, but the door to these joys was closed to Johnny. Johnny had stayed away from Sunday school, and so wasn't legally, morally, or spiritually entitled to join in the merry-making. If boys didn't go to church or Sunday school, then God would see that they didn't go to parties.

So Johnny's mother had patted him on the shoulder, and said, Never mind, son; we'll go together on the top of a thram all round the town, and see th' illuminations and the flowers and the flags; betther than any oul' magic-lantern or tea-fight, with its stale buns and wathery tea.

They had to try to fight their way into the tram, for it looked as if the whole district had poured out to see the sights. Mrs Casside put Johnny in front of her, and shoved him steadily forward, crying out to the crowd that surged around her, Give a breathin' space, there, to a poor delicate child whose eyes are fit to look at things only durin' the first few weeks of the year. It'll be a sorry day for Dublin when no one has a thought for a poor boy sufferin' the terrible handicap of ill-health.

The conductor leaned forward from the porch of the tram, stretched out a sudden hand, and pulled Johnny and his mother on, pushing them up the narrow stairs to the top, as he planked himself in front of the others, perspiring and pushing their way on to the platform.

—A man 'ud want St Pathrick's crozier to knock a little decency into yous, he said viciously as he tried to turn the pushing into an orderly parade. A nice way the whole of yous musta been reared, with your pushin' an' shovin', like a horde of uncivilized savages that has never seen anything beyond the rim o' their own land! I don't know th' hell why Parnell's wastin' his time thryin' to shape yous into something recognizable as men an' women. Honest to Jasus, I'm gettin' ashamed of me life to mention I'm Irish in front of anyone showin' the meanest sign or vestige of dickorum. And all of yous riskin' the breakage of your bodies to see a few twinklin' lights set over your heads to do honour to a famine queen rollin' about in a vis-à-vis at a time the Irish were gettin' shovelled, ten at a time, into deep an' desperate graves.

—You mind your own business be pullin' the bell for decent people to get on the thram, an' decent people to get off the thram, said a man, having a wide watery mouth with a moustache hanging over it like a weeping willow; an' don't be so sure that the personalities thravellin' are set on givin' a delicate or delirious show of loyalty to anyone or anything thryin' to devastate the efforts of our brave Irish Party fightin' for us on the floor of the House of Commons!

Johnny turned and pulled his mother's sleeve.

That oul' fella, he whispered, is Georgie Middleton's da. Whenever he appears in the street, the boys shout afther him, Georgie Middleton's ma wears the pants of Middleton's da.

—Thrue for you, mister, said a fat woman with a big bustle on her big behind, puffing her way as well as she could on to the tram; for a man who starts fluttherin' idle thoughts in front o' people's faces, accusin' them of hidin' the harp behind a gaudy crown, is just takin' advantage of a special time; an' ought, if things were in a settled state, to be walkin' close to the danger of a sensible castigation.

—Speakin' for meself only, said the man carrying the wide watery mouth with a drooping moustache hanging over it like a weeping willow, I've serious business to deal with in the heart of the town; an' if th' illuminations were brighter than even all the comets terrifyin' the sky, an' blazin' along at the same time, I'd sit with me face fast in front of me, seein' only the need for Home Rule, an' the green flag with the sunburst in the centre, wavin' everywhere the thram brings me.

—A prime lot of pathriots yous all are, to be sure, said the conductor sarcastically as he pulled the bellstrap for the tram to start; but I notice once yous get safe in, none of yous get out till the cruise is over. It's waitin' a long time I'll be to see yous busy bandagin' your eyes to keep at a distance the signs an' shows of revelry when the thram penethrates into the sthreets, alive with the flags of all nations, save our own.

—That conductor's a very sensible man, and shrewd, said Johnny's mother, as they settled themselves into a seat on the top of the tram, giving them a grand view of everything before, behind, and around them.

—The conductor didn't seem to be feelin' very gay over what's takin' place in the city, remarked Johnny, even though he manoeuvred us safely up to a good place on the top of the thram. I don't suppose he understood what he was sayin'. It's ignorance, only just ignorance, isn't it, Ma?

—Just ignorance, Johnny. He was really kind, though; and we must always remember that kind people are to be met everywhere; for though people often think wrong things, they can often be quite good.

—Even among the Catholic Fenians, Ma? questioned Johnny.

—Specially among the Fenians. Your poor father often said that Fenians were all honest, outspoken men. One of them lived in our house before he had to fly the country, ere you were born; an' he an' your father were great friends. The little table with the drawer, at home, was bought be us when he was sellin' the few things him an' his wife had, just as they were hurryin' off to America. Besides, some of the Fenians were Protestants too.

—But we're not really Irish, Ma; not really, you know, are we?

—Not Irish? echoed his mother. Of course, we're Irish. What on earth put it into your head that we weren't Irish?

—One day, an' us playin', Kelly told me that only Catholics

were really Irish; an' as we were Protestants, we couldn't be anyway near to the Irish.

His mother's face reddened and her breath came in little pants.

—Th' ignorant, cheeky, little Roman Catholic scut! she ejaculated venomously. I could tell the whole seed, breed, and generation of the Kellys that the O'Casside Clan couldn't be more Irish than they are; and that when the Irish ruled in Ireland, the Clan Casside was just as important an' princely as the Clan Kelly. If your poor father was alive, he'd show from documented histhory that the Cassides stretched back farther than the year of one. And Protestants are Catholics, too; not Roman Catholics, but Catholics, pure an' simple; real Irish, without a foreign title like Roman stuck on to it. If your poor father was alive, he'd show you in books solid arguments, never to be gainsaid, that St Patrick was really as Protestant as a Protestant could be; and that the early Irish didn't hold with many things Roman Catholics now make a part of their creed; but preached and taught only the pure an' unadulterated gospel that we Protestants believe today.

The tram circled into North Frederick Street, and Johnny forgot about St Patrick and the Protestants. The paths were packed with people, and many who couldn't find room on the paths walked along in streams beside the slow-moving tram, forging ahead like a lighted barge in the centre of a living river. Johnny saw gleaming lights and waving flags stretching out before him as far as his eyes could reach. Proud he felt, and full of delight that he could feel himself a living part of this great display given to show the Irish people's fond attachment to mighty England's Queen.

—Looka the Orange Lodge, Ma, exclaimed Johnny enthusiastically; oh, looka the Grand Orange Lodge!

From every second window floated a Royal Standard or a Union Jack. Lights gleamed behind the window blinds, coloured with the Orange and Blue of Nassau. In one window, with the blinds up, several radiant orangemen-faces could be seen staring down at the teeming crowds below. Right across the face of the building stretched, in gleaming gas-lights, the flaming cry of *God Save the Queen*; and above this, surrounded by a bronze laurel wreath, the steadily-gleaming gas-light date of 1690. Over opposite was the stately church built for the Presbyterians by Alexander Findlater, Gentleman Grocer and Wine Merchant

of the city of Dublin, with its great flag flying from its spire, and
its heavy railings, coloured a vivid blue with golden spear tops,
shining gloriously in the gleam of the illuminations all around it.
Every head in the tram leaned forward and every neck was
stretched to gaze at the brilliant and wonderful sight.

—Isn't it all lovely, murmured Mrs Casside, her face aglow,
showin', if ever anything can show, that the best people in the
land an' the poorest people in the land are hand in glove with the
respect an' loyalty that has diapered the city in light an' colour
in honour of our Queen.

—Y'Orange gets! shouted a voice below, and Johnny saw two
policemen seize a shouting man who was shaking his fist at a
window in the Orange Lodge.

—There's goin' to be a row in a minute, said Johnny excitedly;
looka the man gettin' taken be the police.

—He's only a dhrunken rowdy, said his mother. You'll always
get some fool ready to complain of the silence of peace. But one
among so many can't count for much.

The conductor came up the stairs with a scowl on his face,
and moved along between the rows of passengers, collecting the
fares. The passengers, gazing on the gleaming lights, the fluttering
flags, and waving festoons, offered their fares in outstretched
hands to the conductor without taking their ravished eyes from
the garnished streets. He took the money from the outstretched
hands, punched the tickets, and dropped them into the hands
rigidly held out to receive them; the passengers never turning a
head so that the vision of colour and light and jubilation wouldn't
be lost, even for a moment. The conductor kept shaking his
head scornfully as he went from one outstretched hand to
another.

—Poor Wolfe Tone, poor Wolfe Tone, he kept murmuring, as
he mouched along, poor Wolfe Tone.

Johnny watched the conductor going over to the top of the
stairs after he had collected the fares. He stood there, with a
hand on the stair-rail, staring at the passengers gaping at the
decorations; then he sang in a low voice, half to himself and half
to those who were in the tram:

> Once I lay on the sod that lies over Wolfe Tone,
> And thought how he perished in prison alone
> His friends unavenged, and his counthry unfreed —
> Oh, bitter, I said, is the pathriot's meed.

I was woke from my dream by the voices an' thread
Of a band who came into the home of the dead;
They carried no corpse, and they carried no stone,
And they stopped when they came to the grave of Wolfe Tone.

My heart overflowed, and I clasped every hand,
And I blessed and I blessed every one of the band;
Sweet, sweet! 'tis to find that such faith can remain
To the cause and the man so long vanquished and slain.

—Who was Wolfe Tone, Ma? whispered Johnny, moved strangely by seeing tears trickling down the cheeks of the conductor as he sang.

—A Protestant rebel who went over to France nearly a hundhred years ago, an' brought back a great fleet to help the Irish drive the English outa the counthry. But God was guarding us, and He sent a mighty storm that scatthered the ships from Banthry Bay.

—What happened to poor Wolfe Tone, Ma?

—He fought on a French warship till it was captured by the British; and then he was put into prison, an' executed there by the English government.

—Why didn' the Irish save him?

—Oh, I don't know. It all happened long ago, an' everyone's forgotten all about it.

—But the conductor hasn't forgotten all about it, Ma.

—Let's look at the lights and the banners, said his mother, an' not bother our heads about things that don't matter now.

The conductor continued to sing, with one hand resting on the stair-rail, half to himself and half to the others:

In Bodenstown Churchyard there is a green grave,
And wildly around it the winter winds rave –
Far betther they suit him – the ruin an' the gloom –
Till Ireland, a Nation, can build him a tomb.

A seething crowd, making for Sackville Street, got wedged together opposite the Rotunda, whose dome was a mass of vivid lights topped by an imperial crown, mixed in the motto of Honi Soit Qui Mal Y Pense. The tram, caught fair in the middle of the crowd, came to a dead stop, and waited patiently for the throng to loosen a little, so that it might go on its way.

—Be God, said the man with the wide watery mouth and the moustache drooping over it like a weeping willow, as he turned his head to speak to all in general, be God, they haven't spared any expense to turn Dublin into a glittherin' an' a shinin' show!

—It's a shinin' sight to the eye that wants to see it so, said the conductor, with a bite in his voice; but to the Irish eye that sees thrue, it's but a grand gatherin' o' candles, lit to look sthrong, an' make merry over the corpse of our counthry.

—If it is, aself, said the man who had spoken before, it's a grand wake, surely. The whole city's out admirin', an' if we could only get the whole counthry to join in, there'd be peace; aye, an' lashin's an' leavin's in the land as well. But it's comin', it's comin', right enough. It's close to us already, for what Dublin thinks today, Ireland says tomorrow.

Mrs Casside leant over towards the man who had spoken, her face bright with agreement.

—You say the solemn thruth, she said. You've only to take a look at the streets to see that everyone's eager to settle down into a government of law an' ordher, with the crown to be at the head of all the people. Only let them alone, an' the people are frantic for quietness. It only needs a sight an' a time like this to bring us to our senses.

—An', said the man, with a flash of anger, what we're all longin' for 'ud be here before we expected it, if it wasn't for the ruffian, Parnell, thrippin' up the counthry into a dismal turmoil.

—Oh, said Mrs Casside reprovingly, whatever Parnell may be, he's far from bein' a ruffian. I'd say he's a son of a grand stock, an' a thorough gentleman.

—Thorough gentleman! sneered the man. The dirty dhrop's in him, or he wouldn't be rallyin' all the gobeens of the counthry against the intherests an' comfort of the few decent people left livin' here. What's he aimin' at, if it's not at becomin' the un-crowned king of Ireland?

Mrs Casside stiffened, and leaned back to get as far as she could from the man with the wide watery mouth, and the moustache hanging over it like a weeping willow.

—If the thruth must be told, said she, after a pause, an' things allowed it, the counthry couldn't have a betther king!

—Hear, hear, said several people in different parts of the tram.

—Well, responded the man, yous'll find him out when you've well forgotten the wise warnin' given be a man who'll hie himself outa the counthry the first chance he gets.

—It's a pity, murmured a soft voice from the upper end of the tram, that a certain person can't hie himself outa the thram as well as outa the counthry.

—I can pass a remark, can't I? asked the man with the wide watery mouth. There's no law agin the passin' of a remark, is there? Bedammit, it's hard lines, if a man can't pass a simple remark in a simple way on a simple subject.

—When a simple remark lengthens out to a pageant of lies, said the soft voice from the upper end of the tram, it's time for someone or another to signal once for silence.

The man with the wide watery mouth stood up from his seat, his face flushed, and his eyes sparkling.

—I say, he shouted, that an unbelievin' Protestant's no kind of a man to be the leadher of the Irish Race! I'm not goin' to let meself be limited. What the people want's a fair an' quiet way of differin' from each other, without heat or haughtiness, an' a decent regard for everybody else's opinion; an' fists shaken in me face won't frighten me! I say that Parnell's moonlightin', police-stonin' gang's ruinin' the counthry!

The conductor's head appeared above the top of the stairway. The scowl on his face had settled. He glared at the rows of people sitting on the top of the tram. He shook the satchel round his shoulder, rattling the money in it to attract attention.

—Look here, he said loudly, I can't have these goin's on on the top of me thram, disturbin' the passengers in the inside of the vehicle! If yous are so loyal as yous are anxious to show yourselves, yous ought to be able to keep the Queen's peace.

Down the conductor went again, as the crowd suddenly moved on, and the tram, finding room to go forward, glided slowly past the Rotunda over the crossing of Great Britain Street, giving all just time for a swift glance at Mooney's pub, with its well-known clock circled with lights, right into the glowing heart of the decorations and illuminations of the glorious thoroughfare of Sackville Street, the widest street in the whole of civilized Europe. There they were, the lights in their millions, the flags in their thousands, flaunting, flying, and fluttering from windows low down and windows high up; from roofs flat and roofs steep; blue, red, yellow, green, white, and purple flags; with Dublin's blue banner, endorsed with three flaming castles, holding many a place of honour.

Ay, and in many a place, too, swung the flag of Germany, with its black cross stretched over the field, or its savagely-beaked eagle ready to peck the eye of the world out; for Germany had conquered France only a few years ago, and she and England were going along, arm in arm; with the House of Saxe-Coburg-Gotha, and the House of Mecklenburg-Schwerin, and all the other Houses in Germany held in great esteem by all the rich and poor respectable Protestants, Johnny's mother told him. And Johnny remembered once, when a German ambassador had visited his school, all the children, after months of preparation, and countless slaps, had sung, in his honour;

> Dear Fatherland,
> Each child of thine,
> Faithful and true, will guard, will guard the Rhine!

There, too, was the flag of Denmark, for since the Prince of Wales had married Alexandra, the Danish flag and England's henceforth flew side be side.

Every shop, warehouse, bank, and building fluttered with flags; and walls flamed with rose, shamrock, and thistle, harps here and crowns there, with lions and unicorns in special places. It was a gorgeous sight as the tram moved slowly through the street, walled with fire; with copings, pillars, pediments, balconies, and balustrades swathed in purple and crimson cloths, edged with the finest gold; and garlands of red, white, and blue joining them all lovingly together; fair and fine linen, taffeta, and tabinet of gentle weave, brought out and displayed with great cunning in honour of England's valiant Queen.

On the tram crawled between the people crowding the street, the driver constantly blowing his whistle as a reminder to the people to keep a way clear; over the Carlisle Bridge, into, and up, Westmoreland Street, Johnny pointing to the brightly-lit clock, surmounted by a sparkling crown, slung out of the office of the *Irish Times*.

—It's a great thing, said Johnny's mother, to see such enormous crowds so orderly, beset only with the one thought of enjoyin' themselves. If the Government 'ud establish a Royal Residence here, there'd be no more loyal and law-abidin' people in the whole livin' world than the Irish people. We're comin' now to the heart of it all, she added – Thrinity College an' the Bank of Ireland.

The tram slowly glided, with the crowd around it, into a wide well of gleaming, glittering, rippling lights, turning the night into a laughing day. Through the first few streets, Johnny had seen the jewels hanging from Dublin's ear and a shimmering circle of gems around her neck; but here he stared at the beautiful crown set lovingly on her head. Trinity College and the Royal Bank of Ireland were dripping in jewels of light, and the countless banners fluttered like broad blossoms flowering in the midst of flames. The great mass of people stood silent and still, gazing spellbound in the midst of the wonder. The silence was fraught with a quiet passion of esteem and fealty. It was the adorning of the rock of their salvation, and Johnny and his mother pressed each other's hands.

Out in the middle distance, Johnny caught sight of sparkling spots of silver shining out in the darker patches close to less brilliantly lighted buildings. They were the silver-mounted helmets of the police standing in batches, here and there, under the doorways and gateways of the buildings.

Suddenly a crowd of well-dressed young men, arranged in ranks like soldiers, one of them carrying a big Union Jack, began to sing with all the vigour of their voices and all the fervour of their young hearts:

> *God save our gracious Queen,*
> *Long live our noble Queen,*
> *God save the Queen!*

—The College Boys are out, the College Boys are out! shouted the man of the wide watery mouth, jumping to his feet, and hanging half out over the top of the tram. Now we'll see a snatch of the thruth at last!

But the vigour of the lusty singing voices was pushed down to a murmur by a low humming boo from the crowd, growing louder and deeper till it silenced the song and shook itself into a menacing roar of anger. A crash of splintered glass was heard, and pieces of a broken college window fell tinkling on to the pavement below. The menacing roar mellowed into a chanting challenge, low at first, but gradually growing to the tumbling booming of a great river in flood, as the huge crowd sang and pressed against the police in an effort to come closer to the College Boys:

> *The jealous English tyrant, now, has banned our Irish green,*
> *And forced us to conceal it, like a something foul and mean;*
> *But yet, by heavens! he'll sooner raise his victims from the dead,*
> *Than force our hearts to leave the green and cotton to the red!*

Someone raised a great green flag; there was a great cheer; the crowd pressed forward, and the police were hard put to keep them back; and broken glass from the college windows continued to fall tinkling on to the pavement below, as the song went on:

We'll trust ourselves, for God is good, and blesses those who lean
On their brave hearts, and not upon an earthly king or queen;
And freely as we lift our hands, we vow our blood to shed,
Once and forever more to raise the green above the red!

Johnny saw the singing crowd suddenly surge forward, break the line of policemen barring their way, and attack the College Boys with fists and sticks, driving them back, back, back towards the college gates. He heard a bell tolling inside the college; saw the heavy entrance doors open, and a crowd of other College Boys pouring out, armed with heavy sticks, all cheering and yelling as they hurried on to join their comrades attacked by the people. He saw the police struggling with the crowd, trying hard to keep together, and smiting as hard as they could every head that came within reach of a baton; but one by one they were falling, to be savagely kicked and trampled on by the angry members of the dense crowd. And there in it all stood the tram, like a motionless ship in a raging sea, while the gentle horses stood still together in the midst of the tumult.

Some of the crowd had got a rope, had flung it over the pole carrying a great Royal Standard, flying from a big bank building. Hundreds of hands tugged and tugged till the pole snapped, and the great flag came fluttering down among the delighted crowd who struggled with each other to be the first to tear it to pieces.

—Looka them pulling down the Royal Standard, moaned the man of the wide watery mouth. His mouth slavered with rage, and he could hardly speak. Where's the polish! Why don't the polish do somethin' – the gang of well-clad, well-fed, lazy, useless bastards! If I was betther dhressed than I am, I be down in a jiffy to show them how to jue their job.

—Betther if we hadn't come out at all, Mrs Casside kept murmuring, keeping a tight grip of Johnny's hand. I wish we hadn't come out at all.

A frightened cry rang out as the crowd and the College Boys were fighting, The horse police, the horse police, here's the horse police! Far away up Dame Street, Johnny saw the silvered helmets of the horse police bobbing up and down, becoming brighter and drawing nearer second be second. A great wedge of the crowd pressed back into Grafton Street, pushing, shoving, and fisting its way on to get clear of the oncoming mounted police. Women screamed as they were shoved headlong back, and some men tried to lift terrified children on to their shoulders. In one place Johnny saw a yelling woman savagely trying to fight her way back to the thick of the crowd, screaming out:

Me Tommie's lost; he was pushed out o' me hands; let me back, God damn yous, till I find me Tommie! Oh, please, please, make way for me!

But the crowd was helpless, and she was pushed back and back, till Johnny lost sight of her, still screaming to be let back to find her Tommie.

The mounted constables were followed by a great crowd, booing and yelling, throwing stones, bottles, and even bits of iron; coming as close as they dared to the heels of the horses. Occasionally some of the police would wheel, charge back, and the crowd following would scatter; to come back again as soon as the mounted police had turned to their comrades. Once, Johnny saw a mounted constable stiffen in his saddle, give a little yelp, letting go his hold on the long truncheon so that it hung by the thong on his wrist, turn his face backwards, showing that his right cheek had been cut open by the jagged end of half a bottle, flung by a hating hand in the crowd. Other constables ran to help the wounded man from his horse; and one of them tied up the gaping cheek with a large handkerchief borrowed from a comrade.

Some of those fighting the College Boys shouted a warning as the mounted men came curvetting into College Street; the fighters broke conflict, and the enemies of the loyal College Boys retreated down Westmoreland and College Streets, some running with a limp and others with bent heads, and hands clasped over them. The man carrying the long green banner ran with them, but the weight of the pole and the folds of the flag fluttering round his legs hampered his running. The police, angry at the fall of their comrade, came forward at a hard gallop in pursuit of the fleeing crowd. One of them, galloping by the man with the flag, leaned over his horse, swung his long baton, and brought it down on the man's head, tumbling him over to lay him stretched out near the centre of the street, almost hidden in the folds of his green banner.

Johnny shrank back and pressed close to his mother, feeling her body shudder deep as she saw.

A mounted police officer came trotting over to the tram, leaned over his horse, and touched the driver on the shoulder with a slender whip.

—Take your tram to hell out of this, back to where it came – quick! he ordered.

The driver lepped down off his platform, unhooked the tracing-pole with one hand, turned the horses to the opposite end of the tram by the reins with the other, hooked the tracing-pole again, and climbed on to the platform. The conductor pulled his bell, and the tram moved slowly back the way it had come; out of the gas-glittering homage to a Queen; out of the purple and crimson and gold; out of the pomp on the walls and the bloodshed in the street; out of sight of the gleaming crowns and beaming blessings, back to the dimness of Dorset Street and home.

The last sight that Johnny saw, as the tram moved slowly away, was the mounted police making a galloping charge towards Dame Street, in the middle of a storm of boos and stones and bottles; and a lone huddled figure lying still in the street, midway between the bank and the college, almost hidden in the folds of a gay green banner.

I KNOCK AT THE DOOR

JOHNNY'S MOTHER was very concerned about his education. So was Archie in a hazy and bullying kind of way; and so was Ella, who was nursing her first baby and whose husband was soon to bid goodbye to the Army for ever. Ella's education of her own husband was a failure, as Johnny said grumblingly, and now she wanted to fix her teeth in him. Many and mighty were the collogin' that went on between her an' her mother about poor Johnny's ignorance of all things.

One day Ella came, bringing a bundle of clothes for her mother to wash; when the washing was over, they sat down to a cup of tea and a crumpet, to start the talk all over again.

—I know he can't be let go on as he's goin', said Mrs Casside, or, when he's a man, he won't even know the number on his own hall-door. He must be taught something, even though he can't go to school. The last thing throublin' your poor father's mind, before he died, was that Johnny was bound to grow up a dunce.

Ella sipped her tea, and thought for a moment.

—I can't help thinking that he should have been kept to school, in spite of his eyes, she said. Oh, I know the doctors said he mustn't, she went on swiftly, to forestall her mother who was opening her mouth to speak; but the doctors haven't to rear him. A common labourer is all he'll be able to be when the time comes for him to take his place in life.

Your own husband won't be much more, thought her mother; but she held her tongue.

—A common labourer, went on Ella, if he's sthrong enough even for that. It was a sad mistake not to have let him go to the Blue-coat School, afther all the trouble the rector and Mr Purefoy took to get him admitted.

Her mother's mouth hardened.

—That's all over an' done with, she said. As long as I live, the boy'll never set foot in an institution.

—He'd be well fed an' clad, anyway, retorted Ella.

—They're a lot, but they're not everything. The boy hasn't much here, but he has a home.

There had been a great how-do-you-do about this Blue-coat School for Johnny. Ella and Archie had fed him with the grandeur of the boys' lovely blue uniform, with its deep collar and cuffs of chrome yellow, long trousers, glengarry cap, blucher boots that were fastened with buckle and strap, and lastly, a natty cane to be carried under the arm. The brothers in the Army had written home to say the idea was a grand one; and Johnny, himself, had pressed his mother to agree. But his mother had stood out against them all; and every time Johnny pleaded all the good things about the school, she put him off with, You're far betther off as you are, here.

—They'd teach him his religion, went on Ella.

—They'd hammer it into him, Ella. Every turn he'd take would be chronicled; and if one wasn't done as they had planned, the boy'd be broken into their way of doin' it; an' Johnny's my boy, an' not theirs. If they're anxious to feed him, let them feed him here; if they're anxious to clothe him, let them clothe him here. I'm not goin' to have the life in him cowed out of him, as long as I can prevent it. There's no use of harpin' on the Blue-coat School, for me mind's made up – the boy won't go into it.

—I'm arguin' only for the boy's own good, said Ella righteously.

—Everyone advisin' me about the boy says he's arguin' only for the boy's own good.

—You've only to look at him, said Ella, to see what's happening – he has hardly any forehead at all.

—I'm doin' all I can about that, an' it's certainly a little betther than it was, said the mother. Three times a day I brush it off his forehead as hard as I can for more'n quarter of an hour; an' the hair growin' close to his eyes is bound to wear away in time. An', afther brushin' it at night, I put a tight bandage to keep a pull up on the hair while he's asleep. Even if his eyes prevent him from learning much, aself, I'll not let him go through life with a low forehead. I'd like to do something for his teeth, but they'll have to take their chance.

Ella went over to rummage among the books left behind as unsaleable out of her father's fine store. She brought back a Superseded Spelling-book, by Sullivan, who held that by learning affixes and suffixes, Latin and Greek roots, you could net words in hundreds, as against the old method of fishing one word up at a time; a Reading Lesson Book; a Primer of Grammar; and simple Lessons in Geography.

—Here, she said, is all he'll need for the present. Make him learn the parts I've marked in each book, an', if he learns a like lot every day for a year, he'll know a little at the end of it.

Johnny was brought in from the street, and told what he had to do.

—I'm not goin' to do it, he said viciously; I won't do it. I'm good enough as I am.

—Very well, said his mother firmly, at the end of the week, no penny for your *Boys of London and New York*. Remember, no lessons, no penny for your paper.

Johnny was beaten. He'd as lief lose his life as lose the stories of Old King Brady, the Wonder Detective, Red Eagle, the Friend of the Palefaces, or From Bootblack to Broker, the story of business life in New York, all of which his mother helped him to read when he brought the paper home.

After Ella had read the big words for him, he put on his cap, and sauntered gloomily off to where there was a strip of waste ground near the railway, covered with coarse grass, dandelions, daisies, dead-nettles, plantains, rag-worts, an odd scarlet pimpernel, and patches of scarlet poppies. Choosing a fair spot of grass, bordered with poppies and daisies, he sat down, opened his books, watched, for a moment, bees busy in a clump of clover; and then began his studies.

Grammar, he tried to read, is the art of speaking, reading, and writing the English language correctly. It is divided into four parts, namely, Orthography, Etymology, Syntax, and Prosody. Orthography deals with the art of spelling; Etymology with the origin and derivation of words; Syntax with the proper construction of sentences; and Prosody with the laws and rules of poethry.

—Curse o' God on it! he muttered, isn't it terrible!

He opened the Reading Book, and found that Ella had marked the first few verses of *The Brook*, by Tennyson.

—Who the hell's Tennyson? he asked himself, as he slowly recited:

> *I come from haunts of coot and hern,*
> *I make a sudden sally*
> *And sparkle out among the fern,*
> *To bicker down a valley.*

—Coot an' hern, he murmured; I wondher what they are? Must be some kinda birds, ma says; but what kinda birds? He knew well the kinda birds sparrows were; not worth a tuppenny damn, for even Jesus said that two of them were sold in Jerusalem for a farthing; indeed, you wouldn't get even that for a dozen of them in Dublin. He had seen a redpole, a green linnet, a thrush, a blackbird, and a goldfinch, all in cages; they were all the birds he had seen so far; but he had never even heard of a coot or a hern. But this kinda mopin'll never get on with the work; and he started to recite again:

> *By thirty hills I hurry down,*
> *Or slip between the ridges,*
> *By twenty thorps, a little town,*
> *And half a hundred bridges.*

> *Till last by Philip's farm I flow*
> *To join the brimming river,*
> *For men may come and men may go,*
> *But I go on for ever.*

—Only one more verse, murmured Johnny, only one more river to cross.

> *I chatter over stony ways,*
> *In little sharps and trebles,*
> *I bubble into eddying bays,*
> *I babble on the pebbles.*

Sharps an' threbles – what did they mean? He knew that to be sharp meant to have an edge on anything that would cut, if you weren't careful; but what had sharp to do with the running water of a brook? And what was a threble? He sighed. The useless and puzzlin' things they made him learn. He knew what the sea was, because he had seen it at Sandymount. And a river, too, for one flowed through the city. What was the use of askin' him to learn what things were when he knew what they were already? But what about their own river, the Liffey? Where did it make its start? No one could tell him. His mother didn't know; Ella didn't know; Archie didn't know. Somewhere or another, was all they could say. Didn't he know that himself! An' they're cross with you over something you don't know, an' just as cross when you ask them something they don't know themselves. Take the Tolka. That was called a river, yet it was only the size of a brook, for he had paddled in it, and had filled a jar with minnows out of it. Yet it was the river Tolka. Puzzle, puzzle, puzzle. Of course he remembered the time it flooded the rotting little white-washed cottages on its bank, and swept away swift the statue of the Blessed Virgin standing in the muddy space beside the river. The statue had floated back again against the flow, like bread cast upon the waters, returning after many days, and stayed floating beside the houses, till it was taken up, cleaned, painted blue and white, and put back on its pedestal again. Yes, when it was in flood, the Tolka was a river; but every other time, it was only a brook.

A slender shadow fell across the poppies and the daisies. Johnny looked up, and saw Jennie Clitheroe standing beside him. Each eyed the other for a few moments, shyly, in silence.

—Just comin' from school? he asked.

—Yes, she answered, just back from school. What are you doin' with the school books?

—Just havin' a little look at them.

She made a place beside the poppies, passed a hand along her skirt to tuck it in, sat down beside him, and fingered the books.

—Oh, I'm in the fifth standard, now, she said, and I passed out of these years ago. I'm learnin' Euclid an' everything.

Johnny gathered the books up and stuffed them into his pocket.

—Y'know the river Liffey? he asked.

—'Course I do.

—Well, where does it start from?

—How where does it start from? she asked vaguely.

—Where does it begin; where can you find it a thrickle before it swells into a river?

—It's not mentioned in any of my books, said Jennie, so it mustn't much matter. D'ye know yourself?

—'Course I do.

—Where does it start, then?

—Ah, said Johnny mockingly, let the great scholar go an' find out.

Jennie picked a daisy, and began to pluck the petals off, one by one, murmuring, this year, next year, sometime, never; this year, next year, sometime, never; this year – and she let the last petal fall on the grass.

—This year, what? he asked.

—I'm goin' to be married, she said roguishly.

—Who'r you goin' to marry?

—Ah, she said mockingly, let the great scholar go an' guess.

He caught her by the shoulders, and pulled her back towards him.

—Tell me who'r you goin' to marry, or I'll hold you like this for ever.

—You couldn't hold me a second longer, if I thried to break away, she said defiantly.

He pulled her back till her brown curls were pressed against his chest, and her deep brown eyes were looking up into his.

—You just thry to get away, he mocked.

She moved, but put no big effort into it, and then lay quiet, looking up into his face, smiling. Suddenly he bent down and kissed her twice hard on the mouth. Then he shoved her away in sudden shame, his face flushing. He jumped up and made off through the poppies and dead-nettles, frightened at what he had done.

—I'll tell me mother, she cried out after him.

—Tell her, then, he said defiantly, looking back at her, still sitting among the poppies, with a white butterfly fluttering near here. I don't care whether you do or no.

Girls tell their mothers everything, he thought, resentfully, as he walked away. Why did she let him kiss her, anyway? She could easily have broken away, if she wanted. She was more to blame, really, than I was. Oh, let her tell, if she likes.

He took the Reading Lesson-book out of his pocket, opened it, and recited:

I chatther, chatther as I flow
To join the brimming river,
For men may come and men may go,
But I go on for ever.

Well, he'd learned poethry and had kissed a girl. If he hadn'
gone to school, he'd met the scholars; if he hadn' gone into the
house, he had knocked at the door.

'A most beautiful and sweet country as any under Heaven' –
EDMUND SPENSER

'Put an Irishman on the spit, and you can always get another Irishman to turn him – GEORGE BERNARD SHAW

Whatever your view of Ireland you'll delight in these magnificent authors.